Literary

Chicago

A Book Lover's Tour of the Windy City

Greg Holden

First Edition

LAKE CLAREMONT PRESS

4650 North Rockwell Street • Chicago, Illinois 60625
www.lakeclaremont.com

917.731
HOL

Literary Chicago: A Book Lover's Tour of the Windy City
by Greg Holden

Published 2001 by:

4650 N. Rockwell St.
Chicago, IL 60625
773/583-7800; lcp@lakeclaremont.com
www.lakeclaremont.com

Publisher's Cataloging-in-Publication
(Provided by Quality Books, Inc.)

Holden, Greg.
    Literary Chicago : a book lover's tour of the Windy
City / Greg Holden. — 1st ed.
    p. cm.
    Includes bibliographic references and index.
    LCCN: 00-104567
    ISBN: 1-893121-01-1

    1. Literary landmarks—Illinois—Chicago.
2. American literature—Illinois—Chicago—History and
criticism. 3. Walking—Illinois—Chicago—Guidebooks.
4. City and town life in literature. 5. Chicago (Ill.)
—In literature. 6. Chicago (Ill.)—Intellectual life.
7. Chicago (Ill.)—Guidebooks.   I. Title.

PS144.C4H65 2001   810.9'977311
                                  QBI00-901621

**Printed in the United States of America by United Graphics,
an employee-owned company based in Mattoon, Illinois.**

05 04 03 02 01   10 9 8 7 6 5 4 3 2 1

To my parents for instilling me with the love of history and literature;

To my best friend, Ann Lindner, for helping me every step of the way;

To my daughters, Zosia and Lucy, for keeping me inspired.

Publisher's Credits

Cover design by Timothy Kocher. Drawings by Jeff Hall. Maps by
Michael Polydoris. Interior design and layout by Sharon Woodhouse.
Editing by Bruce Clorfene. Proofreading by Sharon Woodhouse, Karen
Formanski, Ann Lindner, and Amy Formanski. Index by Karen Formanski.
The text of *Literary Chicago* was set in WoltonCondensed,
with heads in KaggishCond.

Note

Contents

Foreword

by Harry Mark Petrakis

Greg Holden's literary tour of Chicago—particularly about the South Side where I grew up, went to school, first loved, first married, and wrote my first novel—filled me with a pervasive nostalgia.

I attended the parish school of my father's church at 6105 S. Michigan Ave. Our Greek/English curriculum was taught to the rhythm of the ubiquitous stick. Both Greek and English teachers used the stick gleefully, but the Greek teachers struck with greater passion and fervor.

From the lake west to Cottage Grove, from 87th north to 47th, the green expanses of Washington Park, Jackson Park, and the Midway Plaisance were our boundaries. On the weekends, we would gather on the Midway. Under the shadow of the towering University of Chicago buildings, which were as foreign to us as buildings in Italy or France, we'd play football and soccer, baseball and wrestling, all paced by numerous foot races that the fleetest among us won.

When I began courting Diana, the girl I would marry, she lived with her parents in Hyde Park and I lived in Woodlawn. We had no car in those days, so after a date I'd take her home on the Illinois Central train or the Stony Island bus.

Most of the time, because she lived less than half a block from the 55th Street I.C. station, I'd just put her on the train to Hyde Park. On one such night, watching the red tail lights of the train receding into the distance, I understood with a surge of longing how much I loved her.

We were married by my Greek Orthodox priest father in his church in September of 1945, a small, unpretentious wedding befitting the last year of the war. The first six months we lived with my parents in their old city apartment, confirming my father's wry prediction about his children, "one by one moving out, and two by two moving back in." At the end of that time, we moved with great anticipation into our first apartment in Kenwood near 47th Street. This cramped third floor studio with a Murphy bed that swung out of the closet looked across a courtyard containing the windows of a hundred other apartments. On summer nights, a cacophony of celebrations and altercations filled the courtyard. Through the unshaded windows, one saw clearly the figures of men and women loving, dancing, fighting.

When our first son was born, I worked nights at the South Chicago steel mills. To allow me a few hours of sleep during the day in our small compound, my wife took our son, less than a year old, to the park in the buggy where she walked for hours or rested on a bench visiting with other young mothers.

From that Lilliputian apartment, we moved back into a house on 76th and Ridgeland Avenue that we bought with my parents. Not long after we'd rejoined them, my father became ill and entered the Woodlawn hospital for the final three months of his life. During that illness, when he felt strong enough to get out of bed he'd sit by his window where he could see people passing in the street below as well as the steeple of his church. He talked longingly of recovering and our family moving to the sunshine of California that reminded him of his home island, Crete. But he never recovered and died on Memorial Day, in 1951.

My father didn't live to see the publication of my first story in April of 1956. But he always had faith based on nothing more than his love that I would write and become an author someday.

In 1957, after our second son was born, my wife and I left the city for a stay in Pittsburgh where I took a job with a steel company writing speeches that I loathed. By this time I had sold half a dozen more stories and had also published my first novel and, resonating with unjustified confidence, and undaunted by the birth of a third son in Pittsburgh, we returned to Chicago where I'd try my hand at freelance writing.

That adventure wouldn't have been possible were it not for the love and assistance of my nephews—Leo, Frank, and Steve Manta. Their father owned an old house near the lake on 75th Street, an edifice whose stained glass windows and great mahogany stairwell were the only remaining vestiges of its days of gaslight elegance at the turn of the century. Now, vacant and forlorn, it awaited the wrecker's ball.

My nephews and I, joined by a few workers from their father's company, repaired and painted the old beauty that became our rent-free habitat for the next two years. I would never have survived those first precarious years as a writer were it not for the bounty of my nephews' love.

Beginning in 1966, we spent two years in California while I worked on the screenplay of one of my novels that had been sold to film. I didn't enjoy that seasonless interlude but the spacious houses we rented in the San Fernando Valley left us with a yearning for space. We returned to Chicago, sold our small house on the South Side, and moved into the dunes of Northwest Indiana that my wife and I had been attracted to from childhood. We had even honeymooned in a rented house in Grand Beach, Michigan. Now we bought a house near the towns of Chesterton and Porter on the Indiana shore. At twilight when the air was clear of haze, I could look across the lake and see the glowing skyscrapers of the city where I had grown up. When the sun descended behind them, the buildings glittered like pillars of fire extending into the sky.

We have lived in this Indiana house for more than three decades now. As beautiful as the dunes, pines, and lake are, and as pleasant as I find the conviviality and warmth of the small towns close by, an inseparable part of me remains linked to the city where I grew up. Perhaps it is simply that I spent my formative years there. The wellspring events of my life—the death of my father, my first love and marriage, the birth of our sons, the writing of my first stories—all took place there. Whatever the reason, wearing the raiment of a Hoosier for three decades now, the years I spent in the city across the lake decree my fate. I live in the lovely dunes but, somehow, I remain a stranger in an alien land.

In the writing of my novels and stories, I often return to those South Side streets, to the alleys and byways I knew as a boy. I recall that, in response to my strident shouts, my friend Martin would descend from the building next door to our apartment. We'd join our motley crew and begin our wanderings east to the lake or north to the Midway. We'd play, sprawl, talk, exchange fervid stories, bluster, and boast, returning home at twilight in time to hear the shrill voices of our mothers calling us into our varied ethnic kitchens for supper.

So many years ago . . . yet so easy to recall. Reading Greg Holden's journeys across the city, I journey with him and beyond him back into a magical time when my parents, brothers, and sisters lived like sentries in the rooms around me, a time when my friends were valorous and fleet, and when, as we roamed and played, we never suspected that the sun might not shine upon our youth and vigor for as long as we lived.

Acknowledgments

I'm a Chicagoan born and bred who loves my city. In a way, my smitten condition reminds me of parenthood. Not normally a very outgoing fellow, I now seem to gravitate toward other parents who understand my pride in my children's every accomplishment, and my doting over their everlasting cuteness. I tromped up and down a lot of streets doing this book, finding around just about every corner somebody nearly as passionate about the city as I. You'll find some of these names in other places in this book. In other cases, a benefactor was anonymous or represented the efforts of an entire staff. But here, with apologies to the many I'm leaving out, is a representative sample of folks that I just have to say thanks to one more time:

First, thanks to someone who, like me, left an office job to make a living as a freelance writer in one of the greatest cities for writers. I'm talking about Harry Mark Petrakis, who contributed a foreword to a guy he doesn't even know and who came to him out the blue.

I appreciated the encouragement and generosity of a guy who, like me, is enjoying fatherhood in middle age, the poet David Hernandez.

Michael Polydoris (maps) and Jeff Hall (drawings of authors) took time they could have been spending on more lucrative projects to contribute original artwork to this book; it must have been a labor of love for them, too.

Thayer Lindner spent hours driving all over the city and taking (sometimes retaking) many good photos. He was ably directed by Joan Turk, who knows the city like the back of her hand.

Sharon Woodhouse gave me the chance to do this book in the first place, and her helpful staff made sure it was accurate and readable.

Bruce Clorfene not only copyedited the text but contributed his own extensive knowledge of the city and its writers.

Melvin Skvarla of the Cliff Dwellers Club was generous with his time and introduced me to Burnham Bottomless Pie, which is a wonder in itself. Steve Diedrich provided information on the Bloomsday readings at the Cliff Dwellers Club.

Michael Leonard and the staff at the Sulzer Regional Library provided support and gave me access to their excellent collection of Chicago literature.

Michael McCready provided legal advice when I really needed it.

Alzina Stone Dale, author of another good Chicago literary book, *Mystery Readers' Walking Guide: Chicago,* gave me and a group of book lovers a tour of Hyde Park and was receptive to my questions.

Stephanie Scott of the Omni Ambassador East hotel set up photos and provided information about their authors' suite.

Sonya Booth, editor of *UICNEWS,* the weekly newspaper of the University of Illinois at Chicago, contributed many good suggestions of Chicago writers to profile as well as photos.

Debra Levine and the staff of the Department of Special Collections at the University of Chicago provided photos from the library's archives and helped me verify the date of William Butler Yeats's visit to campus, a question that had been nagging me for years.

Frank Lipo, executive director of the Historical Society of Oak Park and River Forest, guided my search through the society's photo archives and other collections.

Linda Bubon and Ann Christopherson of Women & Children First bookstore let me look through *their* photos and told me about the many writers who've visited their wonderful establishment.

Molly Daniels, longtime Chicago writer and teacher, gave me firsthand experience of why this city is a good place for writers to get their start.

Gelek Rinpoche, Ann Lindner, and Betty Contorer continue to provide essential support and guidance in all aspects of my life and work.

Literary Chicago

A Book Lover's Tour of the Windy City

Introduction

Chicago seen through the eyes of its writers is a magical place. The streets through which we hurry, the houses that we glance at only casually, the bodies of water we're scarcely aware of as we run our everyday errands acquire new possibilities—romance, fantasy, even occasionally drama—when we peek through the special lenses that our local novelists, poets, journalists, and playwrights provide for us.

Literary Chicago is a guide—not a comprehensive guide, but a selective guide, a set of starting points—to an assortment of places of significance to writers, book lovers, and tourists alike. This is, after all, the place where Carl Sandburg lived and worked, where *Playboy* magazine was born, where Harriet Monroe founded *Poetry* magazine, where Richard Wright and Nelson Algren and Margaret Walker and Studs Terkel were all employed by the WPA while they were struggling to learn their craft. It's where Ana Castillo and Scott Turow and Sara Paretsky now live and write. It's the home of Oprah and her book club, the Cliff Dwellers, R. R. Donnelley, and the Encyclopaedia Britannica. By touring Chicago's literary venues and historic landmarks you glimpse not only the city's rich history but also its present opportunities for wonder for anyone who loves books and the artists who create them.

My primary goal in writing this book is not to drop names or churn out an exhaustive list of every writer who's ever lived or worked here, but rather to illuminate this city's literary past by guiding you to a selection of places you can enjoy here and now. I have created walking and driving tours that take you past the homes where many of the city's legendary writers—Carl Sandburg, Edna Ferber, Ernest Hemingway, and Saul Bellow, among others—once lived. I've also tried to include the places where they and some of the lesser-known literary lights have worked, dreamed, complained, commiserated, and loved. I've also thrown in some of the libraries, bookstores, salons, and coffeehouses you can visit in order to foster your own literary interests.

Chicago doesn't like to think of itself as a snobbish, book-lover's town. Yet, by my purely unscientific count, it has more bookstores than London and a comparable amount to New York.[1] Practically every night, you can find a poetry-reading open mic going on. And references to literary figures are everywhere. Driving down the street, you might pass a delivery truck from Big Shoulders Bakery, Hemingway House, or Finley Dunne's Tavern. Finley Peter Dunne who? Nonchalantly mentioning that he was the author of the Mr. Dooley columns, a billiard-playing friend of Mark Twain, admired by President Teddy Roosevelt, and as famous as any journalist in his day just might impress the person sitting on the bar stool next to yours.

The literary face of the city is not always what the world sees first. Outsiders associate Chicago with Al Capone and Mayor Daley. Those notable citizens became famous through their own words and deeds, no doubt, but they became legendary through W. R. Burnett's *Little Caesar* and Mike Royko's *Boss.*

Sometimes it seems that when you are tracking down literary sites in Chicago you are chasing ghosts. The characters who used to make the Fine Arts Building a lively place are all gone now, for instance. Nelson Algren's home (where he wrote *The Man with the Golden Arm* and romanced Simone de Beauvoir) is now in the center of the Kennedy Expressway. But getting there is half the fun and on the way you discover things you never would otherwise. You see the real city, in other words.

In "The Real City Tour," a column included in Bill Granger's *Chicago Pieces,* a collection of his columns from the *Chicago Tribune,* he writes about taking a colleague on a tour of the "real" Chicago: "I like to show neighborhoods and the strong, ethnic beauty of the city that lives nestled on the other side of viaducts and expressway crossings, the part of the city where the tallest buildings are either the horrible monoliths of the public housing projects or the starkly beautiful churches."

He goes down Maxwell St.; to Pilsen; to Red's, a bar which he places around 22nd and Western ("Everyone stops at Red's for a beer sometime in his life"); to the Criminal Courts Building and the County Jail at 26th and California; to the Italian area at 24th and Oakley; to Bridgeport, where Mayor

Daley (Richard J.) lived on Lowe St.; past Comiskey Park; to Kenwood; to Berkeley Ave. where Daley grew up; to 47th St. in Hyde Park; to Chinatown; to Kelly's Pub on Western Ave.; to Lincoln Park; to Greek Islands on Halsted St.; finally ending up at O'Sullivan's on Milwaukee Avenue. These are all places that mean something to him and that play important roles in his writing.

What is the "real" city? The answer is as varied as the people who visit and reside in Chicago. For me, it's the part of the city that writers have known and written about, where they lived, where they went shopping, where they tossed back a few after work, and where they did everyday things.

My Chicago Literary Tour

If I were conducting a Writers' Tour of the city, I would go to places that mean something to me personally—to the Fine Arts Building, with its hidden Italian-style fountain; to South Halsted St. in Bridgeport; to O'Gara & Wilson and Powell's Books on 57th St. in Hyde Park; to the bridge over the Calumet River to have some French-fried shrimp or scallops; to Fontano's Subs; to the Newberry Library; to the Chicago Historical Society; to the open mic poetry readings at Café Aloha or Café Chicago. I'd have a beer at Lottie's in Wicker Park, which was frequented by Nelson Algren; I'd look in the windows of the Berghoff downtown; I'd also go to Borders on Michigan Ave., then walk a few blocks west and visit the Abraham Lincoln Book Shop on Chicago Ave. I'd admire the golden statue of The *Republic* in Jackson Park and stand on the Clarence Darrow bridge and remember the World's Columbian Exposition of 1893, too. These are all very real places to me, places that inspire me and make me happy to be living and working in this city.

Chicago Through Writers' Eyes

Many of the Chicago novels written around the turn of the century play on the rags-to-riches themes popularized by Horatio Alger, Jr. Alger, in fact, set one of his books in Chicago: *Luke Walton or The Chicago Newsboy.*

According to Carl Smith, the golden age of Chicago literature was an "aesthetic response," repeated in other cities besides Chicago, to "the rise of the modern industrial city in America." In this period, he says, "life and art became modern."[2]

Chicago was given the title of literary capital of the United States by H. L. Mencken in "Civilized Chicago," an article first published in the *Chicago Tribune* in 1917, and subsequently in a second article, "The Literary Capital of the United States." It was later reprinted and expanded in *The Nation* (London, England), April 17, 1920, and was reprinted in the *Chicago Daily News*, May 12, 1920. He said it was "the most thoroughly American" of all big cities and also "the most civilized." But later he called it only a "pianissimo revolt"[3] and Sherwood Anderson called it a "Robin's Egg Renaissance": "It had a pale blue tinge. It fell out of the nest."[4]

The growth and rise of Chicago seemed miraculous. Chicago represented a place where dreams could come true, particularly those that involved making or spending money. The city was perfectly situated so that it could serve as a hub for both railroad and water transportation, plus it was the right time due to an unrestricted immigration policy, the high tide of a free enterprise economy, and, Smith notes, "a series of revolutionary inventions in building, transportation, and communication."

The three factors that writers inevitably faced in the golden age were the city's railroads, the large buildings, and the stockyards. Most of the buildings are still there. The other two are of limited importance now. What is important and lasting? The dreams, dramas, and tragedies captured by writers who made this turbulent city grist for their imaginative mills.

The first novel set in Chicago was published in 1856: *Wau-Bun: Early Days of the Northwest,* written by Juliette Magill Kinzie, which was a romanticized view of her father-in-law John Kinzie's exploits in the days of Fort Dearborn.

The image of Chicago as a dream city of the future was expressed by Mark Twain in *Life on the Mississippi:*

We struck the home trail now, and in a few hours were in that astonishing Chicago—a city where they are always rubbing the lamp, and fetching up the genii, and contriving and achieving new impossibilities. It is hopeless for the occasional visitor to try to keep up with Chicago—she outgrows his prophecies faster than he can make them. She is always a novelty; for she is never the Chicago you saw when you passed through the last time.

The primary issue facing writers at the turn of the last century was the collision of traditional forms of art with the influx of new cultures and the new industrial environment. The authors of the golden age, according to Smith, saw Chicago "as a place of primary cultural consequence, a new kind of capital of American civilization (for better and for worse) born out of the heartland of the continent and the Industrial Revolution."

Not Just History, But 'Is'-Story

Today, the city is in flux again as new "immigrants" flood into neighborhoods being transformed by real estate market forces, and blue-collar industries steadily decline. Writers at the dawn of the twenty-first century face the same sorts of challenges to establish art forms as their predecessors did.

Plenty of scholarly works chronicle the history of Chicago literature. I did not attempt to cover the ground already plowed by Kenan Heise in *Chaos, Creativity, and Culture* or Clarence A. Andrews in *Chicago in Story: A Literary History.* If you're looking for a comprehensive list of all books that use Chicago as a setting, you can't do better than the two-volume bibliography *Illinois! Illinois!*

Rather, I've tried to make *Literary Chicago* a practical, selective starting point for writers, readers, editors, or anyone who lives here and wants to appreciate the city from the perspective of local writers. These are the "good old days" for Chicago writers, as far as I am concerned. The confluence of both historical and present-day literary atmosphere still makes it an inspiring place for young people to find their own muse.

When I worked at the University of Chicago I once interviewed an English major named Campbell McGrath. He spoke a mile a minute in a low voice that was somewhere between a whisper and a mutter. "Chicago, the city, is a good place for writers because Chicago is just a good place to write about . . . *The Chicago Literary Review,* which I edit, gets a lot of submissions from Hyde Park and other South Side people, because there's an interest and concern here with the arts in general. And there's a real core of student writers on campus." Mr. McGrath has gone on to write books of poetry like *American Noise* and *Spring Comes to Chicago* and recently won a Guggenheim Fellowship and a MacArthur Fellowship.

Authors respond to the experience of living in Chicago by using their literary imagination. You, the reader, can borrow a bit of that imagination to enrich your stay in Chicago. Whether you are just traveling through or living here permanently, you can appreciate the city more by understanding what's behind the geography and the architecture through looking at its history.

Let's face it. Those of us who are lucky enough to make a living from writing have our pick of locations. With our laptops and modems and calling cards for communicating with our editors we could be breathing the clear air of Taos or hiking up Potrero Hill in San Francisco. Why be a Chicagoan?

What you will discover as you read this book is that classical notions of metropolitan beauty do not necessarily breed creativity. Chicago has what poet Michael Anania describes as "a commitment to grit." It is the landscape of tension and activity that fosters all sorts of literary and intellectual pursuits. Rudyard Kipling described it as the most genuine of American cities, meaning it as both a compliment and an insult:

> I have struck a city—a real city—and they call it Chicago. The other places do not count . . . This place is the first American city I have encountered. It holds rather more than a million people with bodies, and stands on the same sort of soil as Calcutta. Having seen it, I urgently desire never to see it again. It is inhabited by savages. Its water is the water of the Hugli, and its air is dirt. Also it says that it is the "Boss" town of America.[5]

Indeed, Chicago is known for the artists who have left it to go to either the East Coast or the West Coast or to Europe. (Strangely enough, although they identify themselves as expatriates, they keep on writing about Chicago.) But although it is possible to leave it and love it both at the same time, those who choose to linger today will be part of a resurgence of literary activity in Chicago. Poetry in particular is hot and, with more than 120 troupes, Chicago's thriving theater scene may now be the best in the world.

If you are a writer, Chicago will provide plenty of places for inspiration. There is an active community of writers to give you support. And even if you haven't won the Pulitzer Prize, you can find venues to read your stuff and get published.

The Nelson Algren Challenge

All of the writers I profile in this book are busy, hard-working people. Rather than bombarding them with a series of questions, I chose a quote from Nelson Algren's *Chicago: City on the Make* and asked them to comment on it. Their responses are scattered through the book. Here is the quote they are responding to:

> You can belong to New Orleans. You can belong to Boston or San Francisco. You might conceivably—however clandestinely—belong to Philadelphia. But you can't belong to Chicago any more than you can belong to the flying saucer called Los Angeles. For it isn't so much a city as it is a drafty hustler's junction in which to hustle a while and come on out of the draft.

What This Book Is About

You have a much richer and more stimulating experience if you are among people who are thinking and breathing writing, who are looking to become literate in a new vocabulary, who are on the cutting edge, who are hungry for knowledge. Actually, only a particular type of person is looking for this type of experience. If you have picked up this book, it's likely you have some of these qualities. You love books, you are interested in being a participant in your city rather than sitting at home every night watching the tube. The life of the mind—the examined life—is what you are looking for.

Some literary groupies might favor New York or San Francisco where their pursuit tends to be a little more straight forward. But people in Chicago pride themselves on being tough. If you do just a little looking, you find the venues that match your interests. You find the inspiration you need to write your own poetry or make furniture or change your life in some way. If that's what you want, you can do it here. Chicago is nothing if not a city where people can go to remake themselves. Literary characters from Sister Carrie onwards, after all, have made a tradition of it. Chicago is for people who are learning and changing even if their student ID expired long ago.

In *Chicago: City on the Make* Nelson Algren called it a hustler's town, a place where writers and fighters alike get along by settling grudges: grudges against big business, crooked politicians, and whoever oppresses the downtrodden. It is a poet's town because it is at the same time a "working stiff's town," he says. Because there are slums, because there are "useless nobodies who sleep behind the taverns, who sleep beneath the El." The city's "troubled heart" is why it is a good place for writers.

I also think of Sherwood Anderson, and imagine him walking around the snowy streets of the Near North Side, looking at passersby, then returning to his humble rooming house on North Wabash Avenue and writing a story called "Hands," which became the opening of his great collection (and one of my all-time favorite books) *Winesburg, Ohio.* Anderson said:

> When I visit any other great city of the world I am a guest. When I am in Chicago I am at home. It is a little what I am. I am more than a little what Chicago is. Not many can escape this city.
>
> I am not proud of it. Chicago will not be proud. But it is a real city—my city.[6]

In his own prose poem *Chicago,* Algren's friend Studs Terkel observes that Chicago is a city both blessed and cursed by Janus, the two-faced god, a city with "double-vision, double-standard, double-value, and double-cross."[7] Algren, he observes, had a clear vision of the town's doubleness—one face for winners, one

one for losers.

What Makes Chicago a Literary Capital?

Why do we writers grip our sheaves of paper against the "hawk" winds of winter, wipe our sweat off our keyboards during the blistering heat waves of summer? Why do we endure the loss of beloved neighborhood booksellers and look the other way as historic homes are turned into parking lots or broken up into condos with price tags guaranteed to induce sticker shock?

It's because this is a town with a spirit that stretches to encompass the imaginative worlds we create. It's a town whose lack of pretension gives us room in which to grow and build careers on our own terms. Chicago is the city of big shoulders, yes, but it's also the City on the Make, the Boss City that ain't ready for reform, the city of Judge Hoffman and Council Wars. All of this gives us something to grind willingly against so we can carve out a space for ourselves. Chicago writers are tough; they love a challenge.

The peculiar quality of Chicago literature emerges from the conflicts and contrasts in the city—the hurly-burly political mix; the juxtaposition of ethnic groups competing for their share of the American dream; the contrast between rich and poor sharing the same space but having different forms of reality; the city block that is the site of a blue-collar industry, a white-collar business, and quiet residences. Anyone in Chicago is aware of the cars, trains, and airplanes bringing people to and from its attractions, but the roles of the lake, the river, and the canals are also significant. Yes, Chicago is a big city in the North, but overhearing conversations in any café will reveal accents from across America and overseas as well.

Who This Book Is For

I am hoping aspiring writers find this a particularly good resource. There are so many benefits to be found by reading your own poems, listening to other people read poems, and just hanging out with people who love literature and writing.

On the other hand, you don't have to be a writer, or an aspiring writer, to make literature an integral part of your life. You can be an accountant, a painter, a secretary, or a computer programmer. This book is for anyone who wants to be part of the literary scene by going to salons or joining reading groups, or by following authors about whom they are especially passionate.

There is a contagious excitement in knowing how Chicago's neighborhoods have inspired writers in the past and continue to inspire young writers in the present who are working to find their literary muse.

Even if you don't plan to visit all the sites described in *Literary Chicago,* just knowing that they are out there may enlarge your perception of the city. Maybe you commute to work the same way every day and have never taken the time to notice the significance of the locations that you pass. Maybe you will be heading for a Cubs game when you see the unassuming house at 4646 North Hermitage Ave. and remember "this is where Carl Sandburg once lived," or maybe you will distract the kids in the back seat from their argument about which movie to see by pointing out that 1667 N. Humboldt Blvd. "is where *The Wizard of Oz* was written."

Literary Chicago is not meant to be a follow-the-leader, step-by-step dictation of where to go and what to do. Rather, my hope is that you will take the ingredients provided as a starter and make it happen for you. It's up to you to stir the pot and come up with your own new mixture.

Part I

Literary Tours

DOWNTOWN

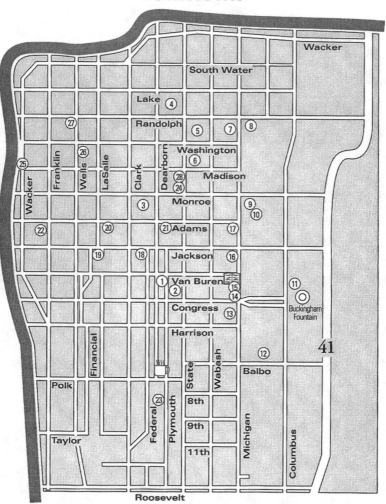

Map by Michael Polydoris.

Downtown

Drawing by Jeff Hall.   *Theodore Dreiser's "Sister Carrie"*

Like a compelling, beautifully designed book jacket, Chicago's lakefront and downtown area attract readers, casual browsers, and visitors from all walks of life. For the most part (with the glaring exceptions of the Art Institute and McCormick Place), the city's downtown lakefront has been "forever open, clear, and free" in the famous words of Montgomery Ward, and in accordance with the vision put forth in one of Chicago's most important literary works, architect Daniel Burnham's 1909 *Plan of Chicago*. As Burnham wrote:

> The Lake front by right belongs to the people. It affords their one unob-
> structed view, stretching away to the horizon, where water and clouds seem
> to meet . . . these views of a broad expanse are helpful alike to mind and body.

They beget calm thoughts and feelings, and afford escape from the petty things of life. The Lake is living water, ever in motion ... In its every aspect it is a living thing, delighting man's eye and refreshing his spirit.[1]

In terms of literature, the lakefront and the Loop have provided settings for many Chicago novels. Fictional characters have come here for romance, to make their fortune, to develop their art. Writers, too, have found the lakefront to be an inspiring vista. Harriet Monroe, the editor of *Poetry* magazine, grew up in a house on South Michigan Avenue, where she could watch dazzling sunrises and moonrises:

> Long ago when I was little more than a child, a sudden moonrise over Lake Michigan seized me with a kind of terror, so grand was the huge red sphere suddenly emerging out of the water and trailing the little waves with flame.[2]

By taking a walking tour of the city's Loop, you follow in the footsteps of some of the most famous Chicago writers and characters. A visit to the Art Institute of Chicago takes you to the paintings by Cezanne that inspired the young Ernest Hemingway; it's also where poet Vachel Lindsay studied and where Willa Cather's characters visited. The Fine Arts Building transports you to where the Little Theatre held performances, where influential literary magazines such as *The Dial* and *The Little Review* were edited, where the characters of *The Wizard of Oz* books were drawn, and much more.

A reference to the "Loop" may mean the area inside the elevated train loop that runs along Wabash Avenue, and Van Buren, Lake, and Wells Streets. But you're also talking about the north Loop, the south Loop, the Loop, the new East Side, the near West Side ... they all go by a lot of different names. For the sake of simplicity, this section uses the lake and the Chicago River, which have provided natural boundaries and transit routes since the city's earliest days. As Frank Cowperwood pointed out in Theodore Dreiser's *The Financier:*

> That white portion was Lake Michigan, and there was the Chicago River dividing the city into three almost equal portions—the north side, the west side, the south side. He saw at once that the city was curiously arranged, somewhat like Philadelphia, and that the business section was probably an

area of two or three miles square, set at the juncture of the three sides, and lying south of the main stem of the river, where it flowed into the lake after the southwest and northwest branches had united to form it.[3]

How to Get There

All forms of public transportation lead to the Loop. We are talking about the trains to Union Station, the CTA's subway and elevated lines, and lots of buses everywhere. Perhaps the best option is a CTA El to the Van Buren stop next to the Harold Washington Library, where the tour starts. If you choose to cruise on Lake Shore Drive, you can park downtown in the Grant Park Garage South. From there, walk up onto Michigan Avenue at Van Buren Street, then walk two blocks west on Van Buren to the tour's beginning.

Walking Tour

1.
Studs Lonigan's walk
Dearborn and Van Buren Sts.

Pretend you are Studs Lonigan and start your tour where he did in Chapter 2 of *Judgment Day,* the final novel in the classic Chicago trilogy by James T. Farrell. After taking the train downtown with his friends from his South Side neighborhood near Washington Park, Studs stood beneath the El on Van Buren at Dearborn, looking through the window of Marcel's Restaurant at a group of men eating inside. He had half an hour to kill before meeting his girlfriend Catherine at the Chicago Public Library. Let's follow him on his journey around the Loop.

The 'L' As Poetry

If you're tired or in a hurry (which you probably are if you are rushing to or from an appointment or work), the El is an adversary. It's slow. It's noisy.

If you're a poet or writer, the El is magical. Here's how Edgar Lee Masters described the El in "The Loop":

> Around the Loop the elevated crawls,
> And giant shadows sink against the walls
> Where ten to twenty stories strive to hold
> The pale refraction of the sunset's gold.

In his 1947 collection *Iron Pastoral,* poet John Frederick Nims includes the poem "Elevated":

> Three stories up the town is Venice: there
> the streets' abrupt and windy rivers run
> Among the badland brick, the domes of tar,
> The mica prairie wheeling in the sun.

2.
Harold Washington Public Library
400 S. State St. 312/747-4300

Ironically, Studs's walk starts at the back of what is now the main branch of the Chicago Public Library, which contains a bust of novelist Saul Bellow, a statue of poet and writer Gwendolyn Brooks on the seventh floor, plus numerous other kinds of literary resources including:

• A Literature and Languages section is on the seventh floor, as well as an Authors Room that is used for small-scale meetings.

• Go to the ninth floor to find the Beyond Words Café. It is next to the Winter Garden, one of the most unusually beautiful rooms in the city. The Special Collections area, also on the ninth floor, is open to the public and is particularly strong in materials on the Civil War and on the administration of the city's first black mayor, Harold Washington.

- The library's Great Books Discussion Group meets every second Monday of the month on the seventh floor to exchange views on shorter works of fiction. Call Mark Cwik (773/582-5273) or email mcwik@speedsite.com.

Library hours are Mon.-Thurs. 9 A.M.-7 P.M., Fri.-Sat. 9A.M.-5 P.M., and Sun. 1 P.M.-5 P.M.

Earlier in the trilogy, Studs Lonigan had come with his pals from his old Washington Park neighborhood to State and Van Buren to celebrate the end of World War I:

> The Chicago Loop was like a nuthouse on fire. The sidewalks were swollen with people, the streets were clogged, and autoists honked their horns, and motor men donged bells in vain. Tons of paper and confetti blizzarded from the upper stories of buildings and sundry noise-makers echoed an insistent racket. People sang, shouted until it seemed that their lungs would burst from their mouths.[4]

Studs looks in the window of Hassel's Shoe Store and wishes he could purchase the fine wares he sees. But, like so many fictional Chicago characters, he realizes that his meager funds must be spent on more important things like food. He crosses Van Buren and walks north on Dearborn to Jackson Boulevard. Cars fly past. He looks at a newspaper photograph of Charles Lindbergh, the hero of the time, and feels "measly and insignificant." Some athletes pass him; a bum asks him for some spare change.

Studs continues walking north on Dearborn; you should, too—but first, take a look at the CNA Plaza at 55 W. Jackson. Sara Paretsky reportedly worked for CNA Insurance in the marketing department while writing her first novel, *Indemnity Only.* Her success should be a model to other aspiring writers laboring in uninspiring jobs. You can do it, too.

3.
Site of *Chicago Inter-Ocean* newspaper
57 W. Madison St.

On Madison just west of Dearborn, a young reporter named Theodore Dreiser learned much about the city while working as a reporter for a long-vanished newspaper called the *Chicago Inter-Ocean*. A number of stories that crossed his desk reappeared in *Sister Carrie*, such as an account of a restaurant manager who stole money from the company.

At Dearborn and Randolph, you see something in the Civic Center Plaza that Studs wouldn't have seen: the steel sculpture called *Chicago Picasso*, which was created by Pablo Picasso and dedicated August 15, 1967. At the dedication, Gwendolyn Brooks read a poem "The Chicago Picasso," from her collection *Blacks*. It ends:

> Observe the tall cold of a Flower
> which is as innocent and as guilty,
> as meaningful and as meaningless as any
> other flower in the western field.

At Randolph, Studs Lonigan turns east, "the Loop noises bursting upon him with a sudden increase of volume." He is excited by the sounds of the Lake Street El trains, a jazz band playing, a movie theater. *Judgment Day* is set in 1931 at the height of the Depression, so if he looked to his left as he reached State, Studs would have seen the . . .

4.
Chicago Theater
175 N. State St. 312/443-1130

In Meyer Levin's novel of Jewish life in Chicago, *The Old Bunch*, the Moscowitz family attends the opening night show of the first production staged at the Chicago Theater:

> As they turned into State Street, the Chicago sign blazed at them. Boy, was that a sign! It made daylight of the whole block. Eight stories high. Three thousand bulbs spelled CHICAGO!

The historic Chicago Theater's sign was rebuilt recently but the design is exactly the same so that the exterior appearance of the building is very similar to what it was in the twenties.

State Street is also described in *The True American*, a 1976 novel by Melvin Van Peebles. The book's hero, Dave, is wandering through a forest in the nineteenth century when he is killed by Indians. He wakes up at the same spot, but it is many years later and now he is beside State Street in the busiest and noisiest part of downtown Chicago: "He stood and watched the cars whiz past for a while, then he began to wander down the street gaping at the sights. State Street is proudly billed as 'The Longest Street in the World' by Chicagoans, maybe it is, at any rate it runs the length of the citizenry, from the rich roses sprouting at the top of the heap on the North Side to the crumbiest derelicts at the bottom on the South Side."[5]

5.
Marshall Field and Co.
111 N. State St. 312/781-1000

Studs would certainly have passed the famous Marshall Field clock at State and Randolph Streets, installed in 1897, and could have met his girlfriend there like countless couples have over the years. By the time Studs gets to the eastern part of the Loop, away from the financial district, he is happy, "keyed up," and full of life again. He admires the young women he sees and is impatient as he hurries the last block between Wabash and Michigan Avenues.

6.
Carson Pirie Scott
1 S. State St. 312/641-7000

It's worth taking a detour south down State Street to gaze upon the wonders of the Louis Sullivan-designed entryway of the Carson Pirie Scott department store. Caroline Meeber, the heroine of Theodore Dreiser's *Sister Carrie*, looks in the window of Carson Pirie and dreams of being able to purchase the fine clothes displayed here. The store, which was located on Lake Street in the late nineteenth century when the events of *Sister Carrie* take place, moved to this location in 1904.

7.
Department of Cultural Affairs, The City of Chicago Cultural Center
78 E. Washington Blvd. 312/744-6630

This structure, built in 1897, was the main building of the Chicago Public Library until it moved to 400 S. State. The main wonders are upstairs where domes and mosaics are the work of Louis Tiffany. There is also an enormous Grand Army of the Republic Memorial Hall with a statue of a young Lincoln.

The entrance to the Cultural Center from Washington leads you through the Museum of Broadcast Communications, where you can relive the glory days. Features among the archives and displays include Studs Terkel's show *Studs' Place* and a tribute to writer Irna Phillips, who created the first radio soap opera *(Painted Dreams)* along with many TV soap operas such as *Guiding Light* (see p. 57).

The Chicago Cultural Center is open Mon. and Wed. 10 A.M.-7 P.M., Thurs. 10 A.M.-9 P.M., Fri. 10 A.M.-6 P.M., Sat. 10 A.M.-5 P.M., and Sun. 11 A.M.-5 P.M. Closed holidays. Admission is free.

Walk through the Cultural Center and out the Randolph Street doors. To your right you see the Metra stairs.

8.
Metra Entrance
Randolph St. and Michigan Ave.

You can watch crowds of commuters enter and leave the Metra Station steps at Michigan and Randolph. Although the name of the electric train has been changed from Illinois Central (I.C.), the scene is pretty much the same as in Ben Hecht's day when he wrote in his *Chicago Daily News* column *1001 Afternoons in Chicago*:

> ... as the I.C. trains rush their thousands to work and home again the citizens and breadwinners let their imaginations gallop toward a faraway horizon. And these imaginations come galloping back again and the breadwinners are saddened—by a memory. Yes, they were for a moment rovers, egad! Swashbucklers, gentlemen and ladies of fortune free of the rigamarole burdens that keep

them on the I.C. treadmill. And now they are again passengers. Going to work. Going home to go to work again tomorrow.[6]

The Great Chicago Trivia & Fact Book reports that one of the *Chicago Tribune's* top crime reporters was shot to death at this Metra station entrance. After Jake Lingle's death "a large bundle of cash was found in his rooms, and his close ties to Al Capone and other gangland figures became known—much to his employer's embarrassment."[7]

But Studs has no such worries because Catherine is waiting for him on the steps of the Public Library (now the Chicago Cultural Center) at Randolph and Michigan. They have dinner at Charlus Restaurant on Randolph. They then walk south on Michigan, which was as inspiring a walk in 1931 as it is today: "Behind them the avenue was brilliantly lit, and the street seemed like a fog of electricity and mist between the massive piles of stone." At Monroe and Michigan, Studs and Catherine would have walked past the . . .

9.
Art Institute of Chicago
111 S. Michigan Ave. 312/443-3600

In *A Moveable Feast,* Ernest Hemingway writes about going nearly every day to the Musée du Luxembourg in Paris to see "the Cezannes and to see the Manets and the Monets and the other Impressionists that I had first come to know about in the Art Institute of Chicago. I was learning something from the painting of Cezanne that made writing simple true sentences far from enough to make the stories have the dimensions that I was trying to put in them."[8]

The Burnham Library Collection in the Art Institute was established in 1912 in memory of Daniel Burnham. Although it is used primarily by members, students, and alumni of the Art Institute, others may use it by appointment.

Vachel Lindsay left medical school to study art here with the goal of becoming an illustrator or cartoonist. Instead he discovered a talent for poetry, and one of his most famous works is the poem "General William Booth Enters into Heaven."

In Willa Cather's novel *Lucy Gayheart* (1935) a young girl from Nebraska

A Chicago Author's Mysterious Life —and Death

The works of Eugene "Guy" Izzi (including *Bad Guys, A Matter of Honor,* and *The Criminalist)* are notable for their terse, no-nonsense style and the violent, premature ways in which so many of his characters meet their fates.

But one of the most puzzling mysteries concerning this crime novelist is his own death. Early on December 7, 1997, the 43-year-old author's body was spotted hanging outside his office in room 1418 at 6 N. Michigan Ave. He was wearing a bulletproof vest and the contents of his pockets included $481, brass knuckles, and transcripts of what seemed to be threatening phone calls he had received. There was also a canister of Mace-type spray, just as one of his own characters had carried. A .38 caliber revolver lay on the floor of his office.

Did Izzi commit suicide or was he murdered? His wife, Theresa, agreed to the closing of the police file as a suicide. But his friends and family knew of no reason why he would have killed himself. He had just signed a three-book contract with Avon Books. Yet a *Chicago Tribune* article about his death

Did Izzi commit suicide or was he murdered?

reported that he lived in constant fear. He claimed he had been beaten up by, in his own words, "people who knew their business," and that he had equipped his condominium with two burglar alarms and a guard dog.

Perhaps the clue is found in his books, but as of the writing of this book, the criminal—if indeed there was one—remains unpunished.

comes to Chicago to pursue a career in music. Much of the story takes place on or near Michigan Avenue; the cold wind blowing off the lake itself is a constant presence. She is in love with a singer named Clement Sebastian who has a studio in the "Arts Building" (probably the Fine Arts building). She remembers seeing him coming out of the Art Institute: "She thought of the steps leading down from the Art Museum as perpetually flooded with orange-red sunlight; they had been like that one stormy November afternoon when Sebastian came out of the building at five o'clock and stopped beside one of the bronze lions to turn up the collar of his overcoat, light a cigarette, and look vaguely up and down the avenue before he hailed a cab and drove away."[9]

The Art Institute is open Mon., Wed., and Thurs. 10:30 A.M.-4:30 P.M., Tues. 10:30 A.M.-8 P.M., and Sat.-Sun. 10 A.M.-5 P.M. Admission is $8 for adults; $5 for students, children, and seniors. Tues. are free.

Cross Michigan at Monroe and walk across the Metra tracks. At Columbus Drive, turn right.

10.
Chicago Stock Exchange Trading Room/Poetry Center of Chicago
Columbus Dr. between Randolph and Madison Sts. 312/899-1229

Here, on the east side of the Art Institute, you find the School of the Art Institute of Chicago (SAIC) and the original Trading Room of the Chicago Stock Exchange, designed by Dankmar Adler and Louis Sullivan. Adler and Sullivan designed the Stock Exchange, which was built in 1893 and 1894 at 30 N. LaSalle Street and demolished in 1972. (You can also get to the Trading Room through the Art Institute itself; just walk all the way to the Columbus Drive entrance.)

The Stock Exchange is one of the central locations for Frank Norris's *The Pit: A Story of Chicago.* Norris had nothing but contempt for dealers in wheat who made money in this room while the poor were getting more poor all around them, saying: "And besides, it's wrong; the world's food should not be at the mercy of the Chicago wheat pit." It's hard to match the beauty and serenity of the Trading Room with the description of the activities that went on there as filtered through Norris's imagination:

Endlessly, ceaselessly the Pit, enormous, thundering, sucked in and spewed out, sending the swirl of its mighty central eddy far out through the city's channels.[10]

The Poetry Center of Chicago is part of the School of the Art Institute of Chicago. It holds poetry workshops and sponsors readings by both new and well-known poets and writers. (For more information, call 312/899-1229, or visit www.artic.edu/saic/art/poetcntr/.)

Continue walking south on Columbus; cross Jackson; then turn east toward the lake. About half a block east of Columbus, you come upon the Rose Garden; turn right and take time to smell the roses along the way.

Studs and Catherine also headed to Buckingham Fountain, where Studs mused on how many new structures have been built along the lakefront. A cold wind blows, and they hear a train coming from the train tracks to the west. Catherine says:

> Isn't it so, and you know I can remember when North Michigan was not at all built up like it is now. They certainly have built up Chicago, and with the World's Fair coming in a couple of years, it's certainly going to be the most wonderful city in the world.[11]

They walk all the way to the lake and stand looking at the whitecaps. Studs has been changed: he wants to marry Catherine and have her with him during "the real fight of his life." They return to downtown Chicago but now he is "tired and happy and determined" and eager to "make a success out of his life."

11.
Buckingham Fountain and the Lakefront

When Studs admired the light show on the dancing waters in 1931, the fountain was new. This pink marble fountain was given to the city by Kate Buckingham in honor of her brother, Clarence, in 1927. It is still lit up on summer nights and provides quite a wonderful show, especially when downtown festivals like the popular Taste of Chicago or the free Grant Park concerts are also occurring at the same time. The fountain runs from 10 A.M. to 11 P.M. daily from May 1 to October 1 (though those days are often extended if weather permits). The fountain area also provides the first of a seemingly endless series of opportunities to enjoy coffee or other refreshments. The Buckingham Café and Grill just east of the fountain offers hot dogs, pizza, desserts, espresso and cappuccino to fuel the rest of your downtown literary walk. Then walk south to Balbo Drive and head east back to Michigan.

12.
Grant Park
East of Michigan Ave. between Balbo Dr. and the Eisenhower Expy.

In Norman Mailer's *The Siege of Chicago,* he has a view from the window of his hotel room in the Chicago Hilton of thousands of young people camped out in the park. They had come from all over the country to Chicago to protest the war in Vietnam during the 1968 Democratic Convention that eventually resulted in the nomination of Hubert H. Humphrey for president. You may remember seeing photos of young people grouped on and around the statue of John A. Logan just east of Michigan Avenue across from 9th Street. Violence that erupted between protesters and Chicago police was televised live during the convention and replayed for years afterward; 641 persons were arrested and numerous protesters, as well as 198 police officers, reported injuries.

13.
Blackstone Hotel
636 S. Michigan Ave. 312/427-4300

The faded lobby recalls the glories of an earlier time. In Chicago native Ana Castillo's 1990 novel *Sapogonia,* she describes a concert given for "the gentility of Chicago's Latin American community" at the Blackstone Theatre. Afterwards the performing castanetist Pastora "waited for her adoring public that had brought her to that cold American city."[12]

14.
Auditorium Theatre
430 S. Michigan Ave. 312/922-3432

Designed by Adler and Sullivan, this *fin de siècle* masterpiece opened in 1889 and was the first building to be electrified in Chicago.

At the beginning of *The Pit: A Story of Chicago* by Frank Norris, the protagonists are outside the Auditorium Theatre waiting to attend a performance. The opening paragraph gives a glimpse of the upper crust of Chicago society 100 years ago:

> At eight o'clock in the inner vestibule of the Auditorium Theatre by the window of the box office, Laura Dearborn, her younger sister Page, and their aunt—Aunt Wess—were still waiting for the rest of the theatre-party to appear. A great, slow-moving press of men and women in evening dress filled the vestibule from one wall to another. A confused murmur of talk and the shuffling of many feet arose on all sides, while from time to time, when the outside and inside doors of the entrance chanced to be open simultaneously, a sudden draught of air gushed in, damp, glacial, and edged with the penetrating keenness of a Chicago evening at the end of February.

Part of the Auditorium Theatre building today is home to Roosevelt University; go up to the tenth floor and visit the library, which occupies the space that was originally a hotel dining room. The design of its barrel-vaulted ceiling owes a lot to Louis Sullivan and his staff. Monthly tours are given by the Chicago Architecture Foundation on a Sat. at 10:30 A.M. Call 312/922-TOUR or visit www.architecture.org for more information. Admission is $8 or $3 for foundation members.

15.
Fine Arts Building
410 S. Michigan Ave. 312/939-3700

Originally called the Studebaker Building, the structure was renamed the Fine Arts Building in 1898. In the early part of last century this place was a hub of literary activity. Head to the upper floors in the elevator, which has extra charm because it's still operated by a real elevator operator. On your way up, you're likely to encounter music students or teachers heading to or from lessons, or little girls dressed up for ballet classes. (Corthell, the singer Thea Kronberg falls in love with in Willa Cather's *Lucy Gayheart*, had a studio in the Fine Arts Building as well.)

If you wait a few minutes for the elevator and ask the attendant to let you off at the tenth floor, you step back into Chicago history. A literary magazine called *The Dial* was published here until 1918, when it moved to New York. *The Little Review*, edited by Margaret Anderson, had its office in Room 917. Later, when finances dwindled, she moved to a cheaper studio, Room 834, "on the Renaissance court where the fountains and the pianos tinkled all day." Anderson spoke fondly of the bookstore designed by Frank Lloyd Wright (now demolished) on the fourth floor. She also remembered a fountain; you can visit the art gallery on the fourth floor, which opens onto the newly-restored fountain, a hidden place of tranquillity in the midst of the city.

Anderson published T. S. Eliot, James Joyce's *Ulysses*, Ernest Hemingway, Gertrude Stein, William Carlos Williams, and many others. Anderson recalls hearing a knock on the door of Room 917 and encountering Harriet Monroe with the poet Amy Lowell, a woman "of such vastness that she entered the door with difficulty." Lowell offered to work on *The Little Review* and pay Anderson $150 a month for the privilege; the fiercely independent Anderson refused.[13]

The tenth floor of the Fine Arts Building was designed for artists with skylights and high ceilings. Walk down the hall and let your imagination go wild as you read the inscriptions on the plaques that are found outside many of the studios. At the end of the hall is the home of the Rose Bindery, which was there between 1905 and 1913. Ralph Fletcher Seymour, designer and publisher, occupied 1025. Cartoonist John T. McCutcheon was in 1022 between 1898 and 1925; he was a cartoonist for the *Chicago Tribune* for 40 years, won the Pulitzer Prize in 1932, and his famous cartoon "Injun Summer" has been reprinted annually in the *Tribune* since it first appeared in 1912. He collaborated with humorist George Ade on books such as *Chicago Stories*, and he wrote his own book, *Congressman Pumphrey, the People's Friend* (1907). At 1021, William W. Denslow worked on the drawings for L. Frank Baum's *Wizard of Oz* books. At 1038, Lorado Taft worked on his sculptures.

The Little Room was a gathering of artists and writers that met in Ralph Clarkson's studio following Friday afternoon Chicago Symphony Orchestra concerts. Harriet Monroe writes about the period around 1910 (she is not exact):

There were friendly groups of artists in Chicago at this time, and they were less divided by cliques and professional barriers and jealousies than in certain other cities. The Little Room, named from a story by that painter, metal-worker, embroiderer, storyteller and all-round artist Madeline Yale Wynne, was an informal association of workers in the arts. We used to meet on Friday afternoons in Ralph Clarkson's fine two-story studio to talk and drink tea around the samovar, sometimes with a dash of rum to strengthen it, and every visitor to Chicago who was anybody in any of the arts would be brought to the Little Room by some local confrere. On Twelfth Night, and perhaps another date or two each season, we would have a hilarious play or costume party. There was no lack of wit in the club for concoction of parodies, with such famous word fanciers to call on as Henry B. Fuller, Roswell Field, Hobart C. Chatfield-Taylor, John and George McCutcheon, Edith Wyatt, Fannie Bloom-field Ziesler the pianist, Irving Pond the architect, Lorado Taft the sculptor, and others whose names are less conspicuous.

Frank Lloyd Wright designed a bookstore in the Fine Arts Building that was architecturally (and perhaps intellectually) a generation ahead of its times. The walls were of a light oak plywood and dominated by the straight functional lines Wright was to make famous. In connection with the store was a reception room with a large fireplace where visiting literary celebrities gave occasional talks.

The Little Theatre, conducted by Maurice Browne and Ellen Van Volkenburg, was the first little theater in America. Its 91 seats were arranged to resemble a miniature Grecian temple. The group, whose credo was "Create your own theater with the talent at hand," presented plays by Shaw, Strindberg, and Schnitzler, among others.

Photo by Thayer Lindner.

The Fine Arts Building.

The Chicago Architecture Foundation occasionally gives 45-minute walking tours of the Fine Arts Building. For more information call the foundation at 312/922-TOUR or visit their Web site at www.architecture.org.

Just two doors south of the Fine Arts Building at 404 S. Michigan, you'll find **Rain Dog Books**, an antiquarian bookstore. Around the corner at 418 S. Wabash, students of architecture can find all sorts of books at **Prairie Avenue Bookshop**, the largest architectural bookstore in the country.

16.
Encyclopaedia Britannica
310 S. Michigan Ave. 312/922-0869

The *Encyclopaedia Britannica* has been published in Chicago for many years. In 1952 they published Great Books of the Western World, a collection of the classic works of Western literature.

The first floor of 310 S. Michigan is the home of The Savvy Traveler, which sells travel guidebooks and fiction about travel, as well as books about culture and politics around the world.

A traffic jam on Michigan across from Grant Park on a hot summer's afternoon is memorably lamented in Bernard de Voto's *We Accept With Pleasure:* "Prairie heat was a wall he forced himself against. He walked through jagged clamor. Chicago screamed, whore of cities."

Before you leave Michigan and turn left on Jackson, take a look north. A. C. McClurg's Bookstore was located at 218 S. Wabash, a local literary landmark and gathering spot. Writers such as Eugene Field, Dr. Henry Ward Beecher, and many others held lively book discussions there. (The bookstore in the Newberry Library, 60 W. Walton, 312/255-3520, is now called A. C. McClurg's.) A little farther north on Michigan is another famous gathering place for writers and artists. Between 2 P.M. and 5 P.M. on weekdays, you can take the elevator to the top floor and visit the home of . . .

There's No Place Like Home
A Brief History of the Cliff Dwellers

The Cliff Dwellers still adheres to its original charter, which calls for it to be "a congenial place for artists and writers, a rallying point for the Midland arts." The group was first incorporated in 1907 as the Attic Club, then formed as The Cliff Dwellers Club in 1909. The first meeting in the "khiva" or main quarters of the club featured a fire-lighting ceremony that would have alarmed present-day fire inspectors.

From 1907 to 1996, the Cliff Dwellers were located in the top floor of the Orchestra Hall building (now called Symphony Center). The quarters in Orchestra Hall were known for their fireplaces, old grandfather clock, and terrific view of Lake Michigan; the present quarters down the street live up to those qualities as well. During Prohibition days, alcohol was available in the club because the waiters also worked as train conductors and were able to procure it from Canada. Former Chicago Mayor Carter Harrison II was a member and came there to lunch.

Amid much controversy, the club picked up its original furnishings, including the desk at which famed architect Louis Sullivan wrote *The Autobiography of an Idea* and a fireplace surrounded by oak paneling, and moved to the top of the Borg-Warner Building in a space that also has an outdoor terrace and magnificent view of the Lake Michigan shoreline. Their former home is now used for gatherings of donors to the Chicago Symphony Orchestra.

> "a congenial place for artists and writers, a rallying point for the Midland arts."

Sullivan's small writing desk is in a corner of the Louis Sullivan Room, where you can also see a bust of the architect as well as a bas-relief taken from one of the buildings he designed. Sullivan frequently labored at this desk until two or three o'clock in the morning only to show up at the office seemingly fresh and ready for work the following day. The ecstatic, often feverish enthusiasm of *The Autobiography* might be attributed to the legend that the architect was addicted to morphine in his later years. He writes (in the third person) of arriving in Chicago in 1873, just two years after the Chicago Fire:

> The train neared the city; it broke into the city; it plowed its way through miles of shanties disheartening and dirty gray. It reached its terminal at an open shed. Louis tramped the platform, stopped, looked toward the city, ruins around him; looked at the sky; and as one alone, stamped his foot, raised his hand and cried in full voice:
>
> THIS IS THE PLACE FOR ME![14]

Finishing *The Autobiography* was one of the things that kept Sullivan going through the illnesses, bad nerves, and poverty that marked his tragic later years. A copy of the book was placed in Sullivan's hands on his deathbed just three days before he died on April 14, 1924, at age 67. At the time of his death he had less than $200 in his bank account and was several weeks behind in his rent. Friends, including his partner Dankmar Adler, convinced the hotel where he had lived to forego the rent and paid for his monument at Graceland Cemetery.

According to Chicago publisher and Cliff Dwellers historian Henry Regnery, the quintessential Cliff-Dwellers member is "witty, friendly, cultivated, and thoroughly competent in his profession."[15] (Henry Blake Fuller, author of the novel that gave the group its name, was never a member himself; he was a thorough pessimist as to the future of the arts in Chicago.)

On the evening of March 1, 1914, William Butler Yeats was honored by *Poetry* magazine at a banquet held in the Cliff Dwellers' quarters. The great Irish poet was upstaged by Chicago poet Vachel Lindsay, who was perhaps reacting to a question Yeats had asked him: "What are we going to do to restore the primitive singing of poetry?"[16] Lindsay stole the show with an impassioned recitation (partly read, partly sung) of his poem "The Congo," which begins:

> Fat black bucks in a wine-barrel room,
> Barrel house kings, with feet unstable,
> Sagged and reeled and pounded on the table,
> Pounded on the table,
> Beat an empty barrel with the handle of a broom,
> Hard as they were able,
> Boom, boom boom

With a silk umbrella and the handle of a broom,

Boomlay, boomlay, boomlay, boom.

On June 16, 1999, the annual Bloomsday festival was held for the first time in the quarters of the Cliff Dwellers; the year 2000 Bloomsday event was held there too. The program consists of readings from James Joyce's *Ulysses,* a monumental work that follows the adventures of Leopold Bloom and Stephen Daedalus around Dublin on the single day, June 16, 1904. It's one of the few events held by the Cliff Dwellers that is open to the public. For more information on Bloomsday, call the event's organizer, Steve Diedrich, who teaches a course on Joyce at the Newberry Library, at 773/973-3716.

17.
The Cliff Dwellers
200 S. Michigan Ave. 312/922-8080

The Cliff Dwellers is a private club for about 350 writers, architects, musicians, and others associated with fine arts organizations or performing groups.

Don't miss the statue, *Bird Girl* by Sylvia Shaw Judson, that stands before the east-facing windows of the club. It has quite a history. The model for the statue was a poor girl named Lorraine Greenman who studied dance at a Chicago settlement house. It is the original mold of the statue that was used on the cover of the bestselling 1994 novel *Midnight in the Garden of Good and Evil: A Savannah Story* by John Berendt. *Bird Girl* also appears in the first scene of the film version of the book.

Four bronzes were cast of the statue; one went to a Savannah cemetery, where a photographer snapped it for the cover of Berendt's book. The producers of the 1997 movie adaptation (directed by Clint Eastwood) asked to make a fiberglass copy of the statue, and the current copyright holder, the sculptor's daughter Alice Judson Hayes, gave permission on the condition that the copy be returned to her. It now resides in the Cliff Dwellers Club, where the sculptor's father, Howard Van Doren Shaw, was once a member. Shaw is a distant relation of the famous family that includes poet Mark Van Doren and disgraced professor and quiz show contestant Charles Van Doren, and . . . well, that's probably everything you need to know about *Bird Girl.*

Art exhibits, which are a regular feature of the Cliff Dwellers, can be viewed Mon.-Fri. from 2 P.M. to 5 P.M. To be admitted to the club at other times, call for an appointment. If you're lucky enough to be hosted for lunch by a member, be sure to ask for the Burnham Bottomless Pie, named in honor of the savior of Chicago's lakefront.

Walk west on Jackson from Michigan, returning to the Loop.

18.
Monadnock Building
53 W. Jackson Blvd.

The beautiful 16-story Monadnock Building, built in 1890, is one of the early skyscrapers that not only made Chicago famous as a center for architecture around the turn of the twentieth century, but that have inspired writers and poets as well. The Monadnock was designed by the originators of the Chicago School of Architecture, Daniel Burnham and John Wellborn Root, and uses masonry-bearing walls that are six feet thick in places, but the addition just to the south (you can see it if you walk half a block south on Dearborn) was designed by Holabird and Root using steel skeleton construction.

In Sara Paretsky's novel *Blood Shot,* detective V. I. Warshawski meets a reporter named Murray Ryerson at her favorite bar, the Golden Glow, which is supposed to be located on the ground floor of the Monadnock. Carl Sandburg, who worked as a reporter in the Loop for the *Chicago Daily News* as well as other publications, frequently wrote about skyscrapers. He may not have been writing about the Monadnock specifically in his poem "The Skyscraper Loves Night." He might well have been thinking about the 1896 Fisher Building at 343 S. Dearborn or the Manhattan Building at 431 S. Dearborn. But in his poem, he endows one of these tall buildings with a heart and soul:

> One by one lights of a skyscraper fling their checkering cross work on the velvet gown of night.

I believe the skyscraper loves night as a woman and brings her playthings
she asks for, brings her a velvet gown,
And loves the white of her shoulders hidden under the dark feel of it all.
The masonry of steel looks to the night for somebody it loves,
He is a little dizzy and almost dances . . . waiting . . . dark . . .

Sandburg's "Prayers of Steel" uses the construction worker as metaphor:

Lay me on an anvil, O God.
Beat me and hammer me into a crowbar.
Let me pry loose old walls.
Let me lift and loosen old foundations.

Lay me on an anvil, O God.
Beat me and hammer me into a steel spike.
Drive me into the girders that hold a skyscraper together.
Take red-hot rivets and fasten me into the central girders.
Let me be the great nail holding a skyscraper through blue nights
into white stars.

In *The Cliff-Dwellers,* the eternal pessimist Fuller takes the opposite view
of downtown skyscrapers. He puts his characters in a fictitious building called
the Clifton. They lead unhappy lives because of the materialistic culture that
built such buildings.

There is a coffeeshop and fine fountain pen shop on the ground level of the
Monadnock Building. You'll also find the Midwest Women's Center Library.
This noncirculating collection of books and periodicals on women's issues is
especially strong in employment and culture.

19.
Chicago Board of Trade
141 W. Jackson Blvd. 312/435-3500

If nearby early in the morning or at lunchtime, you'll see CBOT workers going
around together. Their activities and spirit are the forces that have driven the
commerce and development of much of Chicago.

Scott Turow

Scott Turow was born in Chicago in 1949 and started writing when he was a teenager. Even though he is the bestselling author of such books as *Presumed Innocent* and *Personal Injuries,* he still commutes from his home in the north suburbs to his office as a partner in the Chicago law firm of Sonnenschein, Nath & Rosenthal.

Turow had a succinct response to the "Nelson Algren Challenge" mentioned in the Introduction:

Photo by Sigrid Estrada.

Scott Turow.

> I do not agree with Algren. I think one belongs to Chicago, more than many other cities, because you have to put up with our winters and some of our urban ugliness to call it home; it's a commitment.

Laura, the heroine of Frank Norris's *The Pit,* is attracted to Jadwin, the trader:

> He was a heavy-built man, would have made two of Corthell, and his hands were large and broad, the hands of a man of affairs, who knew how to grip, and, above all, how to hang on. Those broad, strong hands, and keen, calm eyes would enfold and envelope a Purpose with tremendous strength, and they would persist and persist and persist, unswerving, unwavering, untiring, till the Purpose was driven home.

The day-traders fixed on their computers, addicted to speculation, were described a century ago in this novel: "But by now the real business of the morning was over.... Nobody listened. The traders stood around in expectant attitudes, looking into one another's faces, waiting for what they could not exactly say; loath to leave the Pit lest something should 'turn up' the moment their backs were turned."

Another description gives the building a menacing air:

And this was her last impression of the evening. The lighted office buildings, the murk of rain, the haze of light in the heavens, and raised against it the pile of the Board of Trade Building, black, grave, monolithic, crouching on its foundations, like a monstrous sphinx with blind eyes, silent, grave,—crouching there without a sound, without sign of life under the night and the drifting veil of rain.

Compare Norris's dark vision with Scott Turow's more detached description of a fictitious trading house (not supposed to be in Chicago, and not based on the Board of Trade) called Maison Dixon, as observed by the protagonist of *The Burden of Proof* (1990), Alejandro Stern:

Outside, the vast trading room of MD burned on, eighty young men and women, casually dressed, each behind a telephone console blinking with the action on twenty lines, and a pillar of cathode-ray tubes. Across these glowing screens darted figures, flashing by briefly like fish in the sea, a matrix of dollars and cents, beans and oil, fast markets and bulletin items, high, low, open, volume, change.

Free tours of the Board of Trade are offered Mon.-Fri. 9A.M.-1 P.M.

20.
The Rookery Building
209 S. LaSalle St.

Curtis Jadwin, one of the main characters in Frank Norris's *The Pit,* has his office in the Rookery Building. "LaSalle Street swarmed with the multitudinous life that seethed about the doors of the innumerable offices of brokers and commission men of the neighborhood. To the right, in the peristyle of the Illinois Trust Building, groups of clerks, of messengers, of brokers, of clients, and of depositors formed and broke incessantly." Much of what Jadwin describes still remains today. (The "Illinois Trust Building" probably refers to the

Sister Carrie's Chicago Journey

One of the greatest of all Chicago books, *Sister Carrie,* which was published in 1900, achieved a variety of milestones. It was Theodore Dreiser's first novel; he began work on the book in the fall of 1899 while living in New York, but had earlier lived in Chicago, working as a reporter, laundry driver, and bill collector, among other things.

Sister Carrie was also the first truly great Chicago novel. Its story about a small-town Wisconsin girl who comes to the big city and transforms herself into a successful actress paved the way for countless subsequent books that described the fortunes of small-towners who are attracted to Chicago as a place to escape narrow provincial mores and discover new opportunities.

The events of the Chicago part of *Sister Carrie* take about a year to transpire. Along the way, Carrie Meeber takes her own journey around Chicago's downtown and West Side sights. The story is framed by two train trips:

Chapter 1: Carrie is on the train to Chicago; she has only four dollars to her name. She encounters a handsome stranger, Drouet, who gives her his card:

Sister Carrie gazed out of the window. Her companion, affected by her wonder, so contagious are all things, felt anew some interest in the city and pointed out the marvels. Already vast networks of tracks—the sign and insignia of Chicago—stretched on either hand. There were thousands of cars and a clangor of engine bells. At the sides of this traffic stream stood dingy houses, smoky mills, tall elevators. Through the interstices, evidences of the stretching city could be seen. Street cars waited at crossings for the train to go by. Gatemen toiled at wooden arms which closed the streets. Bells clanged, the rails clacked, whistles sounded afar off.

Chapter 2: Carrie goes to live with her sister and dour brother-in-law in a tiny flat on West Van Buren Street. She immediately feels "the drag of a lean and narrow life."

Chapter 3: Carrie goes job-seeking and literally pounds the pavement all day. "Upon street-lamps at the various corners she read names such as Madison, Monroe, LaSalle, Clark,

Dearborn, State, and still she went, her feet beginning to tire upon the broad stone flagging."

Chapter 4: She takes a poorly paid, exhausting job at a shoe factory at Adams and Fifth (now Wells Street).

Chapter 6: Drouet appears and takes Carrie to dinner at the Windsor House Hotel, Washington and Dearborn.

Chapter 8: Drouet buys Carrie new clothes at Carson Pirie's, which is now called Carson Pirie Scott.

Chapter 10: Scandal! Carrie leaves her sister and takes up with Drouet, living in his three-room apartment on Ogden Place, facing Union Park on the West Side! (Dreiser himself had lived near Union Park in the summer of 1892 while working on the *Chicago Globe*.)

> The best room looked out upon the lawn of the park, now sear and brown, where a little lake lay sheltered. Across the park were Ashland Boulevard and Warren Avenue, where stood rows of comfortable houses built and occupied by a middle-class who were both respectable and moderately well-to-do. Over the bare limbs of the trees, which now swayed in the wintry wind, rose the steeple of the Union Park Congregational Church.

Photo by Thayer Lindner.

The Union Park Congregational Church referred to in *Sister Carrie* is still standing.

Chapter 12: Carrie and Drouet go to McVicker's Theatre where they see *The Mikado;* G. W. Hurstwood, the manager of Fitzgerald and Moy's Restaurant, shows interest in Carrie.

Chapter 13: While Drouet is out of town, Carrie and Hurstwood go riding along Washington Boulevard.

Chapter 20: Dilemma: Carrie finds herself wavering between her two lovers.

Chapter 24: Drouet leaves Carrie.

Chapter 28: Kidnapped! Hurstwood spirits Carrie away to the Michigan Central Station, 24th and the lakefront. He takes her away on an eastbound train; they eventually end up in New York.

Sister Carrie attracted controversy for many reasons, not the least because it depicts an independent woman striking out on her own and making her own way. Just as controversial was the fact that Carrie does not end up paying for her flagrant moral transgressions; in fact, she achieves success on her own terms, apparently without lasting consequences. Dreiser's editors—particu-

larly his wife, who typed and re-worked the original manuscript—anticipated criticism and excised many passages even before the book went to press.

After novelist Frank Norris, a staff reader at Doubleday, Page and Company, recommended the book, the company agreed to publish it. Legend has it, however, that after Frank Doubleday's wife looked at the manuscript, she urged that it be turned down. Since the firm had already agreed to publish the book, it did so; but only 1,000 copies were printed in a plain red cloth binding, and another publisher was not found until 1907.

Illinois Trust and Savings Bank building in the 200 block of South LaSalle, designed by Daniel Burnham and demolished in 1924.)

On the carriage ride home from an evening at the Auditorium Theatre in the opening pages of Frank Norris's *The Pit,* the main characters pass the Rookery and then the Chicago Board of Trade, which is described as a "somber mass" with a "black and formidable façade" at the base of LaSalle Street. Laura sees people still working late at night.

21.
Berghoff Restaurant
17 W. Adams St. 312/427-3170

For a taste of history to accompany your stroganoff and beer, you'll find The Berghoff to be an excellent choice. In the manuscript of his novel *Sister Carrie,* Theodore Dreiser originally called the restaurant that G. W. Hurstwood manages Hannah & Hogg. There were, however, real restaurants on the South Side of the city with that name and the publisher insisted that it be changed. Dreiser then called it Fitzgerald and Moy's, and it was supposed to be located on Adams between State and Dearborn, where the Berghoff is today.

Driving Tour

22.
Sears Tower
Franklin and Adams Sts. 312/875-9696 (Skydeck)

A visit to the observatory at the top of the world's second-tallest building (actually, that skyscraper in Malaysia is only the tallest because its antennas are higher than the Sears Tower, but we won't get into that controversy) is always fun. The literary connection comes in the form of a mural, part of the tower's "The Sights and Soul of Chicago" exhibit that includes the likenesses of Ernest Hemingway, Ana Castillo, and other Chicago writers and figures of note.

Open daily 9 A.M.-11 P.M. $9.50 adults, $6.75 children 5-12.

23.
Printers Row area
Dearborn St. south of Eisenhower Expy.

The **Dearborn Street Station**, 47 W. Polk, 312/554-8100, has been transformed into shops, offices, and restaurants. But its exterior is little changed from when it was called the Polk Street Station and poet Edgar Lee Masters, the author of *Spoon River Anthology,* arrived here from the small Illinois town of Lewistown. He was met by his uncle at the station and expected to be taken to a fine residence, but was disappointed when he landed in a dingy rooming house. Masters worked at a succession of jobs until he became a lawyer in Clarence Darrow's firm and started making the big bucks.

The Printers Row Book Fair is held along South Dearborn every summer and is not to be missed. Also, don't miss the terra cotta decorations on the entrance to the old Second Franklin Building on Dearborn. There are plenty of pleasant restaurants nearby, plus **Sandmeyer's Bookstore**, 714 S. Dearborn, 312/922-2104, and **Gourmand Coffee Shop**, 728 S. Dearborn, 312/427-2610. **Powell's Books** has a branch at Burnham Park Plaza, 828 S. Wabash, 312/341-0748.

24.
Shubert Theatre
22 W. Monroe St. 312/977-1710

The Shubert is one of the few theaters in the Loop itself, and with its ornate terra-cotta decorations and a real stage door alley, it recalls the old McVicker's Theatre mentioned in Dreiser's *Sister Carrie*. The musical named after the city, *Chicago,* played here in 1997 during its successful revival. *Chicago* was originally produced in 1975 with music by John Kander and Fred Ebb and choreography by native Chicagoan Bob Fosse. The original dramatic version of *Chicago,* however, actually dates back to 1926, when it was written by Maurine Watkins to complete an assignment for her drama class at Yale University. Presumably, she got an *A.* The first film version was in 1927, and in 1942 the story was filmed with Ginger Rogers as Roxie Hart and with Adolphe Menjou.

25.
Civic Opera House
20 N. Wacker Dr. 312/419-0033

Thea Kronberg, the heroine of Willa Cather's *Song of the Lark* (1915), comes to Chicago from Moonstone, Colorado, and achieves some initial operatic success at the Civic Opera House before becoming a bigger star in New York.

26.
Site of Schlogl's Restaurant & Saloon
37 N. Wells St.

For many years Schlogl's was the hangout of choice for newspapermen and

The Chicago River in Literature

The River surfaces again and again in Chicago literature as a focal point for the imagination. Writers and their characters tend to look at the river and think of other things: often, they dream of being transported to another time and place.

> ## The Chicago River: A focal point for the imagination

This being Chicago, you get both terribly cynical and ugly views of the river as well as romantic ones.

The River As History: Wolf Point

The point of land that juts out into the river at the point where the North Branch splits off from the South Branch, near the Orleans Street bridge, was the subject of a book called *Wolf Point: An Adventure in History,* by Leonard Dubkin. The narrator, who professes to be a businessman in the nearby Merchandise Mart, is astonished when he hap- pens on the narrow path on the tip of land at the river's edge called Wolf Point. It seems to him an undisturbed bit of the city's past:

Here was a whole new unsuspected world, as unbelievable as though I should suddenly come upon a dense tropical jungle while walking in the Loop—I stopped to look about me, and to heave a deep sigh of pleasure and happiness. How beautiful all this was, and how wonderful to come upon it so unexpectedly, to find here in the midst of the city a little spot that was wild and untouched by civilization, and teemed with natural beauty.

Throughout the rest of the book the narrator travels back in time to discover how Wolf Point played a role in the city's history.

The River and the Chicago Economy

Pause on the Madison Street bridge over the Chicago River. A tunnel under the river suffered damage and caused tons of flooding in the 1990s. It was one of a series of transportation tunnels that go beneath the Chicago River itself. A complete tunnel system was built underneath the Loop around the turn of the century to permit underground deliveries to stores and office buildings. The Chicago Tunnel Company ran freight cars that carried packages roughly 40 feet below the sidewalk; in 1914 there were 62 miles of working tunnels beneath the downtown streets. These tunnels play a role in Theodore Dreiser's *The Titan.* Frank Cowperwood, the hero, builds a new transit line under the river using these very tunnels.

In his historical novel *Homeland,* bestselling author John Jakes follows the fortunes of the Crown family, who own a brewery in Chicago. One passage recalls the river before the Sanitary and Ship Canal helped with drainage:

> Paul found his cousin piling up sacks of hops on the brewery loading dock. The spring afternoon was mild and clear, with a pleasant breeze blowing out of the south. Unfortunately such breezes always picked up the stink of sewer waste and garbage in the Chicago River. Paul could even smell the cattle, hogs, and sheep in the Union Stock Yards, miles away.[17]

Death and Chocolate: *Going Down Fast*

The Blommer Chocolate Factory, which still sends out a delicious aroma, is mentioned in a scene in *Going Down Fast* by Marge Piercy, in which a character passes over a bridge dedicated to Mayor Carter H. Harrison: "Historians' favorite. Handsome and less the gouger than most." The narrator adds:

> Along the mushy shores stripped sumacs and cottonwood saplings stood ankle deep in frozen gray scum. Fish reeked from a processing plant on the bank he had left, and overlying all floated a strong aroma of chocolate from a factory a couple of blocks south. Streetlights cast his reflection on the garbage laden water. Sluggish, peristaltic. Would anyone drown himself in that?[18]

River As Lifeline: *Show Boat*

One of the most evocative views of the Chicago River and its connection not only to the city but to the Midwestern rivers that eventually lead to the Mississippi is contained in Edna

Ferber's *Show Boat* (1926). Magnolia is terrified by her first brief glimpse of the city. She tries to comfort herself by comparing it to the environment with which she is most familiar:

> After all, she told herself, as the astounding roar and din and jangle and clatter of State Street and Wabash Avenue beat at her ears, this city was only an urban Mississippi. The cobblestones were the river bed. The high grim buildings the river banks. The men, women, horses, trucks, drays, carriages, street cars that surged through those streets; creating new channels where some obstacle blocked their progress; felling whole sections of stone and brick and wood and sweeping over that section, obliterating all trace of its former existence; lifting other huge blocks and sweeping them bodily downstream to deposit them in a new spot; making a boulevard out of what had been a mud swamp—all this,

Magnolia thought, was only the Mississippi in another form and environment; ruthless, relentless, Gargantuan, terrible.

The River and the Stockyards: *The Dean's December*

Albert Corde, the main character in Saul Bellow's *The Dean's December*, is reminiscing with an old friend about his college days, when the stockyards were still active, and says:

> Odd, in Chicago, where the South Branch of the river, you remember was called Bubble Creek because the blood and tripes and tallow, the stockyards' shit, made it bubble in summer.

> **"the blood and tripes and tallow ... made it bubble in summer."**

literary figures. Regulars included Henry Justin Smith, Carl Sandburg, John Gunther, and Ben Hecht. One incident sheds light on the respect Chicago shows traditional Old World literary figures. As related by Smith in his book *Chicago's Left Bank*, Ben Hecht and another journalist, Henry B. Sell, had the famous English author Hugh Walpole to lunch at Schlogl's, "having previously sawed through the legs of the chair upon which Mr. Walpole was to sit." Hecht later remarked that stitches might have to be taken as the result of the affair.

27.
Ernest Hemingway's office job
128 N. Wells St.

In the days between leaving Oak Park and marrying his first wife Hadley and going to Europe, Ernest Hemingway lived with a succession of friends on the near North Side around Division and State Streets. For a while, he worked at 128 N. Wells. for a monthly magazine called the *Cooperative Commonwealth,* which was published by the Cooperative Society of America. Hemingway turned out huge quantities of copy for a salary of $40 a week. He wrote to his mother that he would dutifully use his first paycheck to purchase new underwear as well as outerwear.[19]

28.
Site of McVicker's Theatre
Madison St. west of State St.

McVicker's Theatre is a long-lost piece in the puzzle of Chicago history. The original burned down in the Chicago Fire of 1871; three more theaters were built on the site, the last being torn down in 1922 and replaced by a movie palace. Whatever the incarnation, McVicker's Theatre has turned up in literature many times after it was built by James H. McVicker in 1857. Sarah Bernhardt created a sensation when she was on its playbill 100 years ago. She starred in a series of classic plays, including *Adrienne Lecouvreur* and *Phaedre.* John Wilkes Booth played there in Shakespeare's *Richard III* in 1862. Harriet Monroe remembered seeing his brother, Edwin Booth, on that stage in *Hamlet.*

In Frank Norris's *The Pit,* Laura Dearborn and her family have come here from Boston and are enjoying Chicago to the hilt. "Now it was another opera party, now a box at McVicker's, now a dinner, or more often a drive through Lincoln Park behind Jadwin's trotters."

Bookstores

Art Institute of Chicago Bookstore, 111 S. Michigan Ave. 312/443-3535.

Barbara's Bookstore, 333 S. Wacker Dr. 312/466-0223,
2 N. Riverside Plz. 312/258-8007.

Bariff Shop for Judaica, Spertus Museum of Judaica,
618 S. Michigan Ave. 312/322-1740.

Borders Books Music & Café, 150 N. State St. 312/606-0750,
830 N. Michigan Ave. 312/573-0564.

Brent Books & Cards, 309 W. Washington St. 312/364-0126.

Columbia College Bookstore, 624 S. Michigan Ave. 312/427-4860.

Crown Books, 105 S. Wabash Ave. 312/782-7667,
144 S. Clark St. 312/856-0613.

Powell's Books, Burnham Park Plaza, 828 S. Wabash Ave. 312/341-0748.

Prairie Avenue Bookshop, 418 S. Wabash Ave. 312/922-8311.

Rain Dog Books, 404 S. Michigan Ave. 312/922-1200.

Robert Morris College Bookstore, 180 N. LaSalle St. 312/836-4856.

Sandmeyer's Bookstore, 714 S. Dearborn St. 312/922-2104.

Secondhand Prose, Harold Washington Library Center,
400 S. State St., 1st Floor. 312/747-4112.

The Savvy Traveller, 310 S. Michigan Ave. 312/587-0808.

Coffeehouses and More

Beyond Words Café, Harold Washington Library Center,
400 S. State St., 9th Floor. 312/922-7743.

Buckingham Café and Grill, just east of Buckingham Fountain, between Columbus Dr. and Lake Shore Dr. 312/922-6847.

Corner Bakery Café, 224 S. Michigan Ave. 312/431-7600, Chicago Cultural Center, 78 E. Washington Blvd. 312/201-0805, Field Museum, Lake Shore Dr. and Roosevelt Rd. 312/588-1040.

Gourmand Coffee and Teas, 728 S. Dearborn St. 312/427-2610

Torrefazione Italia, 30 N. La Salle St. 312/920-9024.

Other Places of Interest

Adler Planetarium, 1300 S. Lake Shore Dr. 312/322-0300.

Art Institute of Chicago, 111 S. Michigan Ave. 312/443-3600.

Blackstone Hotel, 636 S. Michigan Ave. 312/427-4300.

Buckingham Fountain, Grant Park, across from Congress Blvd. Open daily Oct. 1-May 1.

Chicago Cultural Center, 78 E. Washington Blvd. 312/744-6630. Department of Cultural Affairs. 312/744-6630. Museum of Broadcast Communications. 312/629-6000.

Chicago Hilton & Towers Hotel, 720 S. Michigan Ave. 312/922-4400.

Chicago Symphony Orchestra, 220 S. Michigan Ave. 312/294-3000.

Columbia College, 600 S. Michigan Ave. 312/663-1600.

Field Museum, Lake Shore Dr. and Roosevelt Rd. 312/922-9410.

John G. Shedd Aquarium, 1200 S. Lake Shore Dr. East. 312/939-2438.

Soldier Field, McFetridge Dr. and Lake Shore Dr.

Spertus Museum of Judaica, 618 S. Michigan Ave. 312/222-1747.

NEAR NORTH SIDE

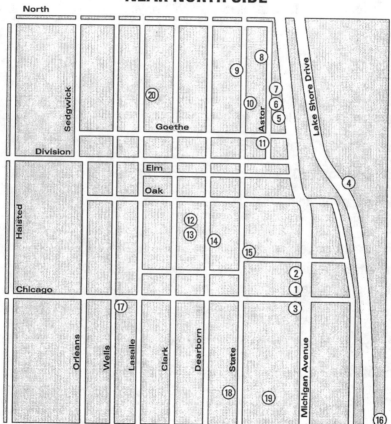

Map by Michael Polydoris.

Near North Side

Around the time of Chicago's so-called "literary renaissance" (which took place 1912-1925, according to Chicago's own *Encyclopaedia Britannica*) the neighborhood immediately north of downtown was a gathering place for poets, *By Jeff Hall.*

Harriet Monroe

novelists, journalists, and others who made their living by the written word, as well as artists and other Bohemians. The Near North Side was the place to hang out and occasionally perform one's work, just as trendy areas like Wicker Park and Bucktown are today.

After leaving their Loop offices at the end of the day, some struggling young writers whose names are now household words would walk up State or Dearborn to head for their apartments—or, just as likely—to kibbitz, perform, and share ideas at their favorite cafés, parks, or watering holes. It could happen on any given night in the area just north of Division Street.

Harriet Monroe commuted from her *Poetry* magazine offices at 543 Cass (which has since been renamed Wabash) to her home on Astor. Carl Sandburg and Ben Hecht, after the *Chicago Daily News* was put to bed, might have dinner at a favorite journalists' hangout called Schlogl's on North Wells Street and then head for some hijinks at the Dil Pickle Club. This tiny club was set up in a barn just off of North Dearborn Street, around the corner from the Newberry Library. They were often joined by future playwright Charles MacArthur, critic Maxwell Bodenheim, and, when he was in town, the novelist Sinclair Lewis (the author of *Babbitt* and *Main Street*).

After he fled what he once described as the "wide lawns and narrow minds" of Oak Park, young Ernest Hemingway got a job as a copywriter in the Loop and lived with a series of friends around Clark and Division. He and his first wife Hadley took an apartment on North Clark that was so dreary that they eventually acted on their dream of moving to Paris and became charter members of the Lost Generation.

These days, the Near North Side has an altogether different character. The area today is called the Gold Coast because it contains some of the world's most valuable real estate. When realtors talk about "location, location, location," they're referring to places like this.

In terms of history, at least, the real estate boom has taken a toll. The rooming house where Sherwood Anderson wrote *Winesburg, Ohio* has been replaced by a parking garage. No trace of the Dil Pickle Club remains. Sleek apartment and condo buildings far outnumber coffeehouses such as the Red Star Inn or the Black Cat Club that Hemingway used to visit.

Although Potter Palmer's famous mansion, Michigan Ave. and Oak St., which reportedly had no doorknobs on the exterior (everyone, including the Palmers themselves, had to be admitted by butlers or maids), was torn down in 1950, many of the other magnificent structures that were built for the rich and famous do remain. The combination of past literary history and present-day elegance makes the Near North Side a stimulating place to visit. The walking tour described in the pages that follow is pleasant all by itself but it can be easily combined with additional excursions to North Michigan Avenue just to the south, or Old Town just to the west.

How to Get There

Parking around here is difficult to find and expensive when you do find it. Public transportation serves you better. If you're taking the CTA's Red Line, exit at the Division Street subway stop, then walk east on Division. Or, take the 146 or 151 bus and exit between Walton and Oak Streets.

Walking Tour

1.
Chicago Water Tower
Chicago and Michigan Aves. 312/751-1600

This Chicago landmark, originally built in 1869, is one of the few structures in the area to survive the Great Chicago Fire of 1871. It earned the scorn of Oscar Wilde when the English playwright toured America in February, 1882, and began a brief but torrid love-hate affair with the city. First, he was greeted with head-lines such as the following in a daily newspaper (now defunct) called the *Chicago Inter-Ocean:*

> SAINT OSCAR DE WILDE
> ARRIVES, LILIES AND
> ALL, IN CHICAGO

Not to be outdone, the *Chicago Daily News* her-alded his presence with a poem entitled "Wilde Oscar" that began:

> The simpering Oscar comes,
> The West awaits his wonder.
> As bullfrogs list to beating drums,
> Or hearken to the thunder...[1]

OSCAR WILDE.

The Esthetic Apostle Greeted by an Immense Audience.

Chiefly Drawn to Central Music-Hall by a Marked Curiosity.

"The Chicago Water-Works Tower a Castellated Monstrosity."

"Only an Oriental Beauty Can Wear the Sunflower."

Chicago Tribune, *Tuesday, February 14, 1882.*

When Wilde dined at a private Chicago home, young boys milled outside, jeering and waving sun-flowers and lilies; the hosts had to smuggle him out through a back alley—though a few urchins continued to pursue him there as well.[2]

Wilde was lounging in his hotel suite when he commented to reporters that Chicago society was mildly passable but the city itself was "too dreary for me." Of the city's buildings, he remarked: "Why don't you get some good public dwellings?"[3] Wilde's most notorious barb was aimed at the venerable Water Tower, which was revered by many because it had survived the Great Fire. In a lecture called "The Decorative Arts," Wilde outraged Chicagoans when he described this structure as "a castellated monstrosity with pepper-boxes stuck all over it."

A local grifter named Hungry Joe Lewis allegedly relieved Wilde of several thousand dollars during his time in the United States—a swindle mentioned by Nelson Algren in his famous prose poem *Chicago: City on the Make.*[4]

Chicago seemed to grow on Wilde, and he even modified his initial evaluation of the Water Tower by admiring its machinery and describing it as "simple, grand, and natural." When he left, he complimented the handsomeness of the Chicago women and the hospitality of its citizens.

The mood of the press, however, did not seem to mellow. When Wilde left town, a newspaper gave him the following fond farewell: "Go, Mr. Wilde, and may the sunflower wither at your gaze."

2.
Borders Books Music & Café
830 N. Michigan Ave. 312/573-0564

I have mixed feelings about Borders. On the upside, this particular location features a beautiful café overlooking Michigan Avenue; capturing one of the highly-prized seats along the windows provides free entertainment (i.e., terrific people-watching). You can also attend more official functions such as readings and musical performances. And I can't ignore the fact that their huge selection includes my computer books.

On the downside, any longtime Chicago resident who laments the passing of small independent bookstores such as Guild Books on Lincoln Avenue or Booksellers Row can point directly to big national bookstore chains as the culprit. Suggested compromise: buy your coffee here, and shop for books at places such as **Brent Books & Cards** (see p. 73), **Barbara's** (see p. 73), **Powell's** (see p. 48), or the other local merchants who contribute so much to the life of the city and its neighborhoods.

3.
American Girl Place
111 E. Chicago Ave. 312/943 9400

My daughters wouldn't forgive me if I failed to mention this mecca of girldom. In terms of literature, the series of books on each of the dolls that make up the American Girls Collection is pretty good. Each girl's make-believe life growing up in a particular time and place in American history is described in a series of books that are all written by the same author. The books about Kirsten take place in the mid-nineteenth century and are written by Janet Shaw, for instance. The ones about Molly are set during and after World War II and are written by Valerie Tripp. There is a free exhibit about each of the girls in the basement. As for the price tags in other parts of this facility, harden yourself to feminine pleas . . . you're on your own.

4.
Oak Street Beach
Oak St. and Lake Michigan

Walk north on Michigan Avenue; consider having tea at the Drake Hotel; admire the sunbathers at the Oak Street Beach. In *St. Valentine's Night* by Andrew M. Greeley, Neal Connor is attacked in the long Oak Street underpass that pedestrians use to walk beneath Lake Shore Drive to the beach. The perpetrator tries to escape by running across the Drive and is, not surprisingly, killed by an oncoming car.

5.
Home of Harriet Monroe
1310 N. Astor St.

Turn left on Division Street, then turn right on Astor. Astor, located just one block west of Lake Shore Drive between Division and North, was named for John Jacob Astor and has long been identified with Chicago society. It's very pleasant to stroll past all the old homes and townhouses.

Harriet Monroe and her family moved to 1310 N. Astor, which was a house designed by her brother-in-law John Wellborn Root. Root, with his partner Daniel Burnham, founded the Chicago School of Architecture.

Monroe wrote in her memoirs that in the Astor Street house she and "a few of the Little Room writers—Henry Blake Fuller, Edith Wyatt, Margaret Potter, and one or two others—used to meet and try out our stories and poems."

Monroe was the founder and first editor of *Poetry* magazine, which had offices at 543 Cass. She corresponded with, and published, poets such as Ezra Pound, William Butler Yeats, William Carlos Williams, Robert Frost, Vachel Lindsay, and T. S. Eliot. *Poetry* was the first magazine to accept Carl Sandburg's poems—his *Chicago Poems* were published in March, 1914. Its battle was for "freer technique, for stripped modern diction, for a more vital relation with the poet's own time and place . . . "[5] *Poetry* was also the first to publish T. S. Eliot. When *Poetry* first appeared, the *New York World* declared that Chicago was "henceforth to be recognized as the true center of literary art . . . "[6]

6.
Home of Irna Phillips
1335 N. Astor St.

When you hear the word "writer," what probably pops into your head are poets, novelists, and journalists. But another kind of writer lived in the sleek apartment building at 1335 N. Astor who was nonetheless very successful and influential. Irna Phillips is credited with creating the first successful radio soap opera, as well as writing scripts for a vast number of television soaps.

7.
German Poets' streets
Goethe and Schiller Sts.

These two streets are named after the German poets Johann Wolfgang von Goethe and Friedrich von Schiller. And, if you're a real groupie of theirs, you can gaze upon their visages in the form of statues in Lincoln Park.

Queen of the Soaps

Irna Phillips was a consummate writer. For one thing, she could churn out as many as 60,000 words per week. If the occasion demanded, Phillips could come up with as many as three scripts per day. Her secretary would type whatever came out of her mouth as she paced the floor acting out all the parts. Second, Phillips seemed to thrive under deadline pressure. Sometimes, pages would be snatched as they emerged from her secretary's typewriter, rushed to a mimeograph machine, and thrust directly into the hands of actors who were on the air in a nearby radio studio.

Phillips was never content to sit around waiting for others to make their move first. In 1930, she got tired of being a schoolteacher in Dayton, Ohio, and so she took off for Chicago. She somehow persuaded WGN to give her 15 minutes of radio time a day for a family drama she called *Painted Dreams,* which is credited with being the first soap opera. Leaving nothing to chance, she herself played the role of the main character, Mother Moynihan.

Later, she came up with radio soap opera hits such as *Road of Life* and *Woman in White.* She originated the types of plots that are now classics: someone is hit over the head and develops amnesia; someone is kidnapped; someone is put on trial.

> **If the occasion demanded, Phillips could come up with as many as three scripts per day.**

She had more going for her than beginner's luck. For example, her radio show *Guiding Light* was not only the first serial adapted to television, but it also became the longest-running soap opera in broadcast history.

Nor was she the type to rest on her laurels. Phillips astonished industry observers in 1956 when her half-hour drama *As the World Turns* was joined at the top of the ratings by her crime-oriented half-hour *The Edge of Night.*

8.
Patterson-McCormick Mansion
20 E. Burton Pl./1500 N. Astor St.

Some writers manage to preserve more than their words for posterity. The mansion at the northwest corner of Burton and Astor was built for Elinor Patterson, daughter of Joseph Medill, the publisher of the *Chicago Tribune* and a mayor of Chicago. Cyrus H. McCormick bought the building in 1914.

9.
Playboy Mansion
1340 N. State Pkwy.

Walk to North, turn left, and check out the Archbishop's residence and the Chicago Historical Society building across North. Then turn south on State to contemplate the history of a more worldly religion—the religion of sex.

1340 N. State Pkwy. was once the home and office of *Playboy* magazine founder and publisher and all-around swinger, Hugh Hefner. It was so self-contained that during one three-year period, Hef left his urban paradise only nine times. It was also the location for the filming of the *Playboy After Dark* television show.

Hefner, the onetime *Esquire* cartoonist, founded *Playboy* magazine in 1953 and expanded it into a worldwide empire. The Palmolive Building at Michigan and Walton was known as the Playboy Building when the magazine was published there. At this writing, Hefner's daughter Christie is chairman of the board of Playboy Enterprises, Inc. In early 2000, Hefner returned to his old stomping grounds as a portion of West Walton was named Hugh Hefner Way in his honor—over the protests of feminists who took exception to his magazine's treatment of women.

In Richard Stern's story *East, West... Midwest,* an unstable typist named Miss Cameron becomes obsessed with a historian named Bidwell. After four years of regular five o'clock tea at Pixley and Ehler's restaurant downtown, she commits suicide by throwing herself from a 10th-floor window of the Playboy Building. A spokesman for *Playboy* comments that "perhaps the building was chosen as a deranged protest or symbol, but, of course, there was nothing to be done about that."

10.
Omni Ambassador East Hotel Author's Suite
1301 N. State Pkwy. 312/573-6040

For $225 a night, you can stay at the "Author's Suite," in the Omni Ambassador East. This three-room complex on the 16th floor is designed especially for traveling authors who are promoting their books, but it is also a temporary home for editors and publishers. You'll be more than comfy with overstuffed chairs, brass reading lamps, a fireplace, a leather-topped writing desk, and historic paintings. The main attractions, though, are the 150 or so volumes signed by former guests including Jimmy Breslin, Shel Silverstein, Alex Haley, Kirk Douglas, and Danielle Steel. Thomas Hoving, author of *Making the Mummies Dance* and curator of the Metropolitan Museum in New York, learned while staying in the suite that his book had made a bestseller list. But get your reservations in early. The literary crowd keeps the suite booked 90 percent of the time.

11.
Ernest Hemingway residences
1230 N. State St.
1300 N. Clark St.
63 E. Division St.

As a young man, Ernest Hemingway left Oak Park to live with his friend Bill Horne in an apartment at 1230 N. State. They frequented long-vanished watering holes such as the Red Star Inn and the Venice Café.

In a letter written to his first wife Hadley while they were courting, the young writer reported that Lake Shore Drive in winter looks like "white piping on gray ruffles, indistinguishable from the sky."[7] Later, he moved in with another friend, Kenley Smith, at 63 E. Division, on January 7, 1921.[8] One respite from the urban scene was retreating to a cottage in an artists' colony in

Michael Anania

Born in 1939 in Omaha, Michael Anania is a poet, novelist, essayist, ex-steel worker, and professor of English at the University of Illinois at Chicago. His published work includes six volumes of poetry, and he appears in the *Norton Anthology of Poetry.* His novel, *The Red Menace,* was recently released in paperback. He responded to the Nelson Algren *City on the Make* quote:

> Algren invented a Chicago to suit his work . . . a Chicago played by hustlers, con artists, and fixers . . . a nighttime city switched on each evening when the North Side's first "torpedo" reached a cue up to snap on the light above a pool table. It was a dark but oddly romantic place, the capital of "the nation of furnished rooms" and fall guys, lit like a New Masses woodcut by a bulb that stamped out a small space ineffectually on the dark.
>
> What made Algren's Chicago persuasive is that the grifters, pug fighters, dealers, and junkies were all there. But, of course, there was and is much more. Algren's Chicago is not the working city of Dreiser, Herrick, Farrell, or Halper that grinds down its individuals. It's not the capitalist monster of Frank Norris or Sherwood Anderson. It's not Saul Bellow's "raw slangy town" or Harry Mark Petrakis's sometimes regal, always ceremonial, place. And it's certainly not Richard Wright's Chicago or Cyrus Colter's or Gwendolyn Brooks's or Leon Forrest's. The hulking beast Dreiser sees brooding over Sister Carrie the first day that she goes out looking for work in Chicago and the "white matron" one of Colter's characters sees in the Wrigley Building's flood-lit facade are just as persuasive and represent totally different views of the city. Writers invent Chicago as they go. If their invention is both telling and true, then the city—that version of the city, at least—is theirs. They don't so much belong to it, as it belongs to them. For a while, if it gives us a sense of things in the mad welter of the place, slowing it down or spinning it faster, turning our glance once and for all their way, then we belong to their city.
>
> Part of the South Branch of the river is now Stuart Dybek's; West Taylor Street is Tina da Rosa's, the lake breeze Larry Heinemann's; the Hancock Plaza is—until somebody does it better—Jim McManus's; a quadrant of the suburbs belongs to Charles Newman, another to Mary Morris, another to Maxine Chernoff; the South Shore was taken from Farrell by Stanley Elkin.

The South Side has been opened and reopened by Angela Jackson, Sterling Plumpp, and Sandra Jackson; Pilsen by Sandra Cisneros; Near North by Mark Costello and Tony Ardizzone. And on it quite reasonably goes.

Chicago is more exacting than most places for writers because it is a fabled place and because it has been so written so well so many times. Unlike most places that merely ask for description, Chicago seems to tease us toward definition, like Algren's, sweeping formulae that might capture and explain it. It's in the word—or at least in the way we say it—Chicago, as though it were still a mythic place whose essential qualities swirl round its mere saying. Listen to Studs say it, and it's still there, tinged with Dreiser, Wright, Sandberg, Farrell, and Algren, Midway and Grey City, together with a dash of the Beulah-land that promises "sweet home Chicago."

And belonging to . . . ? Well, everyone's family seems more settled than your own, and everyone else's city—Boston, New Orleans, San Francisco—seems more a place of belonging than yours. What matters is how interesting the city is for the writers who live here, how much it still gives back when they push at it, or the extent to which it has become just a place to live and work.

Photo courtesy UIC
Photographic Services.

Palos Park rented by Sherwood Anderson.

After their marriage, Ernest and Hadley lived in a dingy, shabby apartment in the 1300 block of North Clark Street. Their boredom and frustration led to one main form of inspiration: the idea that they should get out of the city. They soon left for Paris, following the advice of Anderson who had recently returned from its more friendly atmosphere. Perhaps in gratitude, the Hemingways bequeathed to him their leftover canned goods when they vacated their apartment. Years later, Anderson recalled the sight of young Hemingway climbing the stairs carrying a sack full of foodstuffs.

12.
Newberry Library
60 W. Walton St. 312/943-9090

Walk west on Division, turn north on Dearborn, and head for the Newberry Library, 60 W. Walton. The Library was founded by Walter Loomis Newberry,

Photo by Greg Holden.

Washington Square Park with the Newberry Library in the background.

who came to Chicago in 1833. The city received half of his fortune after his death on a sea liner bound for Europe. The captain chose to place his body in a cask of Medford rum that was part of the cargo. Cask and corpse were eventually returned to Chicago for burial in Graceland Cemetery.

The Newberry is the place to go in Chicago if you have been bitten by the genealogy bug or are doing scholarly research. The library's holdings include a copy of the First Folio of Shakespeare's works, as well as many other rare and specialized books. Its vast collections of Americana include the history and literature of Native Americans and of the Midwest. The papers of Katherine Mansfield, Ben Hecht, and Sherwood Anderson are at the Newberry. Plus, the library building now houses the office of *Poetry* magazine.

Admission to the reading rooms is free. Sign in at the front gate to register for a reader's card that is valid for one year. The reading rooms are open Tues.-Thurs. 10 A.M.-6 P.M. and Fri.-Sat. 9 A.M.-5 P.M.; the bookstore is open Mon., Fri., and Sat. 9 A.M.-5 P.M., Tues. and Thurs. 9 A.M.-6 P.M., and Wed. 9 A.M.-7:30 P.M.; and tours are given Thurs. 3 P.M. and Sat. 10:30 A.M. For more information on library collections and services, call 312/255-3506.

13.
Washington Square Park

South of Newberry Library, bounded by Walton, Clark, and Dearborn Sts. and Institute Pl.

This was Chicago's first public park. It earned its unofficial name of Bughouse Square in the 1920s when anyone could get up on a soapbox and issue diatribes about the world's problems in the fashion of Speaker's Corner in London. In Ben Hecht's biography of his writing partner Charles MacArthur, he recalls a "monster feast of reason" held in Bughouse Square to raise money for a poet named Lestram Weber. Weber had been fined $600 for throwing an ink pot through the window of a second-hand bookstore trying to hit a police alarm that was keeping him awake with its incessant ringing. The gathering began in Tooker Alley, and the march was led by "Trip Hammer Johnson and the Dil Pickle Symphony Orchestra."[9]

Every July, the Newberry holds a terrific used book sale, during which speakers gather in the park to recreate the old Bughouse Square atmosphere.

14.
Site of the Dil Pickle Club
800 block of N. Dearborn Pkwy.

In the 800 block of North Dearborn Parkway, between Institute and Chestnut, is an unassuming little alley. This is what remains of what was already one of the shortest streets in Chicago in the early decades of the twentieth century: Tooker Place. A barn that opened onto the alley at 18 Tooker Place was the site of the Dil Pickle Club, a favorite hang-out of Carl Sandburg, Ben Hecht, and others. It was founded by a radical soapbox orator named Jack Jones, who put on lectures, poetry readings, and one-act plays. A sign over the entrance read "Step High, Bend Low, and Leave Your Dignity Outside."

In a letter to a woman friend, Sherwood Anderson wrote what could have been ad copy for the Dil Pickle Club:

> Are you a struggling poet, groping your way through a dark and dreary commercial world? Have you written a prose masterpiece that some money-minded publisher will not publish? Are you an eager young feminist longing to lift womankind into a higher life? . . . Jack Jones and the Dill Pickle are looking for you.

Courtesy of the University of Chicago Archives, Joseph Regenstein Library.

Sherwood Anderson.

Jack Jones is the father, the mother, and the ringmaster of the Dill Pickle in Tooker alley, just off Dear-

Chicago's Greatest Sex Writer

You'll never find the name Jack Woodford mentioned in the same breath as Chicago's more highly regarded literary lights. That wasn't the writer's real name, anyway. Due to the nature of the man's work, he used a number of pseudonyms, including Gordon Sayre, Sappho Henderson Britt, and Howard Hogue Kennedy.

Woodford's actual name was Josiah Pitts Woolfolk. He was brought up on the Near North Side by his grandmother, and his parents lived nearby as well. Today, whatever notoriety Woolfolk has is through his pseudonyms, under which he wrote more than 75 pulp fiction books (he himself described them as "sex novels") with titles like *White Heat, Sin and Such,* and *Love in Louisiana.* Some of the stories are set in Chicago; many have lurid covers and are eagerly collected and traded on the Internet auction site eBay.

Woolfolk was a friend of Clarence Darrow and many other Chicago writers. There's even been a memorial edition of some of his works, which includes *My Years with Capone: Jack Woodford and Al Capone, 1924-1932,* in which author Neil Elliott interviews Woodford/Woolfolk about Chicago's most notorious gangster.

Pulp Fiction—Chicago Style

born, north of Chicago Avenue, on the north side.

You may have visited the neighborhood. There is a charming little park just around the corner from the Pickle. It is filled with benches and trees and the big, grim, wise looking Newberry Library looks down on it. Before Jones came to gather together what he calls his "trained band of ants" the poor homeless nuts lived with the squirrels in the park. On warm Sunday afternoons they came forth in droves. One by one they climbed upon soap boxes and talked to the sad-eyed loafers gathered about.[10]

Every Thursday night, Anderson wrote, the Dil Pickle was filled with devotees of the arts. One lecture was given by a woman on "Men Who Have Made Love to Me."

Sandburg played his guitar, read poetry, and took part in political discussions here. Ben Hecht and Charles MacArthur staged a play here. Other visitors included Sinclair Lewis, Vachel Lindsay, and Robert Frost.[11] The Dil Pickle Club was only one of several Bohemian hangouts in the Water Tower-Bughouse Square neighborhood early in the twentieth century, including the Black Cat Club and the Radical Bookshop. Little remains of the former Bohemian-radical character of this area today, despite the presence of the nearby Washington Park and Bughouse Square. In fact, as you stroll down the alley imagining these literary giants striding to and fro, you would be well advised to keep an eye out for Range Rovers and Lexuses backing out of the present-day garages.

To visit the site of another Sandburg hangout, walk south on Dearborn to Chestnut, turn left (east) on Chestnut, and walk one block to State.

15.
Former site of Abraham Lincoln Book Shop
18 E. Chestnut St.

From 1946 to 1990, 18 E. Chestnut was the location of the Abraham Lincoln Book Shop, run by Lincoln scholar and big-time FOS (Friend of Sandburg) named Ralph Newman.

According to Daniel R. Weinberg, who runs the bookstore these days at 357 W. Chicago, 312/944-3085, www.ALincolnBookShop.com, the 18 E. Chestnut location was a place for researchers to work, receive feedback, and even camp out if need be. Weinberg lists such American history scholars as John Hope Franklin, Bruce Catton, and Shelby Foote as having visited the store early in their careers. Carl Sandburg worked on his monumental life of Abraham Lincoln in a room upstairs, bringing the drafts down to the store at intervals for criticism.

When you've breathed in all the rarefied atmosphere you can handle, walk south on Dearborn and turn left (east) on Chicago to head back to the Water Tower.

Driving Tour

16.
Chicago Shakespeare Theater
Navy Pier, 800 E. Grand Ave. 312/595-5600

Although William Shakespeare never visited Chicago, judging by the wild popularity of this theater his spirit feels right at home in the Windy City. The productions are full of modern bells and whistles, but this facility, which opened in fall 1999, is designed to resemble the Globe Theatre, where Shakespeare's plays were originally produced in London. Tickets are hard to come by, but at the very least you can browse through the theater's bookstore and quaff an ale in its English pub.

17.
Abraham Lincoln Book Shop
357 W. Chicago Ave. 312/944-3085

The present-day location of the store is filled with Lincoln memorabilia—some for sale and some just for admiring. You'll find books from Lincoln's own library, some of his handwritten legal briefs, letters to his wife, and even a bed from his home in Springfield. The shop frequently holds autographing parties for authors and lectures on Lincoln and related topics.

18.
Tree Studio
9-11 W. Ontario St.

People come from all over the world to hear music and visit the museums and restaurants that crowd the streets around Ontario and State. But not far from the tourist hubbub surrounding the Hard Rock Café and other sites, you'll find the intricately carved entranceway to the Tree Studio, 9-11 W. Ontario, which provides a quiet and serene place to work for primarily visual artists. Small-scale publishers and aspiring authors, however, were among the literary community that originally gathered in the low-rent studios that Judge Lambert Tree erected in 1894 in the backyard of his house. His goal was to keep alive the innovative cultural milieu that had been created—despite a persistently depressed economy that hampered the arts in general—by the hundreds of young people who were drawn to Chicago by the World's Columbian Exposition of 1893. The now-booming economy threatens the community, as big-scale developers keep eyeing the Tree Studio property and the adjacent Medinah Temple. But architecture and history lovers are continuing the good fight to at least preserve the facades of the buildings. It remains to be seen whether the Judge's vision will continue to be realized. (Note the listing for something called The Rat Pack Club in the directory next to the Tree Studio's front door.)

Photo by Greg Holden.

Tree Studio.

19.
Sherwood Anderson residence
735 N. Wabash Ave.

Sherwood Anderson lived on the second floor of a red brick boarding house at 735 Cass (now Wabash) where he finished writing *Winesburg, Ohio.* Like many of the historic sites in this desirable area, it was bulldozed long ago and is now a parking garage. The reputation of the book, in contrast, continues to thrive, as it contains some of the most influential and striking American short stories ever written.[12]

Anderson moved to the Near North Side to be among the other Bohemian artists and writers who flocked to the area in the 'teens, many of whom were fellow tenants in the same rooming house.[13] He reported that his "first real writing" occurred in this room, and it was his great artistic breakthrough:

I walked along a city street in the snow. I was working at work that I hated. . . . I was ill, discouraged, broke. I was living in a cheap rooming house. I remember that I went upstairs and into the room. It was very shabby . . . I grew desperate, went and threw up my window. I sat by the open window. It began to catch snow. "I'll catch cold sitting here. What do I care?" There was some paper on a small kitchen table I had bought and had brought up into the room. I turned on the light and began to write. I wrote, without looking up . . . a story called "Hands." It was and is a beautiful story.[14]

20.
Carl Sandburg Village
Bounded by North Ave., Division, Clark, and LaSalle Sts.

Carl Sandburg Village, completed in 1965, was intended to function as a city within the city. It's a huge development of townhouses, apartments, and stores that mostly serves young singles. The apartments were converted to condominiums in the 1970s. The Sandburg Village movie theater was torn down in 1983, but you can still buy wine at the **Sandburg Wine Cellar**, 1525 N. Clark; get your shirts cleaned at the **Sandburg Cleaners**, 1355 N. Sandburg; get your nuts and bolts at **Sandburg Ace Hardware**, 110 W. Germania; and—you get the idea.

The tall buildings that line the west side of Clark between Division and North are named after different poets. They include Eliot, Dickinson, and Kilmer Houses.

21.
Old Criminal Courts Building
54 W. Hubbard St.

Completed in 1892, this huge structure housed the Cook County Criminal Courts. Reporters Carl Sandburg, Ben Hecht, and Charles MacArthur came from their *Chicago Daily News* offices to what was known as Courthouse Place to cover trials and write about the criminal proceedings of the day.

It was here that Clarence Darrow defended Leopold and Loeb in 1929 for the murder of young Bobby Franks. The Cook County Jail was across the alley,

Photo by Thayer Lindner.

The former Criminal Courts Building,
now CourtHouse Place.

and Darrow undoubtedly spent a substantial amount of time there visiting with clients.

Clarence Darrow was himself a writer of fiction. His 1905 novel *An Eye for an Aye* is a stark, grim account of a man accused of killing his wife. The entire book takes the form of a first-person narration as the prisoner tells his story to a friend who visits him in jail just before he is to be executed.

The Women's Ward of the Cook County Jail is the setting for Maurine Watkins' classic 1927 play *Chicago,* which was turned into the musical choreographed by Chicagoan Bob Fosse in the 1970s. In the story, Roxie Hart is described as "the prettiest woman ever charged with murder in Chicago."

22.
Horse stables on Orleans

If you are having a hard time imagining the Near North Side as it was when Carl Sandburg and his contemporaries gathered here, visit the stables where the horses who pull the tourist carriages around the Water Tower area are housed. Choose either your feet or the elevated train to transport you while you read this vivid passage from Frank Norris's novel *The Pit.* I guarantee you a trip into the past:

> Outside the weather continued lamentable. The rain beat down steadily upon the heaps of snow on the grass-plats by the curbstones, melting it, dirtying it, and reducing it to viscid slush. The sky was lead grey; the trees, bare and black as though built of iron and wire, dripped incessantly. The sparrows, huddling under the house-eaves or in interstices of the mouldings,

chirped feebly from time to time, sitting disconsolate, their feathers puffed out till their bodies assumed globular shapes. Delivery wagons trundled up and down the street at intervals, the horses and drivers housed in oil-skins.

The neighborhood was quiet. There was no sound of voices in the streets. But occasionally, from far away in the direction of the river or the Lake Front, came the faint sounds of steamer and tug whistles. The sidewalks in either directions were deserted. Only a solitary policeman, his star pinned to the outside of his dripping rubber coat, his helmet shedding rivulets, stood on the corner absorbed in the contemplation of the brown torrent of the gutter plunging into a sewer vent.[15]

23.
Chicago's journalistic tradition
Tribune Tower, 435 N. Michigan Ave. 312/222-3994
Chicago Sun-Times Building, 401 N. Wabash Ave. 312/321-2350
Billy Goat Tavern, 430 N. Michigan Ave., lower level. 312/222-1525

The literary tradition of the wisecracking Chicago newspaperman dates back to Ben Hecht and Charles MacArthur's 1927 play *The Front Page.* The *Chicago Daily News,* which was published from 1876 to 1978, "produced more books by its writers than any other American newspaper," according to Clarence A. Andrews (*Chicago in Story,* p. 326).

Today, some watering holes that newspaper employees used to frequent, like Riccardo's and Schlogl's, are gone, but the Billy Goat Tavern remains and, in the afternoons and evenings, you're still likely to see reporters kibitzing and drinking as they complain, gossip, and try to relax.

The Billy Goat was a favorite stop for columnist Mike Royko. He often wrote about the Billy Goat's owner, Sam Sianis, blaming him for putting a hex on the Chicago Cubs that has prevented them from winning a pennant since 1945. But Royko was only one of a long line of Chicago newspaper columnists who ultimately became famous for writing books, including Eugene Field, Ben Hecht, Ring Lardner, Jack Mabley, Sydney J. Harris, and Bob Greene.

George Ade, a columnist working in the 1890s, moved to Chicago from rural Indiana. He worked for the *News-Record,* which was the morning edition of the *Chicago Daily News.* It was later called the *Chicago Record.* Finley Peter Dunne worked there as well, along with Will Payne, the novelist. Ade, along with the artist John T. McCutcheon, had a column called "Stories of the Streets and of the Town" for seven years beginning in 1893. He experimented with dialogue, short stories, verse, and fables. The *Record* published eight editions of Ade's columns in paperback form.[16] Ade's column "The Advantage of Being Middle Class" contains a detailed description of the Near North Side area 100 years ago:

> Dearborn Avenue leads to the lights and shadows and cool depths of Lincoln Park. First there is a broad, smooth roadway, which shows boldly in the electric glare, and then there's a deeply shaded drive between solid walls of trees. It widens and brings into dim outline a dark statue with a massive pedestal. Each wheelman coursing the drives is marked by a speck of lantern, and the illusion is that of racing fireflies. No carriages disturb the night with a clatter of hoofs. Under the trees, right and left, the shade is so deep that sometimes voices may be heard where no one can be seen. Only a few feet away a flood of light shows every blade of grass and every pebble. All roads into the park lead to some circling pathway which is laced with the black shadows of trembling leaves, while misshapen blotches of the blending light fall on the figures and the benches.[17]

An illustration by John McCutcheon from one of George Ade's collections of columns.

Bookstores

Abraham Lincoln Book Shop, 357 W. Chicago Ave. 312/944-3085.

After-Words, 23 E. Illinois St. 312/464-1110.

Barbara's Bookstore, Navy Pier, 700 E. Grand Ave. 312/222-0890, 1350 N. Wells St. 312/642-5044.

Barnes & Noble, 1130 N. State St. 312/280-8155.

Beck's Book Store, 50 E. Chicago Ave. 312/944-7685.

Borders Books Music & Café, 830 N. Michigan Ave. 312/573-0564.

Chicago Children's Museum Store, Navy Pier, 700 E. Grand Ave. 312/595-0600.

Chicago Rare Book Center, 56 W. Maple St. 312/988-7246. Open 11 A.M.-6 P.M. Mon.-Sat., 12 P.M.-5 P.M. Sun.

Children In Paradise, 909 N. Rush St. 312/951-5437.

Europa Bookstore, 832 N. State St. 312/335-9677.

Moody Bookstore, 150 W. Chicago Ave. 312/329-4352.

Newberry Library Bookstore, A. C. McClurg's, 60 W. Walton Ave. 312/255-3520.

Virgin Mega Store, 540 N. Michigan Ave. 312/645-9300.

Waldenbooks, 900 N. Michigan Ave. 312/337-0330.

Coffeehouses and More

The definition of "coffeehouse" has to be stretched a bit in this neighborhood. It might be worth abandoning coffee for a while, though, to have high tea at the Drake, a cocktail at the Pump Room, or a "cheezborger, cheezborger" at the

Billy Goat Tavern.

Billy Goat Tavern, 430 N. Michigan Ave. 312/222-1525.

Borders Books Music & Café, 830 N. Michigan Ave. 312/573-0564.

Capra's Coffee, 205 E. Ohio St. 312/329-0063.

Caribou Coffee, 1561 N. Wells St. 312/266-7504,
1 W. Division St. 312/664-6789.

Coffee Expressions, 100 W. Oak St. 312/397-1515.

Color Me Coffee, 700 E. Grand Ave. 312/595-5520.

Drake Hotel, 140 E. Walton St. 312/787-2200.
Indulge in afternoon tea with cucumber sandwiches in the Drake's Palm
Court or Oak Terrace restaurant.

Peet's Coffee and Tea, 1000 W. North Ave. 312/475-9782.

Pump Room, Omni Ambassador East Hotel, 1301 N. State Pkwy.
312/573-6040.
The Pump Room was long considered the place to see and be seen in
Chicago.

Savories, 1651 N. Wells St. 312/951-7638.

Seattle's Best Coffee, 42 E. Chicago Ave. 312/227-0885,
701 N. Wells St. 312/649-9452.

Torrefazione Italia, 700 N. Michigan Ave. 312/766-6400,
680 N. Lake Shore Dr. 312/587-8332.

Other Places of Interest

Archbishop's Residence, 1555 N. State Pkwy.
The official residence of the head of the Roman Catholic Archdiocese of
Chicago was one of the first mansions in the area, built in 1880.

James Charnley House, 1365 N. Astor St. 312/915-0105.
Designed by Frank Lloyd Wright when he was just a draftsman in the firm
of Adler and Sullivan. Tours are given Tues., Thurs., and Sun. by the Society
of Architectural Historians.

Chicago Shakespeare Theater, Navy Pier, 600 E. Grand Ave.
312/595-5600.

Patterson- McCormick Mansion, 20 E. Burton Pl./1500 N. Astor St.
Designed by New York architect Stanford White, built in 1893.

Drake Hotel, 140 E. Walton St. 312/787-2200.

Graham Foundation for Advanced Studies in the Fine Arts,
4 W. Burton Pl. 312/787-4071.

International College of Surgeons, 1516 North Lake Shore Dr.
312/642-3555.
This building, designed by well-known architect Charles Van Doren Shaw,
contains the International Museum of Surgical Science, which includes a
collection of exhibits and items related to the history of surgery.

Navy Pier, 600 E. Grand Ave. 312/595-7437.

Playboy Mansion, 1340 N. State Pkwy.

Joseph T. Ryerson House, 1406 N. Astor St.
Designed by David Adler and built in 1922.

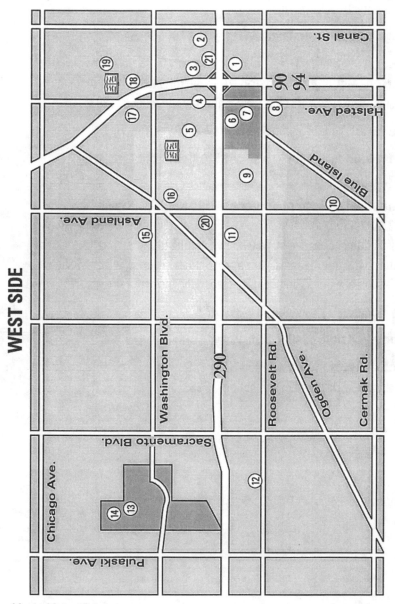

WEST SIDE

Map by Michael Polydoris.

West Side

After the factories, stores, and stockyards closed for the day, the captains of Chicago industry would go home to their mansions on Prairie Avenue, Astor Street, or Lake Shore Drive. Their workers would head home to more humble— but in some ways more colorful and historically rich—areas like those west of the Loop.

By Jeff Hall.   *Ana Castillo*

The West Side has been the Chicago entry point for many, and much of the literature associated with this part of the city has been for or about immigrants. Theodore Dreiser, who first came to Chicago in the 1880s at the age of 12, worked as a cashier in a dry goods store on West Madison until his mother made him quit; later he and his brother found work as newsboys. The family, he writes, lived in an apartment that was "One of a row of cream-colored flats, two blocks in extent, on West Madison Street at Throop."[1] Studs Terkel grew up near Cook County Hospital, 1835 W. Harrison. Stuart Dybek writes about the old Czech neighborhood, and Ana Castillo writes about the Mexicans who now live there. In a recent interview, Castillo said her character Carmen in her novel *Peel My Love Like an Onion* came to her during the Chicago heat wave of 1995, when she worked in the basement of her mother's home. In typical Chicago fashion, Carmen dances her way through the hot and often hostile city streets, overcoming physical problems and creating beauty both inside and out.[2]

Carmen describes a bar where a man tried to pick her up as the only Sapogon restaurant in town, though one that serves only "impostor Mexican food." In the 1980s, Carmen explains, "all kinds of people were moving to

Chicago from south of the border, variations of the Mexicans and Puerto Ricans I was used to when I was growing up." She listens as heartsick Cubans sing "Guantanamera," lonesome Mexicans croon "Cielito Lindo," and so on.[3]

The stories about the West Side contain an abundance of both hope and despair. In "The Books in Fred Hampton's Apartment," Richard Stern recalls the predawn raid on the building on West Monroe Street where Hampton, the chairman of the Black Panther Party's Illinois chapter, was killed in a predawn raid on December 4, 1969. Stern notices that the books in the apartment speak of individuals who were curious and interested in "self-improvement." They include James T. Farrell's *The Face of Time.*

In the classic novel *Knock On Any Door,* much of which is set on the West Side, Willard Motley portrays tough-guy hero Nick Romano, whose motto is to "Live fast, die young, and have a good-looking corpse."

The diversity of the many neighborhoods west of downtown produced literature that celebrates many different cultures; only in Chicago would you find writers and works from such a variety of backgrounds.

How to Get There

A few of the sites covered in this section are within convenient walking distance of the University of Illinois at Chicago. Hull House is virtually part of the campus; Taylor Street is only a few blocks west; and Greektown is only a block or two north on Halsted Street. Take the Halsted bus to the area, or the CTA Blue Line to the Morgan Street stop, and walk west across Harrison Street to enter the UIC campus. The rest of the sites are best reached by automobile.

Walking/Driving Tour

1.
Chicago Fire Academy
558 W. DeKoven St. 312/747-7238

This museum was built on the site of the spot where, according to legend, the Chicago Fire of 1871 started in Mrs. O'Leary's barn.

In response to the catastrophe, Reverend E. P. Roe wrote one of Chicago's first bestsellers, *Barriers Burned Away*, in 1872. His book describes a utopian society created as a result of the Fire, in which social barriers are eliminated.

In Theodore Dreiser's *The Financier*, Frank Cowperwood learns of the Chicago Fire from a newsboy's cries outside his Philadelphia home. When his wife asks what is happening, he reacts with nonchalance: "Nothing much, I hope, sweet," he said. "Chicago is burning up and there's going to be trouble tomorrow. I have to talk to your father." The fire throws Cowperwood's banking house into bankruptcy and threatens his future. A map in a newspaper that shows the burned area of Chicago haunts Cowperwood as he struggles to save what he can of his own ruined business.

2.
Union Station
210 S. Canal St. 312/655-2231

Watching commuters during rush hour at Union Station is an inspiring activity for a writer. Potential stories abound in the faces of the thousands of workers and tourists who hurry up or down the escalators and cross the huge waiting room each day. Sherwood Anderson wasn't writing about Union Station specifically when he wrote this passage from *Marching Men*, his gloomy novel about the labor movement. But the sight of office workers moving toward the station in the evening recalls Anderson's vision of laborers returning home after a hard day's work in a dirtier, harder time:

> The people of Chicago go home from their work at evening—drifting they go

in droves, hurrying along. It is a startling thing to look closely at them. The people have bad mouths. Their mouths are slack and the jaws do not hang right... Clatter, clatter, clatter, go the heels on the hard pavements, jaws wag, the wind blows and dirt drifts and sifts through the masses of the people. Every one has dirty ears. The stench in the street cars is horrible. The antiquated bridges over the rivers are packed with people. The suburban trains going away south and west are cheaply constructed and dangerous.[4]

Union Station itself turns up briefly in *Dead Time,* a 1992 novel by Waukegan mystery writer Eleanor Taylor Bland: Detective Marti McAlister remarks to her partner that her father had once cleaned trains there.

3.
Old St. Patrick's Church
Desplaines and Adams Sts. 312/648-1021

Be sure to visit Old St. Patrick's Church. Built in 1852, St. Patrick's survived the Great Chicago Fire and is now the city's oldest church. This is where Mayor Daley and other Irish politicians go to church on St. Patrick's Day. It was the boyhood parish of Finley Peter Dunne, author of the Mr. Dooley columns (see pp. 11-12).

4.
Greektown
Halsted St. north of the Eisenhower Expy.

The old Greek neighborhood that nestled in the Halsted Street-Blue Island Avenue-Ashland Avenue triangle was decimated by the construction of the Eisenhower Expressway. However, a strip of big restaurants, which are popular with tourists as well as locals, remains on Halsted just north of the Eisenhower.

In Harry Mark Petrakis's novel *A Dream of Kings,* the main character is Leonidas Matsoukas. He keeps part of his spirit in his native Greece even as he gambles and fights his way through Chicago, praying to the gods to save a son who cannot speak and can hardly move.

Sara Paretsky's gumshoe V. I. Warshawski is drawn to Greektown, too. In

Guardian Angel she relates the following:

> I got off Halsted at Jackson, where the remnants of Chicago's Greek commu-
> nity lie. I'd only turned there because Jackson was the direct route to my
> office, but the smell coming from the restaurants on the corners was too much
> for me. It was almost five, anyway, too late to ask Freeman Carter to start a
> search. I settled down with *taramasalata* and a plate of grilled squid and put
> the heat and frustrations of the day behind me.[5]

5.
Skid Row
Madison St. west of Halsted St.

Skid Row isn't what it used to be. Many would say that's a good thing. It
certainly isn't the gathering place for the city's down-and-out that it once was.
The city has erected banners that give the West Madison area a new name—
West Loop Gate. These days redevelopment is doing its usual bit to drive out the
city's homeless population. Loft buildings and the occasional trendy *trattoria*
butt up against traditional restaurant supply stores and greasy spoons like the
Palace Grill Sandwich Shop, 1408 W. Madison, 312/226-9529. 1179 W.
Madison is the site of the fictional hotel where Frankie Machine is found dead at
the end of Nelson Algren's *The Man With the Golden Arm*.

Much of Willard Motley's 1958 novel *Let No Man Write My Epitaph* takes
place on West Madison, which is described as being populated with bums,
hobos, and groups of men standing in doorways and on corners "as uncon-
cerned as horses."

6.
University of Illinois at Chicago
601 S. Morgan St. 312/996-2724

The Chicago campus of the University of Illinois, commonly called UIC, has
long been known as an especially good institution for students who are interested in literature (UIC is the alma mater of the author of this book, after all).
UIC offers a Master's degree in Writing, as well as programs in English and

Theater.

Directly across the Eisenhower, if you stand at the CTA's Morgan Street stop you see a factory building with a colorful mural covering its wall. When I was a student at UIC, this wall advertised the Formfit Bra factory. Today, the mural depicts a far different vision: Daniel Burnham's 1909 *Plan of Chicago.*

The Plan, prepared in collaboration with Edward H. Bennett, called for the lakefront to be "forever open, clear and free." Burnham's strategy for convincing civic leaders of the merits of his plan included the claim that the moral character of the city's inhabitants would improve when city streets were cleaner and better organized. He intended to further ennoble the lives of everyday residents by providing an elaborate design of throughways, parks, and forest preserves. Better citizens would be more productive workers, according to Burnham, which would result in bigger company profits. His entire vision was never realized, but we have his original proposal to thank when we dwell on lofty thoughts while enjoying the magnificent system of lakefront parks.

7.
Jane Addams's Hull House Museum
800 S. Halsted St. 312/413-5353

Hull House is one of the most significant institutions in Chicago history. It was founded in 1889 by Jane Addams and Ellen Gates Starr to serve the poor on the West Side. The house was donated to Addams and Starr by a retired businessman named Charles Hull. The Jane Addams Hull House Association is still active throughout the city, operating programs for parents and children, as well as senior citizens.

Jane Addams's memoir *Twenty Years at Hull House* is a classic examination of the way the city ignored the plight of many of its poor. She describes her admiration for Abraham Lincoln and mentions the time she found solace by visiting the statue of the fallen president in Lincoln Park. During travels in Europe, she conceives of the settlement and her plan to

> . . . rent a house in a part of the city where many primitive and actual needs are found, in which young women who had been given over too exclusively to

study might restore a balance of activity along traditional lines and learn of life from life itself.[6]

The services of Hull House helped Addams and her colleagues affect dramatic changes in Chicago's Near West Side, as they coped with succeeding influxes of Irish, Germans, Jews, and many other immigrant groups:

Halsted Street is thirty-two miles long, and one of the great thoroughfares of Chicago; Polk Street crosses it midway between the stockyards to the south and the shipbuilding yards on the north branch of the Chicago River. For the six miles between these two industries the street is lined with shops of butchers and grocers, with dingy and gorgeous saloons, and pretentious establishments for the sale of ready-made clothing.[7]

One of the young people who was helped by Hull House was Benny Goodman—jazz clarinetist, big band leader, and King of Swing—who took music classes there. His family lived at 1342 Washburne when Benny was born in 1909.

Though Near West Side has lost all traces of its Jewish culture, Willard Motley's evocative description of Halsted Street in *Let No Man Write My Epitaph* still holds:

It is one block from Africa to Mexico, from Mexico to Italy two blocks, from Italy to Greece three blocks . . . Mother Halsted is wise. Is patient. She knows their tastes, their traditions, their beliefs. She puts the immigrant to sleep in his first New World bed. She holds him in her slum arms. Chicago's most humane street, she adopts them all.[8]

Open Mon. - Fri. 10 A.M. - 4 P.M., and Sun. 12 P.M. - 5 P.M. Admission is free.

8.
Maxwell St.
Four blocks south of Roosevelt Rd. between the Eisenhower Expy. and Blue Island Ave.

Maxwell Street, once the center of the Jewish community in Chicago and the site of an open-air market from 1871 to 1994, is barely a shadow of its former self. The whole area bounded by Polk, 16th, Canal, and Blue Island was once full of Jewish merchants with pushcarts and stalls hawking all sorts of wares. The old market was described by Carl Sandburg in "Fish Crier," one of the *Chicago Poems:*

> I know a Jew fish crier down on Maxwell Street with a voice like a north wind blowing over corn stubble in January
>
> He dangles herring before prospective customers evincing a joy identical with that of Pavlova dancing
>
> His face is that of a man terribly glad to be selling fish, terribly glad that God made fish, and customers to whom he may call his wares from a pushcart

In more recent years, before it was closed on August 15, 1994, the Maxwell Street Market was reduced to a Sunday flea market, where Chicagoans could buy almost anything from car parts to household furnishings, while blues musicians played for donations. The area is used as a backdrop in a novel called *The Maxwell Street Blues* by Chicago mystery author Michael Raleigh, one of a series of books featuring private investigator Paul Whelan. Whelan is hired to find a Maxwell Street hustler and flea-marketeer, Sam Burwell, and shows a 20-year-old photo of Burwell around the market and surrounding area.

Today, the University of Illinois at Chicago is expanding to cover most of what was once a busy shopping area on Halsted. The city of Chicago operates a New Maxwell Street Market that is no longer on Maxwell Street itself, but takes place every Sunday on Canal Street between Taylor Street and Depot Place adjacent to the expressway. Although it's only one third the size of the old market, it's still the largest open-air market in Chicago.

9.
Taylor Street
Taylor St. west of Morgan St.

Traces of the Taylor Street Italian neighborhood survive, but construction of the Eisenhower Expressway in the 1960s took the life out of it. The main attractions are the terrific Italian eating places along Taylor, particularly the legendary **Mario's Italian Lemonade**, 1070 W. Taylor.

W. R. Burnett's 1929 novel *Little Caesar,* on which the 1930 Edward G. Robinson movie was based, did much to promote the "boom-boom" image of Chicago as a gangster town. The chase scene near the end in which the police hunt the gangster Rico leads right through this neighborhood. He dies in the gutter, but not before uttering the immortal words: "Is this the end of Rico?"

Just after *Little Caesar* was published in 1929, Burnett left Chicago for Los Angeles, where he worked on scripts for movies such as *The Great Escape* and such television shows as *77 Sunset Strip* and *Bonanza.*

Late in life, Burnett wrote a novel called *Good-bye, Chicago,* in which a character eventually leaves Chicago for Detroit. Burnett's character looks upon the city as someone who has seen only one side of it, someone who never really liked the city but still benefited from its legacy. The character, an attorney named William Macready, feels "immense relief to be out of that huge, sprawling, complex, immense, corrupt, and bewildering city on the shores of Lake Michigan."[9]

10.
Pilsen
Centered around Ashland and Blue Island Aves. and Cermak Rd.

The Pilsen neighborhood is like a step back into history: beautiful old houses and inexpensive apartment buildings provide homes to recent immigrants just as they did at the turn of the century. Today the immigrants are from Mexico and Central America; earlier, they were from Czechoslovakia.

Many of Stuart Dybek's stories center on the Czech neighborhood around 25th and 26th Streets. In "The Cat Woman," he writes about an old woman on Luther Street who "disposed of the neighborhood's excess cats" by drowning them in her washing machine. After she leaves, the area is full of stray cats again within a year. In "The Palatski Man," two young people follow the title character down Western Avenue to the Chicago River, where all the ragmen live and are apparently dressed up for Sunday. "They wore crushed hats of all varieties: bowlers, straws, stetsons, derbies, homburgs. Their ties were the strangest of all, misshapen and dangling to their knees in wild designs of flowers, swirls, and polka dots." They have a procession and conduct an odd kind of mass over a bubbling pot.

In "La Miss Rose," a story by Ana Castillo, Stormy and Carmen are summoned to Chicago from Santa Fe by a fortune teller named Miss Rose. She instructs them to take the train to the Blue Island Avenue stop. "Chicago from the air was big, big with lots of very tall buildings. Stormy had never seen such tall buildings." Carmen looks at the gray all around, "the gray of the asphalt, concrete, brick everywhere," and she longs for the desert. The air is described as smelling of "exhaust fumes and something close to chorizo."[10]

11.
Cook County Hospital
1835 W. Harrison St. 312/633-6000

This is where many of the victims in Chicago crime and mystery novels end up. "County" is just west of the medical center district, which includes Rush-Presbyterian St. Luke's Hospital and the University of Illinois at Chicago Hospital.

Studs Terkel, the city's most prominent and perceptive chronicler, grew up in his family's rooming house at Ashland Avenue and Flournoy Street. Most of their guests were nurses, interns, and technicians who worked at Cook County Hospital. He recalls in his book *Chicago* that his older brother used to have late-night romantic rendezvous with some of their female tenants; Studs would change the bed sheets in exchange for sheets of popular song lyrics that his brother would bring him from the Dreamland Ballroom. Studs attended McLaren School at Flournoy and Laflin Streets, and later McKinley High School, both of which have since been torn down.

Ana Castillo

Poet, novelist, and writer Ana Castillo is the author of such works as *Sapogonia, Loverboys,* and *Peel My Love Like an Onion.* She received an American Book Award from the Before Columbus Foundation for her first novel, *The Mixquiahuala Letters.* Her other awards include a Carl Sandburg Award, a Mountains and Plains Booksellers Award, and fellowships from the National Endowment for the Arts in fiction and poetry. She lives in Chicago with her son.

I was born and educated in Chicago. The city shaped me into the kind of writer I have become. Multiple ethnic presences here prepared me for realizing that the world is not simply black and white or mostly brown (as they do feel sometimes in the Southwest, for example). My first 20 years of life were spent around Taylor Street. The spot where my home was became one of the first parking lots on the UIC campus.

One reason I left the city in the 1980s was that I felt I didn't have the support I needed as a writer. I had written my first novel, but I didn't feel that this was the place for an alternative writer, a woman, a feminist. So I ended up in San Francisco, where they welcomed me with open arms—as if to say another soldier joining our cause. It was wonderful for me. I won the American Book Award during that period. (The people who give out the award are based in the Bay Area.) I also wrote a few reviews for the *San Francisco Chronicle* in addition to teaching.

So things fell into place for me. Times were changing and writers considered radical feminists of color, like myself, were getting some attention. Eventually, I made another leap, when I moved to New Mexico and wrote my novel, *So Far From God.* From then on I've been considered an American mainstream writer. I don't really see that the people who stayed here were able to jump on that same boat.

But I do think that if I had stayed in Chicago it wouldn't have worked out for me as it has. But who knows. I would have ended up being published, but I feel my experience was much richer because I was moving around during those ten years. The *Philadelphia Inquirer* wrote about my short story collection, for example, that I covered more geographical territory than any other American writer the reviewer was aware of. "I came back ten years later because my roots were here, and because my mother was a widow and she didn't get around that well. I didn't plan to stay, but it turned out that way. I had a home in New Mexico, in Albuquerque, in an old adobe. Coming back was a hard switch that immediately affected the stories I was writing. When I am writing, I immediately write "on location." Therefore my characters all moved to Chicago along with me. At the time, I was trying to finish my collection of stories, *Loverboys*.

Photo by Antonio Perez.

Ana Castillo.

My mother passed away in 1997. Then the reasons for staying on in Chicago were pragmatic. My son was just about to start high school. We both decided to stay on. After having moved around for so long, we agreed he should have some stability and this was as good a place as any we had lived in. Chicago's really a great city. Everyone, media, cultural milieu—has been supportive. So now it's OK for me here as a writer, but I don't know how the experience would be for beginning writers.

My environment does feed into my writing as does what is going on in the world at that moment. Chicago does that for me. I think this is a city that is very aware of the rest of the country and the rest of the world. It's really into its local politics but it is also in tune, I think, with how we connect with international affairs. I like the way my hometown has influenced me. It has kept me on my toes. I came from a community where we were always aware of lots of different kinds of people and lifestyles.

However, in my prose, I never am too definite about particular surroundings. In *Sapogonia*, I may mention Milwaukee Avenue, but mostly I am interested in the interior world of my characters. In my stories I make general statements about gentrification and corporate America and don't get nostalgic about the ma and pa shop that used to be on the corner. As a writer I keep an eye to changes. But I am more interested in what goes on with my characters psychologically and politically. When I wrote about Little Village in *Peel My Love Like an Onion* (my most recent novel), a reader was brought to tears when I mentioned the Dollar Mart because that was a place he not only recognized from where he grew up but as an aspiring writer, he couldn't believe something so real to him could be turned into legitimate literature.

I find inspiration in jazz nightclubs like the Green Mill or now and then a blues club because of the ambiance that's so particular to Chicago. We take these places like that for granted here. As a poet and wisecracking feminist, I like the dynamics of the night spots, blues clubs, or small theaters, listening to local vernacular, watching how people interact with each other after a couple of drinks, when they let their hair down. In terms of music, jazz is a mix of cross-cultural influences that speaks to people like me on a visceral and also intellectual level. It's a city with an edge. It has a lot of venues for the arts but it's strongest in music and theatre than in the plastic arts or at this time in its history—literature. Although as everyone knows—it's the home of the renowned poetry slam.

I have a prediction about this town in the coming decade or so: The cultural career of choice will be filmmaking, and Chicago will be a strong place for it. So storytellers with high-tech skills will find good opportunities here.

12.
Lawndale
Around Douglas Park

In the first half of the twentieth century, the Lawndale neighborhood was a vibrant Jewish community. As described in the book *Ethnic Chicago,* Lawndale was full of movie and vaudeville houses where the Marx Brothers, Sophie Tucker, Benny Goodman, and other performers played. Much of the action in the early sections of Meyer Levin's *The Old Bunch* takes place in the Lawndale area around Roosevelt Road, especially at Mrs. Kagen's drug store at Roosevelt and St. Louis Avenue. He writes:

> Turning again onto Independence Boulevard was like walking up the last side of a rectangle bounding that world. Almost everybody lived inside that rectangle. Well, Sam Eisen lived down on Troy Street, and the Meisels over on

Sixteenth; but the half mile square that he had bounded was somehow warmer, full of life, it was the body containing the guts of the neighborhood though there might be limbs spreading outward.

Lawndale, along with the Douglas Park and Garfield Park areas, succeeded Maxwell Street as the Eastern European Jews moved west. In the 1960s the area switched over to a predominantly black population, and virtually no traces of the old Jewish culture remain.

Photo by Thayer Lindner.

Statue of Robert Burns outside the Garfield Park Conservatory.

13.
Robert Burns Statue
Garfield Park

There used to be lots of statues of literary figures around the conservatory, but they have all been stolen or vandalized except for one. Perhaps the statue of Scottish poet Robert Burns remains out of respect for his contribution to New Year's Eve celebrations: he wrote the words to the old ballad *Auld Lang Syne.* In this likeness, however, he is holding a copy of his book *Poems, Chiefly in the Scottish Dialect*—probably because of his famous poem "Coming Through the Rye," on which the title for J. D. Salinger's novel *The Catcher in the Rye* was based. By the artist W. Grant Stevenson, the statue was cast in Edinburgh and unveiled in Chicago in 1906.

14.
Garfield Park Conservatory
300 N. Central Park Ave. 312/746-5100

This conservatory isn't as centrally located as the one in Lincoln Park, but it's the largest in the world under one roof, with more than 5,000 varieties of plants, including orchids, ferns, and cactuses. One especially strange-looking and rare plant has a literary connection: the Boojum Tree. This species was given the name of Boojum from Lewis Carroll's poem "The Hunting of the Snark." Carroll's Boojum was a mythical thing found in desolate, far-off places. The Boojum Tree grows in the wild only in a single area of the world, the Baja Peninsula in California.

Inside the conservatory, you'll also find two marble figures, *Pastoral* and *Idyll,* done by Lorado Taft, the sculptor of *The Fountain of Time* on the Midway Plaisance near the University of Chicago and a charter member of Harriet Monroe's Little Room discussion group.

15.
Edgar Rice Burroughs's birthplace
1943 W. Washington Blvd.

Burroughs, the creator of the Tarzan series of books and associated merchandising, was born in 1875 at 626 Washington, which was later renumbered to 1943 W. Washington. This location reportedly served his father's family well as they watched the Chicago Fire from the roof of the home. Like so many Chicago landmarks, it's now a parking lot, serving the United Center, 1901 W. Madison, just to the south. (For more about Burroughs and his career, see pp. 234-236.)

16.
Union Park
Bounded by Ashland Ave., Washington Blvd., and Ogden Ave.

In *Sister Carrie,* this is where Carrie Meeber lives "in sin" with Drouet after she leaves her sister's flat. Union Park was once a fashionable neighborhood, and the park itself once contained elaborate landscaping, including miniature waterfalls. Few traces of the area's former splendor remain today.

Photo by Thayer Lindner.

Union Park with the Union Park Congregational Church in the background.

17.
Randolph Street Market
Randolph and Halsted Sts.

In his novel *The Pit,* Frank Norris describes South Water Street at 15th and Morgan as "a jam of delivery wagons and market carts backed to the curbs, leaving only a tortuous path between the endless files of horses, suggestive of an actual barrack of cavalry."

There are still a few wholesale food distributors on Randolph around Halsted, but visitors to this area today are more likely to find their veggies under a gourmet sauce in a trendy restaurant.

18.
Haymarket Square, site of the Haymarket Riot
Desplaines and Randolph Sts.

On May 4, 1886, a labor rally was held near Crane's Alley, which was located on the east side of Desplaines, just north of Randolph. A bomb thrown from just south of the alley resulted in the deaths of seven policemen and injuries to both police and spectators. The resultant trial of eight activists gained worldwide attention for the labor movement, and initiated the tradition of "May Day" labor rallies in many cities.

Frank Norris, the author of *McTeague* and *The Pit,* wrote a lesser-known novel called *The Bomb* that centered on the Haymarket Riot. In John Jakes's novel *Homeland,* the Haymarket Riot is also recalled as a Chicago resident takes his cousin to a monument marking the riot, and explains what happened:

> The bomb exploded at the head of the police column. Seven officers died, sixteen were hurt. The police broke ranks, crouching to shoot . . . The rain pelted down. God flashed the lightning every other second, Benno said, and the coppers showed no mercy.[11]

Don't go looking around this intersection for signs of the riot. A marker that was once on the side of the Catholic Charities building was reportedly torn off years ago. The monument to the Haymarket martyrs, a well-known statue by sculptor Albert Weinert, is located not here, but in Forest Home Cemetery in suburban Forest Park. Here, as elsewhere, the real monument is in books that refer to the event and in the memories of those pro-labor activists who still place flowers around the monument each year on the Sunday closest to May 4.

19.
N. Fagin Books
459 N. Milwaukee Ave. 312/829-5252
e-mail: nfagbo@aol.com

From the outside, this bookstore, which is just south of the intersection of Grand, Halsted, and Milwaukee, looks pretty unassuming. It's tucked away in an old three-story brick building whose facade is mostly obscured by a fire escape and security gates covering the windows. But the moment you step inside, you enter another world. First, you're likely to be greeted by Luke the whippet, the beloved pet dog of store owner Nancy Fagin and her husband Ron Weber, who works in the store part time. Then, your eyes are diverted by an astonishing range of obscure old books, mostly in anthropology and related fields, and by masks and artwork from cultures all over the world.

N. Fagin Books is probably better known by anthropologists around the world than by most Chicago residents. The store was started seventeen years ago by Nancy Fagin, who was then working for a small Chicago publisher, after she became disgruntled when she had to wait eight weeks for a book she ordered from one of the big Chicago booksellers.

The store now contains more than 20,000 titles in its two-story facility, and includes works of art from many countries as well. Some of its best cus-

Photo by Greg Holden.

N. Fagin Books.

tomers are scholars and researchers who come to Chicago for conferences and make special pilgrimages to North Milwaukee Avenue, where they can scour the narrow shelves to their heart's content for books about the sciences, particularly botany, zoology, and ecology. They might well discover works on obscure subjects such as lichens that grow on telephone poles, or a field guide to North American bird nests (that's a guide to nests, not to birds). There's a small room containing old lantern slides, and masks from tribes around the world, as well as exotic pottery, baskets, ethnographic art books, and on and on. "It's probably the weirdest bookstore in the U.S.," jokes Weber.

Fully ten percent of N. Fagin Books' business comes from outside the country. The store has both new and used books. It's open Mon.-Fri. 10 A.M.-5 P.M. , Sat. 10 A.M.-3 P.M., and by appointment.

20.
Mayor Carter Harrison home
Jackson Blvd. at Ashland Ave.

Chicago mayor Carter Harrison was assassinated in his home on this corner in 1893. Harrison is particularly notable in a literary guide because he wrote two short novels, *A Summer's Outing* and *The Old Man's Story.* The house has long since been demolished.

21.
Chicago main post office building
433 W. Van Buren St.

The main post office might not look very exciting, but it's been an important place to some writers. Richard Wright worked here, and so did poet and writer Sterling Plumpp, the University of Illinois at Chicago professor profiled in the South Side section of this book (see pp. 204-206). The opening of Eugene Izzi's novel *Bad Guys* describes a tavern a block from the post office on Van Buren, where the postal workers go to drink and shoot pool after cashing their paychecks.

Bookstores

Chicago Textbook Inc., 1076 W. Taylor St. 312/733-8398.

N. Fagin Books, 459 N. Milwaukee Ave. 312/829-5252.

Thomas J. Joyce & Company, 400 N. Racine Ave. 312/738-1933.

Libreria Giron, 1443 W. 18th St. 312/226-1406.

Living Quarters Enterprise, 2724 W. Washington Blvd. 773/265-7450.

Logan Medical Book Store, 1910 W. Harrison St. 312/733-4544.

UIC Medical Bookstore, 828 S. Wolcott Ave. 312/413-5550.

Coffeehouses and More

Café Sol.net, 1134 W. 18th St. 312/666-3594.

Dulce Vida Café & Gallery, 1338 W. Madison St. 312/666-1920.

Fontano's Subs, 1058 W. Polk St. 312/421-4474.

Hot Pot, 2227 W. Taylor St. 312/243-6130.

La Tazza Bella, 1227 W. Taylor St. 312/850-1510.

Lou Mitchell's, 565 W. Jackson Blvd. 312/939-3111.

Mario's Italian Lemonade, 1070 W. Taylor St.

Sip Coffee House, 1223 W. Grand Ave. 312/563-1123.

What's Brewing, 1062 W. Chicago Ave. 312/432-1628.

Other Places of Interest

Chicago Fire Department Training Academy, 558 W. DeKoven St. 312/747-7239.

Haymarket Square, Randolph and Desplaines Sts.

Holy Family Church, Roosevelt Rd. and May St.
Chicago's second oldest church, built from 1857 to 1860.

Hull House Museum, 800 S. Halsted St. 312/413-5353.
Open Mon. - Fri. 10 A.M. - 4 P.M., Sun. 12 P.M. - 5 P.M., free admission.

Jackson Boulevard Historic District, 1500 block of W. Jackson.

Museum of Holography, 1134 W. Washington Blvd. 312/226-1007.
Open Wed. - Sun. 12:30 P.M. - 5 P.M., $2.50 admission.

Randolph Street Market area, between Halsted and Loomis Sts. on Randolph St.

United Center, 1901 W. Madison St. 312/455-4500.
  Home of the Chicago Bulls and Chicago Blackhawks.

PRAIRIE AVENUE - NEAR SOUTH SIDE

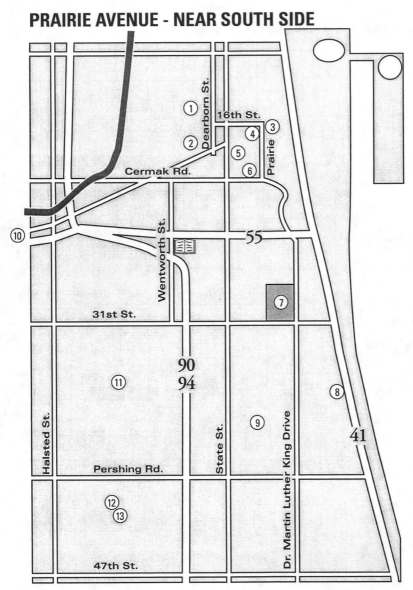

Map by Michael Polydoris.

Near South Side/ Prairie Avenue

By Jeff Hall.   *Gwendolyn Brooks*

Delve into both the city's literary and socioeconomic past south of the Loop. On Prairie Avenue, you can tour Chicago's oldest surviving house and the remnants of a neighborhood that was inhabited by the rich and famous. When novelists like Edna Ferber or Theodore Dreiser wanted to provide a glimpse of where the very wealthy lived in Chicago, they had their characters come to Prairie Avenue.

A bit farther south, in contrast, are the last traces of the Union Stock Yards, where some of the poorest inhabitants of Chicago once toiled, immortalized in Upton Sinclair's crusading novel *The Jungle.* Revisit (in imagination, at least) the city's notorious red light district, the Levee, which was frequented by poet Edgar Lee Masters as well as other writers and journalists. There's also the Bridgeport area—the original enclave of Chicago's Irish that was described in the "Mr. Dooley" newspaper columns of Finley Peter Dunne.

The economic and political power base of this part of the city is diminished, though it's by no means gone completely. Through the power of the printed word, however, this area comes alive with as much character and spirit as it ever had. You get the feeling that when you turn a corner you might bump into Mayor Daley (both Richard J. and his son, Richard M.), George Pullman, shall Field, or transportation tycoon Charles Tyson Yerkes (who funded the construction of Yerkes Observatory in southern Wisconsin, and who served as the model for Frank Cowperwood in Theodore Dreiser's trilogy), along with some of the workers from these businessmen's factories and stores. Parts of the city's Black Belt that inspired Richard Wright to write one of the most famous Chicago novels, *Native Son,* are also here.

How to Get There

To do Prairie Avenue, take the CTA Red Line to the Roosevelt Road station and walk east. The other sites in this section, however, are spread out over a wide area and are most easily reached by automobile.

Driving Tour

1.
South Dearborn Street development
Dearborn St. just north and south of Roosevelt Rd.

In Eugene Izzi's *The Criminalist,* the main hero is a retired detective named Tom Moran. He lives in one of the relatively new houses for young professionals in the South Loop, near downtown and protected from the high-crime areas around it: "It was a walled little community, with one road in and one road out, a guard standing lonely duty in a small shack, to raise the black-and-white electric gate when the cars with the proper sticker in the windshields approached on the blacktopped road."[1]

Chicago's Most Notorious Publication

The unassuming booklet consists of only one page of text. Not a single person is shown in any of its photos. Yet, its appearance in the summer of 1911 infuriated the mayor of Chicago and ended an era of the city's history.

"The Everleigh Club" was a promotional brochure published to advertise the facilities of Chicago's most famous (or infamous) brothel, which had opened on February 2, 1900. By the end of the century's first decade, business was booming. The proprietresses, sisters from Kentucky named Minna and Ada Lester (who renamed themselves Minna and Ada Everleigh), were raking in an annual tax-free profit of $120,000.

Patrons of the club could expect to be serenaded by four-piece orchestras and waited on by valets and maids. Other forms of entertainment were provided by young women who had passed the sisters' elaborate screening process and subsequently attended special courses in culture and manners. It was possible to pay as little as $50, but the total cost for an evening could easily reach $1,500—including generous tips that were not only encouraged but expected.

Habitués of the Everleigh Club included journalists such as Ring Lardner and George Ade, and poet Edgar Lee Masters.[2]

Masters, the author of *Spoon*

The Everleigh Club

WHILE not an extremely imposing edifice without, is a most sumptuous place within. 2131 Dearborn Street, Chicago, has long been famed for its luxurious furnishings, famous paintings and statuary, and its elaborate and artistic decorations. "The New Annex," 2133 Dearborn Street, formally opened November 1, 1902, has added prestige to the club, and won admiration and praise from all visitors. With double front entrances, the twin buildings within are so connected as to seem as one. Steam heat throughout, with electric fans in summer; one never feels the winter's chill or summer's heat in this luxurious resort. Fortunate indeed, with all the comforts of life surrounding them, are the members of the Everleigh Club.

This little booklet will convey but a faint idea of the magnificence of the club and its appointments.

Courtesy of the Chicago Historical Society.

The first page of the Everleigh Club brochure, 1902.

River Anthology, recalled in a 1944 magazine article that Minna was "somehow the larger personality, the more impressive figure of the two sisters." Ada was remarkable for her long golden hair, which Masters observed resembled the color of the Everleigh Club's gold piano. He also remembered that shortly after he rang the bell the door was opened by Minna, who greeted him with a cordial "How is my boy?"[3]

Along with the Everleigh Club's Japanese Throne Room, Moorish Room, and other theme rooms was a library lavishly stocked with Minna's collection of rare books. As a lover of literature, it's not at all surprising that she should turn to the printed word to market her thriving business.

When Mayor Carter Harrison II was shown the Everleigh Club's pamphlet, he was enraged. The anonymous author (could it have been Minna herself?) boasted:

> The Everleigh Club, while not an extremely imposing edifice without, is a most sumptuous place within. 2131 Dearborn Street, Chicago, has long been famed for its luxurious furnishings, famous paintings and stat-

uary, and its elaborate and artistic decorations . . . Steam heat throughout, with electric fans in summer; one never feels the winter's chill or summer's heat in this luxurious resort. Fortunate indeed, with all the comforts of life surrounding them, are the members of the Everleigh Club.

Harrison ordered the facility closed "because of its infamy, the audacious advertising of it, and as a solemn warning that the district had to be at least half-way decent."[4]

The pamphlet provided Harrison with a convenient justification to shut down the club; the activities of the Levee's gambling and prostitution houses had been a source of controversy since William T. Stead's crusading book *If Christ Came to Chicago!*

In 1910, a vice commission appointed by the City Council investigated the activities of the sisters and their competitors, with the ultimate result that October 24, 1911, would be the Everleigh Club's last night. It was one of its busiest ever. Minna told the *Chicago American:* "If the ship sinks, we're going down with a cheer and a good drink under our belts, anyway."[5]

Minna and Ada hoped to make a comeback in 1912 with a second facility, but their plans fell through when the city demanded huge license fees. The sisters re-tired before the age of 40; they moved to New York City, where they lived out their days according to their desire—anonymously and quietly—without ever following up their first, and apparently only, publishing venture.

2.
Site of the Everleigh Club
2131-2133 S. Dearborn St.

This brothel, famous in Chicago lore, was run by two sisters from Kentucky, Ada and Minna Everleigh, in a South Dearborn Street mansion. Minna Everleigh had literary ambitions that may have surfaced in odd ways, most notably the writing of a promotional guidebook to the Everleigh Club that eventually led to its downfall.

Irving Wallace, who tracked down Minna Everleigh late in her life, wrote a 1989 novel called *The Golden Room* about the Everleigh Club.

In 1894, William T. Stead wrote one of the most famous and influential books in the city's history, an exposé of the gambling and prostitution indus-tries called *If Christ Came to Chicago!* This nonfiction book eventually con-tributed to a movement to clean up Chicago. Ironically, the book's immediate effect was to boost the economy of the city's red light area—it included a detailed map of the notorious Levee district that provided convenient directions to "business establishments."

3.
George Pullman house
1729 S. Prairie Ave.

George Mortimer Pullman (1831-1897) was an industrialist who developed the railroad sleeping car and later headed the Pullman Palace Car Company. In the

1880s, he built the complete factory town of "Pullman" for his employees, now a Chicago neighborhood. He was the target of many attacks by Chicago newspaper columnist Eugene Field, especially during the bitter strike at the Pullman factory in 1894.

In Theodore Dreiser's *Sister Carrie,* Drouet takes Carrie to Prairie Avenue to gaze upon the houses of the rich.

> "Say Carrie," he said, "see that house on ahead there?"
>
> He pointed to a rather awkward brick and stone affair not at all beautiful in its decorative effect which was set down in a rather extensive green lawn—a very fair example of the mixed and uncertain architecture characteristic of the city at that time.
>
> Carrie nodded.
>
> "That's Pullman's," he said.
>
> The two gazed at the great sleeping-car magnate's residence with undisguised interest.
>
> "Say, but he's got the money. Twenty million dollars. Think of that!"[6]

Another famous Chicago business figure, Marshall Field, lived a block south at 1905 S. Prairie. Go to the next stop on the tour, Glessner House, to find out more about Prairie Avenue and the illustrious figures who once called the neighborhood home.

A Prairie Avenue mansion.

Photo by Thayer Lindner.

Photo by Thayer Lindner.

Detail, Glessner House.

4.

Glessner House

1800 S. Prairie Ave. 312/326-1480

This beautiful mansion is open for tours and is the logical starting point for a visit to Prairie Avenue. Elizabeth Marsh is one of the female protagonists of Edith Freund's *Chicago Girls*, a novel set at the time of the World's Columbian Exposition in 1893. She lives in a mansion on Prairie and her family is said to be acquainted with the Glessners. Edith walks across the Illinois Central railroad tracks one night and stands on the beach during an electrical storm:

> Anyone who believed Chicago was an inland city had never stood next to the lake like this, close enough to feel the power of it, close enough to sense that the lake was older than anything here and would remain dominant over man's inventions on its shore.[7]

In one of the rags-to-riches stories written by Horatio Alger, Jr., *Luke*

Walton or The Chicago Newsboy, Luke saves a rich woman named Mrs. Merton from being hit by a streetcar. After he is summoned to the Merton home on South Prairie Avenue, his fortunes begin to change.

Were the rich residents of Prairie Avenue really so charitable? Selina Peake, the heroine of Edna Ferber's *So Big,* was another poverty-stricken character who received assistance from Prairie Avenue. A policeman starts to chase her away when she tries to peddle her vegetables on Prairie. Selina fights back with passion: "the vegetables lay scattered all about them on the sidewalk in front of Julie Hempel Arnold's great stone house on Prairie Avenue." Peake's old friend Arnold happens on the scene in the nick of time and rescues her.

In a 1949 novel by Arthur Meeker called *Prairie Avenue,* a young man named Ned comes to live with his Uncle Hiram and Aunt Lydia at 1817 Prairie Ave. Much of the novel takes place in the winter, and bad weather was shown to be a normal part of existence during that time period:

Chicago had a great many different kinds of weather, but as far as he could tell most of the kinds in winter were bad.

Photo by Thayer Lindner.

A Prairie Avenue entryway.

If the wind blew from the east, it might be beautifully clear for days, but so raw that part of Lake Michigan seemed to have got into the house. If it blew from the west—as it generally did—the air was so sharp and dry that it hurt going down.... If it snowed, the streets were buried almost immediately. If it thawed after that, one waded through slush for days. If instead it got colder, ice stuck to the pavement as a month-long menace. If it failed to snow freshly at least three times a week, what lay on the ground grew so loathsomely dirty that one prayed for a storm.[8]

5.
Site of Charles Yerkes mansion
2100 block of S. Michigan Ave.

Frank Cowperwood, the protagonist of Theodore Dreiser's *The Titan,* builds a mansion on South Michigan Avenue. His saga was based on the life of Chicago transportation magnate Charles T. Yerkes whose mansion was once on South Michigan. It was Yerkes who began construction of the elevated railway that would define the Loop. Dreiser's heroes Curtis Jadwin and Cowperwood aren't just financial geniuses who are able to make a lot of money, but are depicted as brooding artists with a special sense of a mission. In contrast, Yerkes didn't display much beyond self-interest.

6.
R. R. Donnelley & Sons' Lakeside Press Complex
350 E. Cermak Rd.

Chicago once had nearly 200 book and job printers, many located on Printers Row (see pp. 42-43). R.R. Donneley's historic Lakeside Press printing complex, built in 1912, is on the National Register of Historic Places. Before Donnelley closed the plant in 1993, many of the country's most popular magazines rolled off its huge presses, as did millions of catalogs and telephone directories. The complex has recently been transformed into the Lakeside Technology Center.

7.
Dunbar Park and High School
3000 S. Martin Luther King Dr. 773/534-9000

Named for black poet and writer Paul Laurence Dunbar.

8.
Stephen A. Douglas Memorial
35th St. and Lake Park Ave.

Stephen A. Douglas was a major player in local, as well as state and national, politics. His own writings include an autobiography, but perhaps his most often quoted words are those he hurled at Abraham Lincoln during their famous debates in 1858. He also promoted literature in a manner of speaking by donating the land and much of the financing as founder of the first University of Chicago in 1855.

Photo by Thayer Lindner.

Chicago Tribute marker at site of Richard Wright's house.

9.
Site of Richard Wright's house
3743 S. Indiana Ave.

Novelist Richard Wright came to Chicago from Memphis in 1927 in search of work. Despite financial difficulties, he stayed until 1937. He found the poverty that surrounded him to be very depressing, but Chicago provided him with camaraderie from other writers and leftists, as well as material he would draw upon for novels such as *Native Son.* It's difficult to briefly summarize Wright's entire Chicago experience, but he wrote about the city in an autobiographical work called *American Hunger* and in articles such as "Early Days in Chicago" and "The Man Who Went to Chicago." In *American Hunger,* he writes:

> My first glimpse of the flat black stretches of Chicago depressed and dismayed me, mocked all my fantasies. Chicago seemed an unreal city whose mythical houses were built of slabs of black coal wreathed in palls of grey smoke, houses whose foundations were sinking slowly into the dank prairie. Flashes of steam showed intermittently on the wide horizon, gleaming translucently in the winter sun. The din of the city entered my consciousness, entered to remain for years to come . . . [9]

Wright's biographer Michael Fabre reports that Wright had read the work of Theodore Dreiser to prepare him "for the ways in which unscrupulous city-dwellers set ambushes for inexperienced provincials; it was like adventuring into a jungle."[10] Wright was struck by the dreary atmosphere of the Bronzeville neighborhood. He washed dishes in the Hotel Patricia on Fullerton; he worked at the central post office, as a street cleaner, a ditch digger, and at many other jobs; his work as a youth club supervisor in the ghetto gave him much material for *Native Son,* as he later acknowledged in an article entitled "How Bigger Was Born."

Wright placed an early story called "Superstition" in *Abbott's Monthly Magazine,* a publication started by *Chicago Defender* founder Robert S. Abbott. Friends at the University of Chicago suggested books to satisfy Wright's voracious desire for reading, and he also got to know Nelson Algren. His concern for the poverty he and other blacks were experiencing led him to join the Communist Party. He did research at various libraries, including the Newberry Library where he would listen to speakers at Bughouse Square. He organized a South Side Writers' Group in 1936 that included Frank Marshall Davis, author of *Black Man's Verse,* and Margaret Walker, author of *For My People.*[11]

Wright and his family lived at 4831 S. Vincennes, 4804 S. Saint Lawrence, 2636 S. Grove, and then (in 1935) at "La Veta," the rundown mansion at 3743 S. Indiana. Here he had his own room for the first time, where he worked on his stories and on a planned history of blacks and racial problems in Chicago.

10.
Mr. Dooley's neighborhood
Archer Ave. in Bridgeport

Martin J. Dooley, the creation of newspaperman Finley Peter Dunne, owned a saloon on "Archey Road" (Archer Avenue) in the city's Bridgeport neighborhood. Mr. Dooley spoke in a thick Irish brogue and displayed wit and wisdom. Father Kelly was the mythical pastor of St. Bridget's Church and the hero of many columns as well. There was a St. Bridget's at one time at Archer Avenue and Arch Street, but there's only an office building there now.

Dunne was born in 1867 and grew up in a home on the West Side, the center of the city's Irish settlement, at Adams and Desplaines Streets. Mr.

Dooley made his first appearance in 1893 in the *Chicago Evening Post,* where Dunne wrote a column. His satires of local persons and events took on Admiral Dewey and his attack on the Spanish fleet off of Manila as well as Teddy Roosevelt's Rough Riders. Dunne's columns were collected in many popular books, including *Mr. Dooley in Peace and War* and *Mr. Dooley in the Hearts of His Countrymen.*

An excellent book about the Mr. Dooley columns is *Mr. Dooley's Chicago* by Barbara Schaaf. Another, *Finley Peter Dunne and Mr. Dooley* by Charles Fanning, contains this quote from Dunne's *Chicago Evening Post* column of November 25, 1893:

> Up in Archey Road the streetcar wheels squeaked along the tracks and the men coming down from the rolling-mills hit themselves on their big chests and wiped their noses on their leather gloves with a peculiar back-handed stroke at which they are most adept. The little girls coming out of the bakeshops with loaves done up in brown paper under their arms had to keep a tight clutch on their thin shawls lest those garments should be caught up by

Photo by Thayer Lindner.

Union Stock Yards Gate.

the bitter wind blowing from Brighton Park way and carried down to the gashouse. The frost was so thick on the windows of Mr. Martin Dooley's shop that you could just see the crownless harp on the McCormick's Hall Parnell meeting sheet above it, and you could not see any of the pyramid of Medford rum bottles founded contemporaneously with that celebrated meeting.[12]

Mr. Dooley's tavern was probably located near the South Fork of the Chicago River near the Bridgeport locks, where it splits with the I & M Canal. If you are hoping to recreate the Mr. Dooley experience, visit **Red's Lounge**, 3479 S. Archer, 773/376-0517, which was mentioned by Bill Granger in one of his *Chicago Tribune* columns: "Everyone has a drink at Red's sometime in his life." Or visit the other famous pub in the neighborhood, **Schaller's Pump**, 3714 S. Halsted, 773/376-6332.

11.
Mayor Richard J. Daley's house
3536 S. Lowe Ave.

Current Chicago Mayor Richard M. Daley grew up in this house. At this writing, his mother, the 96-year-old widow "Sis" Daley, still lives here, so be quiet as you go by in case she is napping. His father, Mayor Richard J. Daley, was the subject of Mike Royko's most famous book, *Boss.* He attended the nearby Nativity of Our Lord Church, 37th and Union.

Harriet Monroe's brother-in-law, John Root, was the architect of another neighborhood institution, St. Gabriel Church, 45th and Lowe, built in 1887. Monroe said the church's design was "as personal as the clasp of (the architect's) hand."[13]

12.
Union Stock Yards Gate
35th St. and Exchange Ave.

Considering the former importance of the stockyards to Chicago, it's amazing to think that this feature of the city is virtually gone.

The most famous vision of the stockyards comes from the novel that everyone read (or was supposed to read) in either high school or college: Upton Sinclair's *The Jungle*, published in 1906. Protagonist Jurgis Rudkus and his friends and family tumble out of their train cars at the Dearborn Street Station and stare in wonder at the big black buildings, "unable to realize that they had arrived, and why, when they said 'Chicago,' people no longer pointed in some direction, but instead looked perplexed, or laughed, or went on without paying any attention." The descriptions of Packingtown and the stockyards themselves are vivid and harrowing. Ashland Avenue just west of the yard is described as "Whiskey Row," being lined with saloons. The corner of Ashland and 47th, "Whiskey Point," is said to have contained "one glue factory and about two hundred saloons."

The gateway to the Union Stock Yards, which is made of limestone is 50 feet wide and more than 30 feet high. It is now a lonely national landmark, the stockyards having closed in 1971.

Norman Mailer, in *The Siege of Chicago*, used the stockyards to represent how the city tries to hide reality:

> But in Chicago, they did it straight, they cut the animals right out of their hearts—which is why it was the last of the great American cities and people had great faces, carnal as blood, greedy, direct, too impatient for hypocrisy, in love with honest plunder.

Rudyard Kipling, no great fan of Chicago, said of the stockyards: "There was no place for hand or foot that was not coated with thicknesses of dried blood, and the stench of it in the nostrils bred fear."[14]

13.
Chinatown
Wentworth Ave. between Cermak Rd. and Stevenson Expy.

In *Loverboys*, a collection of stories by Ana Castillo, one of the "Conversations with an Absent Lover" is a reminiscence of going to Chinatown to an all-night Cantonese restaurant called Lucky's "where Papa always ordered the same thing: egg foo young."

Bookstores

IIT Book Store, 3200 S. Wabash Ave. 312/791-0770.

Modern Bookstore, 3118 S. Halsted St. 312/225-7911.

Paragon Book Gallery, 1507 S. Michigan Ave. 312/663-5155.

Pui Tak Christian Bookstore, 2214 S. Wentworth Ave. 312/328-0987.

World Journal Bookstore, 2116 W. Archer Ave. 312/842-8005.

Coffeehouses and Tea Rooms

Café Sol.net, 1134 W. 18th St. 312/666-3594.

Ten Ren Tea & Ginseng Co., 2247 S. Wentworth Ave. 312/842-1171.

Other Places of Interest

Chinatown Gate, over Wentworth Ave. at South Cermak Rd.

Comiskey Park, 333 W. 35th St. 312/674-1000.
Home of the Chicago White Sox baseball team.

De La Salle High School, 3455 S. Wabash Ave. 312/842-7355.

Glessner House Museum, 1800 S. Prairie Ave. 312/326-1480.

Illinois Institute of Technology, 3300 S. Federal St. 312/567-3000.

On Leong Chinese Merchants Association building facade,
2216 S. Wentworth Ave.

NEAR NORTHWEST SIDE - WICKER PARK

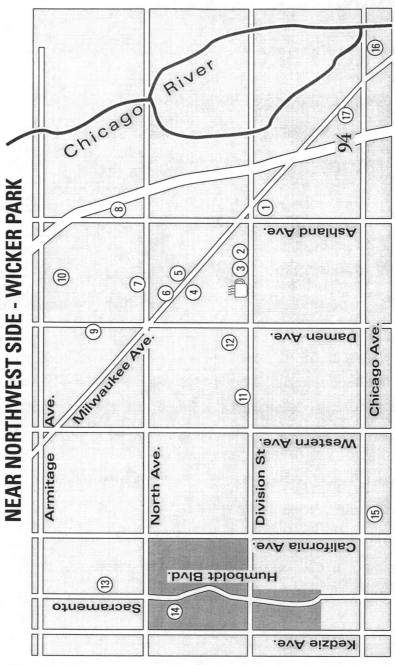

Map by Michael Polydoris.

Near Northwest Side/ Wicker Park

By Jeff Hall.

Nelson Algren

Looking for literary landmarks in Chicago's North and
Near Northwest Side neighborhoods is a matter of hitting
a moving target. Like a new
edition of a classic book, areas
like Wicker Park, Bucktown,
and Lakeview are constantly
being redesigned. Many of
the gritty, ethnic stores and
low-rent apartment buildings that attracted writers like Nelson Algren to these
areas have long since vanished. While hunting down coffeeshops and cruising
past blocks of beautiful old houses, be prepared to dodge the construction crews
and delivery vans that are supplying these areas with new life.

Studs Terkel borrowed the name of one of the area's main drags, Division
Street, for the title of his book *Division Street: America.* He wasn't writing
about the Wicker Park community *per se.* He was looking for a street name that
seemed to symbolize Chicago's cross-section of ethnic, racial, and income
groups. In his preface to this volume he, too, noted the difficulty of pinning
down a single neighborhood in Chicago or any American city: "The nomadic,
transitory nature of contemporary life has made diffusion the order—or disor-
der—of the city. The bulldozer and the wrecking ball have played their roles."[1]

The gentrification of Chicago's ethnic enclaves means past history has to
be balanced with new interests. Some historic sites that show up in Chicago
novels still remain; they tend to be well-known and durable places like the

Photo by Thayer Lindner.

Division Street Russian Baths or Lottie's, a pub on Cortland Avenue. Budding Saul Bellows will find a generous selection of bookstores and coffeeshops that they can frequent for refreshment and for testing out their work at open mics.

Milwaukee Avenue, which was once a plank road and later a streetcar line that delivered Polish, German, and Swedish immigrants from the crowded downtown area to more family-oriented neighborhoods, is still the main road through Wicker Park. The busy intersection of Ashland, Division, and Milwaukee was the spiritual center of Nelson Algren's world, the Polish immigrant community that he explored in such novels as *Never Come Morning* and *The Man With the Golden Arm.* The *Polish Daily Zgoda*, a Polish language newspaper that folded in 1971, was published for many years in the big white tile building on the north side of Milwaukee. Though many of the Polish shops are gone, the intersection's Chopin Theatre still performs some plays in Polish. Damen and Ashland Avenues lead both south to Bucktown and Ukrainian Village, and north to Lakeview, other neighborhoods full of shopping and entertainment options as well as desirable places to live.

Many of the structures that have been around the longest are also among the most beautiful, particularly the Roman Catholic and Russian Orthodox churches. Several churches in particular should not be missed: St. Stanislaus Kostka, at Evergreen Ave. and Noble St., is Chicago's oldest Polish Roman Catholic parish, dating back to the 1880s. Nelson Algren's "biggest drunk on Division Street," Roman Orlov, lived on Noble near the church when he was a boy; Orlov's father played accordion for pennies in the Division Street taverns.

St. Mary of the Angels Church, Hermitage Ave. and Cortland St., is one of Chicago's largest and most beautiful churches. The statues of angels around its roof and bell towers were recently renovated. Holy Trinity Church, Leavitt St. and Haddon Ave., is south of Wicker Park in Ukrainian Village. This beautiful structure was designed by Louis Sullivan and completed in 1901.

Many of the places once associated with Algren himself have vanished due to changes in the area's ethnic and social makeup over the years. Most of the Polish residents and stores left, replaced with businesses serving the newer Latino, mostly Mexican and Puerto Rican, or young and artsy populations.

The result, for those of us who want to follow Algren's footsteps and check out other literary venues, is a mixed bag. On the one hand, you have to use your imagination because most of the businesses Algren frequented are gone. The place where he bought live chickens and killed and plucked them himself, at 1452 N. Milwaukee, is now the site of the People's Gas offices, for instance. But other sites remain. The Flatiron Building and Fairfield Savings and Loan buildings still anchor the busy intersection of North, Damen, and Milwaukee. A house where the pianist Paderewski (1860-1941) is said to have played (2138 W. Pierce) can still be admired, too. Plus there are always new coffeeshops, bookstores, and performances that continue to make Wicker Park a lively literary community.

How to Get There

If you're driving, you can take any one of the main arteries that lead to the area: Ashland, Division, Milwaukee, North, or Damen. If you're taking the El, get on the Blue Line and get off at the Damen stop for the Damen-North-Milwaukee intersection, or the Division stop for the Division-Ashland-Milwaukee intersection. They are a couple of the area's busiest intersections and great places to start exploring Wicker Park.

Walking Tour

1.
Chopin Theatre and Café and Nelson Algren Fountain
Milwaukee Ave., Ashland Ave., and Division St.

One of the big centers of activity in Wicker Park is the Ashland-Milwaukee-Division intersection, an area now also called "East Village." More than a decade after Algren's death, the city of Chicago dedicated the Nelson Algren Fountain as a monument to the Wicker Park neighborhood's most famous writer. It's perhaps fitting that it has been placed on a little island in the center of one the city's busiest intersections, since one of the pivotal incidents of Algren's *The Man With the Golden Arm* is the traffic accident that leaves Sophie Majcinek, Frankie Machine's wife, in a wheelchair.

The **Chopin Theatre and Café**, 1543 W. Division, 773/486-4331, functions as the performance space for the Guild Complex, which holds poetry readings and literary events nearly every night of the year.

Every second and fourth Tuesday of the month, Young Chicago Authors has an open mic reading in the basement of the café. Each Tuesday and Wednesday night, the Guild holds an open mic at 9:30 P.M. You can practice beforehand at **Big Horse**, 1558 N. Milwaukee, a bar and Mexican eatery, which holds its own open mic Tues. 8 P.M.

Young Chicago Authors is a writing program that draws students from public and Catholic high schools all over the city. Students commit themselves to attending workshops and writing classes one day a week. At the end of the year, they receive a $2,000 scholarship. (For more information, call 773/486-4331.)

2.
West Division Street sites

The apartment building at 1860 W. Division where Frankie and Sophie Machine lived in *The Man With the Golden Arm* doesn't exist. However, you can imagine that Algren bought pastries at Sompelski's Bakery on West Division. Or stop in at the **Jinx Café**, 1928 W. Division, 773/645-3667, and imagine Frankie Machine wheeling his wife Sophie up and down this street on their way to or from the Tug & Maul or another bar with a Prager beer sign in the window.

One of Nelson Algren's strongest admirers was another great Chicago writer himself—Mike Royko, columnist for the *Chicago Daily News* and later the *Chicago Tribune,* who wrote frequently about the Polish neighborhood around Milwaukee and Division. Royko's hero, Slats Grobnik, lived a simple life. In "When Slats Caught Santa," a 1968 column, Royko describes Slats's Christmas:

> Every Christmas eve in the middle of the afternoon, Mrs. Grobnik would bundle up Slats and his brother Fats, and they would ride a streetcar to the plant where Mr. Grobnik worked.
>
> When he came out they would greet him and the whole family would ride home together on the streetcar.
>
> It was partly sentiment, but it was mostly a way of making sure Mr. Grobnik didn't stop and blow his Christmas check on Division St.

3.
Division Street Russian Baths
1916 W. Division St. 773/384-9671

Although the Luxor Baths that Nelson Algren used to visit at 2039 W. North Ave. have gone out of business, this old-time bathhouse still remains. (The beautiful facade of the North Avenue Baths building, 2039 W. North, is worth admiring, however.) Take a hot bath here, enjoy a sauna, or get a massage just like the old-timers have done for years (for thousands of years, actually, if you go back to the ancient Roman bathhouses).

The Russian Baths play an important role in Saul Bellow's 1975 novel

Humboldt's Gift. Humboldt's old friend Charlie Citrine, who narrates the story and comes into a legacy that Humboldt has left him, remembers going to the Russian Baths with his father when he was a boy. He describes the facility as seemingly having been at the same location forever, "hotter than the tropics and rotting sweetly." A quarter of a century later, the description still rings true. Citrine goes there to meet a Mafia acquaintance, Rinaldo Cantabile. They are surrounded by old guys "engaged in a collective attempt to buck history."[2]

Photo by Thayer Lindner.

Division Street Russian Baths.

On the corner, just to the west, is Damen Avenue. Here Frankie and Sophie go to see Old Doc Dominowski after the accident that has left Sophie in a wheelchair in *The Man With the Golden Arm.* At Damen and Division, Frankie leaves his friend Sparrow after a long card game and goes to see his drug dealer at 4 A.M.

4.
Nelson Algren's apartment
1958 W. Evergreen Ave.

In contrast to Algren's earlier place on Wabansia, you can actually see the apartment where Algren lived from 1959 to 1975 at 1958 W. Evergreen, this stretch of which has been renamed Nelson Algren Avenue. The city has placed a Chicago Tribute marker in front of the building where Algren lived on the third floor. Look closely and you can see a smaller plaque next to the big picture window on the first floor. It reads:

NELSON ALGREN, Novelist

1909-1981

Lived on the third floor here 1959-1975

"Lyrical, tough, tender, compassionate, he
showed the people's pain."

Nelson Algren Committee

Photo by Thayer Lindner.

Nelson Algren lived here
from 1959 to 1975.

Before he moved from Chicago to Paterson, New Jersey, Algren held a famous garage sale to raise money. He had lost most of his earnings in poker games and at the track. Sale items reportedly included his furniture and some of his manuscripts.

When Algren died in 1981, Mike Royko led a campaign to have the street renamed in Algren's honor. Then-mayor Jane Byrne had a sign prepared, but the alderman of the area received a number of phone calls from residents who complained at having to change their addresses. As a result, the City Council backed out. The renaming wasn't done until years after the writer's death.

According to Doug Moe (writing in *The World of Mike Royko*), Royko once told Algren that the book he admired most was the collection of stories called *The Neon Wilderness*. When a new edition of *The Neon Wilderness* was published in 1967, Algren dedicated the book to Royko. Royko was moved by the gesture, saying it was the nicest thing anyone had ever done for him.

5.
Myopic Books
1468 N. Milwaukee Ave. 773/862-4882

A nice little bookstore that's open late and that provides the browser with lots of tiny passageways and stairways for exploring books. There's food, beverages, and a table in back where you can sit and read.

6.
Occult Book Store
1579 N. Milwaukee Ave., #321, 773/292-0995

If facing writer's block, perhaps some incense or magic talisman from this shop can provide inspiration. They also carry out of print, rare, and used books on subjects ranging from divination, prophecy, and religion to the occult arts and sciences.

7.
Quimby's Bookstore
1854 W. North Ave. 773/342-0910
www.quimbys.com

A quintessential Wicker Park shop—quirky, punky, and self-consciously trying its best to be oh-so-hip. This is a great place for alternative and independently-published books, magazines, 'zines, comics, gay/lesbian literature, pop culture items, posters, and lots of stuff that's just plain bizarre.

8.
Nelson Algren's apartment
1523 W. Wabansia Ave.

Algren's apartment at 1523 Wabansia is described by his biographer, Bettina Drew, as being "almost Siberian in its austerity." It consisted of only two rooms overlooking an Ashland Avenue alley, and the rent was just $10 a month. This is where he was living in 1947 when Simone de Beauvoir first came to visit him during her lecture tour of the United States. Ironically, the friend who gave de

Beauvoir Algren's number was named Mary Guggenheim, a young woman with whom Algren had been having a brief affair. Algren was cooking dinner when de Beauvoir called; he couldn't understand her thick French accent and she had to call back several times. He visited her at the Palmer House and agreed to take her on a tour of Chicago's lowlife, beginning with West Madison Street. Not long after, they became lovers, and young Miss Guggenheim was out of the picture.

This is the apartment depicted in the photo of Algren on the back of the original dust jacket of *The Man With the Golden Arm,* which also includes a laudatory quote from Carl Sandburg, who praises his "great qualities of insight into people, a heart of pity, a gift of cadence and song . . . "

The Wabansia flat was where Algren penned his masterpiece, *The Man With the Golden Arm,* and romanced Simone de Beauvoir. This romantic place now exists only in the imagination, unfortunately; it was bulldozed to make way for the Kennedy Expressway, which cut a swath of destruction through this and other Northwest Side neighborhoods. You can walk under the expressway where the building used to be and see if you can feel what Algren's cronies have felt. A *Chicago Tribune* article reports that "some old friends still feel his ghost in the pavement and concrete pilings."[3]

9.
Damen Avenue shops
Damen Ave. between North and Armitage Aves.

Damen, between North and Armitage, has a long stretch of trendy restaurants and shops. **Minor Arcana**, 1852 N. Damen, 773/252-1389, has a small selection of books on magic, herbs, tarot, palmistry, and witchcraft, as well as a gallery/reading room. **Miko's Italian Ice**, 1846 N. Damen, is a nice place to stop on a warm day for either Italian ice or iced coffee. After you purchase a book at Minor Arcana, enjoy some upscale coffee at the elegant **Caffé De Luca**, 1721 N. Damen, 773/342-6000.

David Hernandez

David Hernandez, a city resident since 1955 who has written several books of poetry and conducts writing workshops around the city, has been dubbed the Unofficial Poet Laureate of Chicago. He performs regularly in the Chicago area with his musical group Street Sounds, an Afro/Cuban/jazz poetry collective. Hernandez regularly turns to the city's multicultural mix and artistic communities for poetic inspiration. "It's a city where you can meet all kinds of people, from Park Avenue to park benches," he says.

One year, for the July 4 celebration in Grant Park, Hernandez read his inaugural poem for Mayor Harold Washington to 1.2 million people, which he calls "the largest audience ever for poetry in Chicago." The city commissioned a David Hernandez poem to commemorate its 150th anniversary, and he has received the Gwendolyn Brooks Outstanding Poet of Illinois Award, as well as other awards and grants.

"Chicago is a good place for writers, especially with the renaissance in the poetry scene that's

Photo courtesy of David Hernandez.

David Hernandez.

been going on for a few years now," says Hernandez.

What's the reason for the resurgence in poetry? It has to do with the way Chicago is changing, both as a place to live and to work. "The city lost its industrial base years ago during the Reagan administration, so Chicago is now more oriented toward the arts," says Hernandez. "Things like the Jazz Festival exist because someone has to bring in the arts to entertain all the white collar workers who are here now. So, because of the change in work here, there's been a renaissance in theater and poetry, too."

Hernandez grew up in Old Town, around North and Wells. In his younger days he frequented the Second City comedy club and folk music clubs such as the Earl of Old Town. He lives in the Humboldt Park neighborhood; for the most part, he works at home, but you might occasionally find him at the Myopic Café on Milwaukee. His favorite bookstore is Bookworks on North Clark, which he calls a "well-kept secret."

To participate in the poetry reading scene in Chicago, Hernandez recommends Chicago Coffee on North Broadway on Friday night, or Café Aloha on North Lincoln on Tuesday. "I just get inspired by the whole artistic community of Chicago, including blues festivals, theater, dance performances, arts shows, and neighborhood carnivals," he says.

> **"Chicago . . . a great place for working poets."**

As an example of the diversity he loves, he mentions that in his poetry workshop in Humboldt Park he gets a real cross-section—from older people to young kids, and from Latinos to Russian ladies. "Once I taught some classes at Trumbull High School, and I discovered that 72 different dialects were spoken there. Another good thing about Chicago being so polycultural is the food in the restaurants here."

Because he does many different things, Hernandez is able to pull off the trick of supporting himself as a poet. "Chicago is a great place for working poets," he says.

10.
Lottie's Pub
1925 W. Cortland St. 773/489-0738

You can honor Nelson Algren's memory by having a shot and a beer at one of his favorite bars. In Algren's day, the upper part of Lottie's was a grocery store, while the stairs that still exist led down to the basement: a low-down-and-dirty drinking hole. Lottie herself is remembered as a no-nonsense woman who didn't hesitate to throw out patrons (including, presumably, Algren) when they got too rowdy. Today Lottie's survives as a sports bar, catering to the young people who now flock to the area.

Photo by Thayer Lindner.

Lottie's, a one-time Algren
watering hole.

11.
St. Mary of Nazareth Hospital
2233 W. Division St. 312/770-2000

Newspaper columnist and writer Mike Royko, a true Chicagoan and local legend, was born here on September 19, 1932. His family owned a bar called the Blue Sky Lounge, which was located at 2122 N. Milwaukee. Royko lived in this part of Chicago until moving to the Edgebrook neighborhood in 1969.

12.
Home of August Spies
2132 W. Potomac Ave.

This unassuming two-story building was a typical workers' home in the 1880s. Spies was one of four men executed for allegedly taking part in the Haymarket

Riot of 1886. After Spies's death, as many as a million people assembled to watch the procession as his coffin was led from this house down Milwaukee Avenue. Frank Norris, author of *The Pit* and *McTeague,* wrote a novel about the riot in 1909 called *The Bomb.* Norris's character Rudolph Schnaubelt sets off the bomb in Haymarket Square, killing eight policemen and 60 people. Discontent with America leads Schnaubelt to join the Chicago Anarchists during the labor unrest of the 1880s. Schnaubelt later escapes to Bavaria, while Spies and the others pay the price for the deed.

Driving Tour

13.
L. Frank Baum house
1667 Humboldt Blvd.

Some Chicago figures in the literary and performing arts were famous themselves, but only a few can be said to have created characters who became cultural icons—characters that people everywhere would instantly recognize. Chester Gould created Dick Tracy in Chicago and the Marx brothers "invented" themselves here; but many Chicagoans don't realize that the Tin Woodman, the Cowardly Lion, and the Scarecrow were also born here, springing from the imagination of a one-time amateur photographer, newspaperman, and shopkeeper named Lyman Frank Baum.

Baum was born in Chittenango, a small town in upstate New York. He tried to make a living running a store and then a newspaper in Aberdeen, South Dakota. When the newspaper went bankrupt, Baum moved with his wife and four sons to Chicago in 1891, where he found work on the *Chicago Evening Post*—the same newspaper that employed Peter Finley Dunne, who would begin writing his famous "Mr. Dooley" columns two years later (see pp. 109-110).

At first, the Baums lived near Campbell Park on the West Side. After publishing two books, including *Father Goose, His Book* in 1899, Baum and his

Photo courtesy of Alexander Mitchell Public Library.

L. Frank Baum reading to his sons in the parlor of their Humboldt Blvd. home.

family were able to move to a home near Humboldt Park. Exactly where this house was located is hard to pin down. Baum biographers Angelica Shirley Carpenter and Jean Shirley list the address as 68 Humboldt Blvd. The city of Chicago itself gives the address as 1667 Humboldt Blvd., but no house with that address exists today. It's generally agreed that the house was just across North Avenue from Humboldt Park.

As Carpenter and Shirley tell it in *L. Frank Baum: Royal Historian of Oz,* one cold winter day as Baum put on his overcoat and prepared to go out to run errands, he was met by a group of children, including his own sons. They beseeched him to come inside and tell them a story. Not anxious to brave the cold winter winds, Baum obliged, and told the story of a Kansas farm girl blown by a cyclone to a magic land. There she encountered a scarecrow, a woodman made of tin, and a lion. Their enemy was a wicked witch. Baum later said that he was possessed by this story, which "seemed to write itself." He shooed the children away and wrote it down hurriedly on scrap paper he had at hand.[4]

Legend has it that when Baum was searching for a name for his magic kingdom, his attention was drawn to the labels on his file cabinet drawers, one of which was marked *O-Z.*

Baum worked with William W. Denslow, an illustrator and fellow member of the Chicago Press Club. Denslow, who had a bushy mustache and wore a bright red vest, had created art for the *Father Goose* book and had a studio on the tenth floor in the Fine Arts Building. The original title for the new work was *The Emerald City,* but fearing a superstition that any book with the name of a jewel in the title would have bad luck, Baum changed the name to *The Wonderful Wizard of Oz.*

After the great success of this book, Baum and Denslow worked on a musical version of the story. Frank turned out a variety of books in succession including *Master Key: An Electrical Fairy Tale, A New Wonderland, The Army Alphabet,* and *The Navy Alphabet.* It took a while before he followed up with another Oz book, *The Marvelous Land of Oz.* This new book included the addition of a new character, a human-being-sized insect named H. M. Woggle-Bug. Dorothy returned to the series in *Ozma of Oz, Dorothy and the Wizard in Oz,* and *The Road to Oz.* Later, Baum created movies of some of the Oz films with the Selig Polyscope Company of Chicago.[5] According to Chicago film historian Arnie Bernstein, the Selig plant was located at Western and Irving Park on the North Side.[6]

Although you can find a statue of the Tin Man in Oz Park on the North Side (see p. 142), the place where he was born and continued to have adventures was near Humboldt and North, a couple of miles to the west.

14.
Fritz Reuter statue

It's quite a step down from L. Frank Baum and the *Wizard of Oz,* but in Humboldt Park near Grower Drive north of Division stands a monument to German novelist Fritz Reuter (1810-1874), who struggled against political oppression, having been imprisoned for seven years for his participation in a student political club.

15.
Chicago Avenue sites

The **Ukrainian Book and Gift Shop**, 2315 W. Chicago, 773/276-6373, is a good place to find a few Russian-language books as well as beautifully decorated eggs and other gifts. **The Autonomous Zone**, 2012 W. Chicago, 773/252-

6019, is a tiny shop with a rack full of obscure little radical pamphlets and literary magazines near the front door. By all means, check out the Ukrainian Coffee with a dash of liquor at **Sak's Ukrainian Village Restaurant**, 2301 W. Chicago, 773/278-4445, which is also a great place to get an authentic Ukrainian meal. **Dixie's Snack Shop**, at Damen and Chicago, has absolutely nothing of literary note, but it's worth a look through the window just for atmosphere. It's the type of gritty place where Nelson Algren himself would have felt at home.

16.
St. John Cantius
825 N. Carpenter St. 312/243-7373

In Nelson Algren's novel *Never Come Morning*, Steffi Rostenkowski has a realization:

> Night after night she heard the iron rocking of the bells of St. John Cantius. Each night they came nearer. Till the roar of the Loop was only a troubled whimper beneath the rocking of the bells. "Everyone lives in the same big room," she would tell herself as they rocked, "But nobody's speakin' to anyone else, 'n nobody got a key."[7]

Be sure to visit this beautiful church, long a center of the Polish community on the Near Northwest Side.

17.
Polish Roman Catholic Union of America
984 N. Milwaukee Ave. 773/278-3210

This worthy organization, which glowers down upon southbound drivers on the Kennedy Expressway, ordered Nelson Algren's first novel, *Never Come Morning*, banned from the Chicago Public Library because it was so highly critical of life in Chicago's Polish-American slums.

Bookstores

Books Plus Publications, 2546 W. Division St. 773/227-5872.

Elohim, 2636 W. Division St. 773/342-5421.

Luz A La Familia, 2425 W. Division St. 773/772-0954.

Minor Arcana, 1852 N. Damen Ave. 773/252-1389.

Myopic Books, 1468 N. Milwaukee Ave. 773/862-4882.

Occult Book Store, 1579 N. Milwaukee Ave. 773/292-0995.

Quimby's Bookstore, 1854 W. North Ave. 773/342-0910.

Socialist Workers' Party, 1223 N. Milwaukee Ave. 773/235-5999.

Ukrainian Book and Gift Shop, 2315 W. Chicago Ave. 773/276-6373.

Coffeehouses and More

Café Cafina, 1588 N. Milwaukee Ave. 773/227-8400.

Caffé De Luca, 1721 N. Damen Ave. 773/342-6000.

Cold Comfort, 2211 W. North Ave. 773/772-4552.

Donofrio's Double Corona, 2058 W. Chicago Ave. 773/342-7820.

Jinx Café, 1928 W. Division St. 773/645-3667.

Little Orbis, 1934 W. North Ave.
Quite possibly the smallest coffeeshop in the city, the remnant of a much larger venue called Urbis Orbis that was once on the second floor of this building.

Sweet Thang, 1921 W. North Ave. 773/772-4166.

Other Places of Interest

Harris Cohn house, 1941 W. Schiller St.
Known as the Wicker Park Castle, this house was built in 1888. It's just one of many beautiful homes in the neighborhood. Also check out the homes in the 1500 block of North Hoyne, the 2100 block of West Pierce, and the 1600 block of North Leavitt.

Division Street Russian Baths, 1916 W. Division St. 773/384-9671.

The Map Room, 1949 N. Hoyne Ave. 773/252-7636.
Browse through a selection of travel maps and books while you're enjoying some liquid refreshment.

Wicker Park, bounded by Damen Ave., Schiller St., and Wicker Park Ave.
This is Chicago's smallest park. It was set aside as a common space in 1870 by two brothers, Charles and Joel Wicker, who had real estate holdings in the area.

LINCOLN PARK

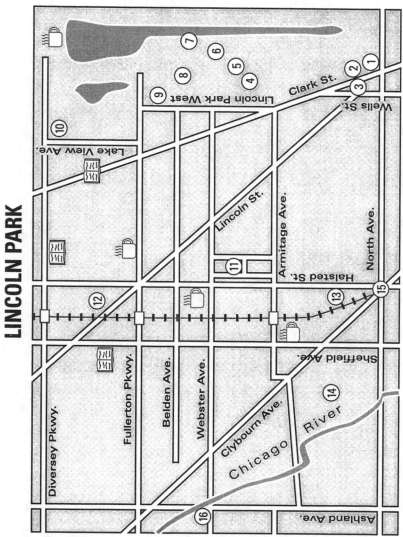

Map by Michael Polydoris.

Lincoln Park

I cross Lincoln Park on a winter night
when the snow is falling.
Lincoln in bronze stands among the
white lines of snow . . .

—CARL SANDBURG, "Smoke and Steel"

Lincoln Park and much of the North Side are dominated by two towering figures: Abraham Lincoln and his biographer, the poet Carl Sandburg.

Lincoln Park actually stretches six miles to the north along the lakefront, making it the city's largest park. The areas around North and Fullerton Avenues are among the most popular green spaces in the city. On every nice day and even some

By Jeff Hall.

Carl Sandburg

that aren't so nice, families with young children migrate to North Avenue Beach and Lincoln Park Zoo, while joggers and bikers crowd the lakefront pathways.

Although most patrons don't go to these recreational havens on a literary mission, you'll find plenty of museum collections and monuments to writers simply by going through Lincoln Park from North Avenue to Diversey Parkway.

How to Get There

The Clark Street, Lincoln Avenue, or North Avenue buses will get you to Lincoln Park. If driving, you'll find parking about a block north of the Chicago Historical Society in the park itself (the entrance is on Stockton Drive). You can also take the CTA's Brown Line to Sedgwick if you're willing to walk a few blocks east on North Avenue until you reach the Historical Society.

Walking Tour

1.
Chicago Historical Society
1601 N. Clark St., at North Ave. 312/642-4600

The Historical Society, formed in 1856, is a gold mine for anyone interested in the city's past in general and its literary heritage in particular. The research areas are open to the public; get a pass from the cashier. Then you can revel in the delights of historic books and photographs to your heart's content.

In the regular display areas of the society you'll find such treasures as John Brown's personal Bible; one of the original broadsides of the Declaration of Independence printed on July 4, 1776; Lincoln's last dispatch to General Ulysses S. Grant (in which he exhorted Grant to end the Civil War by saying "let the *thing* be pressed"); the desk at which Lincoln drafted the Emancipation Proclamation; a first edition of *Uncle Tom's Cabin;* and much more.

At the Big Shoulders Café (the name, of course, from Carl Sandburg's "Chicago"), enjoy menu items like Sheboygan bratwurst and Hobo hash. Café hours are Mon.-Sat. 11:30 A.M.-3 P.M. and Sun. 10:30 A.M.-3 P.M.

The society is open Mon.-Sat. 9:30 A.M.-4:30 P.M. and Sun. 12 P.M.-5 P.M. Admission is $5 adults, $3 students ages 12-23 and seniors, and $1 children ages 6-11. Mon. are free.

2.
Abraham Lincoln statue
North Ave. east of Clark St. (east side of Chicago Historical Society building)

This sculpture was completed in 1887 by August Saint-Gaudens, an Irish-born American sculptor of international renown. While working on this project, Saint-Gaudens also referred to life casts of Lincoln's face and hands. Most people are pretty impressed with the results, but the artist himself preferred his other statue of Lincoln, which is located in Grant Park downtown. Saint-Gaudens visited with Lincoln several time during his lifetime and also came to pay his respects after the assassination when the president was lying in state.

Those of us who live in the Land of Lincoln may get somewhat used to tributes to his accomplishments, but I never fail to feel inspired when I think of his legendary love of books. It's amazing that he composed his timeless prose without benefit of speechwriters, pollsters, and spin doctors. So it shouldn't come as a surprise that he was also a poet. In the first volume of Sandburg's three-volume biography of Lincoln, he quotes a poem called "My Childhood Home I See Again" that the future president wrote in 1846:

> I've heard it oft, as if I dreamed,
> Far-distant, sweet, and lone;
> The funeral dirge it ever seemed
> Of reason dead and gone.
>
> To drink its strains, I've stole away,
> All silently and still,
> Ere yet the rising god of day
> Had streaked the Eastern hill.

This poem, Sandburg reports, was published anonymously in a newspaper called the *Quincy Whig*.[1]

A pedestrian underpass near the statue of Lincoln will take you under LaSalle Street north to Lincoln Park Zoo. This underpass is an obvious place for writers to describe their characters either hiding or being chased. It was used as a setting in a couple of mystery novels, Eugene Izzi's *Bad Guys* and James Michael Ullman's *Lady on Fire*.[2]

3.
Hemingway House
1850 N. Clark St. 312/943-1825

This huge apartment building across from the park bears the name of writer Ernest Hemingway, as does the Hemingway Cleaners next door. But Hemingway himself lived near Clark and Division Streets six blocks south. This is just one of many buildings and sites in the city that use the name of a famous literary figure (another is Hawthorne Place, between Belmont Avenue and Addison Street near the lakefront) without having a real connection to the person.

4.
Hans Christian Andersen statue
Near Café Brauer, 2021 N. Cannon Dr.

Just east of Café Brauer and outside the Lincoln Park Zoo's fence, you'll find a statue of Hans Christian Andersen (1805-1875) and a swan, which recalls Andersen's story "The Ugly Duckling." By John Gelert, the statue shows Andersen sitting on a tree stump and holding a book on his right knee.

In Bill Granger's *The Newspaper Murders,* the two detectives buy hot dogs from a stand near Café Brauer and then walk across the zoo where they throw marshmallows to the polar bears in their swimming area near the Rookery.

5.
Lincoln Park Zoo
Between Fullerton Ave. and Stockton Dr. and east of Lakeview Ave.; the main entrance is 2200 N. Cannon Dr. 312/742-2000

Lincoln Park Zoo is one of the oldest zoos in the country and one of the few that does not charge an admission fee. The Farm-in-the-Zoo near the south end and the Children's Zoo near the west entrance are likely to be there permanently, but one feature that is now missing is an ancient Viking ship. Its absence would have been a big problem for the tormented main character of Saul Bellow's *The Dean's December,* who was searching the city for something eternal. The ship reminded him of his own past—and then of a deeper past:

For old times' sake he had stopped at the Lincoln Park Zoo on his way to the hospital, not to look at the animals but to see whether the Viking Ship was still there. A team of Norwegians had rowed it across the Atlantic ninety years ago and it had been preserved near the waterfowl pond, where he and Dewey Spangler had had their ignorant arguments about Plato. He was sure that there had been Viking shields hung decoratively along the gunwales. If they had been mere ornament they had rotted away, but some of the great oars were still there, laid under the ship.[3]

The Lincoln Park Zoo grounds are open daily at 8 A.M., the buildings daily at 10 A.M.; closing times vary throughout the year.

6.
Eugene Field Memorial

In Lincoln Park Zoo, near the Small Mammal House, you'll find the Eugene Field Memorial (1922) by Edward McCaran. A winged lady drops flowers on two sleeping children who are cuddled at her feet. The statue recalls Field's poem "The Rock-A-By Lady":

> The Rock-A-By Lady from Hushaby Street
> Comes stealing; comes creeping:
> . . . When she findeth you sleeping!

Around the stone base relief panels depict scenes from some of Field's most

Memorial to poet
Eugene Field.

Photo by Thayer Lindner.

famous poems: "Wynken, Blynken and Nod" and "The Sugar-Plum Tree." Smaller reliefs illustrating two more poems, "The Fly-Away Horse" and "Seein' Things," are on the ends of the base above the drinking fountains, which are just high enough for kids. This memorial was provided by donations from public school children and citizens of Chicago, with assistance from the B. F. Ferguson Monument Fund.

7.
Lincoln Park lagoon
East of Cannon Dr., south of Fullerton Ave.

Walk north and then east out the front entrance to the zoo, which fronts on Cannon Drive. Across the Drive you see the Lincoln Park lagoon and a bridle path. The main character in *A Crime Story* by Jay Robert Nash takes his girlfriend walking along this bridle path. In Sara Paretsky's *Blood Shot*, V. I. Warshawski is jogging with her neighbor's dog Peppy along the lagoon when she is kidnapped by thugs who drive her to Dead Stick Pond on the Southeast Side (see pp. 220-221), where they dump her and leave her for dead.

8.
Friedrich von Schiller statue

Just outside the west entrance to the zoo is a large statue of the German poet Johann Christoph Friedrich von Schiller (1759-1805) done by Erns Bildhauer Rau. Cast in Stuttgart, it was erected in Lincoln Park by a group called Chicago Citizens of German Descent and dedicated in 1886. You might be familiar with some of Schiller's work without it; Beethoven used Schiller's poem "Ode to Joy" in his Ninth Symphony.

9.
William Shakespeare statue

The statue of Shakespeare was bequeathed to the Chicago Park District in 1893 in the will of Samuel Johnson, president of Chicago City Railroad Company. The Old English garden just to the north, also called Grandmother's Garden, was

was added to accompany it. It is said to be the first statue in which Shakespeare is shown wearing clothing from the period in which he lived. A plaster model of this statue by William Ordway Partidge was shown at the World's Columbian Exposition of 1893. Partidge was evidently a bit of a perfectionist, visiting Stratford-on-Avon, studying the life of Shakespeare, even making 15 studies of the head before he was satisfied. Finally, the work was cast in bronze in Paris and shipped to Chicago.

Photo by Greg Holden.

Lincoln Park's statue of William Shakespeare.

10.
Goethe monument

Diversey Pkwy. and Sheridan Rd.

Even if you wanted to, you couldn't miss the monument to German poet and dramatist Johann Wolfgang von Goethe done by Herman Hahn in 1913. Prominently located on this intersection's southeast corner, it depicts an idealized gothic figure 25 feet high. On the low wall behind the sculpture is a likeness of Goethe and a quotation in both German and English from *Faust,* his most famous work.

11.
Oz Park
Webster St. and Lincoln Ave.

This park was named in 1976 to commemorate the work of L. Frank Baum,
who wrote *The Wonderful Wizard of Oz*
in 1900 while living in a house on Humboldt Boulevard a mile or two west of here
(see pp. 127-129).

Perhaps in the summer the statue of
the Tin Man on Lincoln just south of Webster gets a kick out of the art fair and plays
that are held under the stars near the hill
at the south end of the park. Kids are sure
to get a thrill when they follow the yellow
brick path and adults will enjoy strolling
through the gardens.

Photo by Greg Holden.

The Tin Man greets visitors to Oz Park.

Driving Tour

12.
Biograph Theater
2433 N. Lincoln Ave. 773/348-4123

One of the most notorious locations in Chicago is where Public Enemy Number
One John Dillinger went on a hot night on July 22, 1934, to see a movie called
Manhattan Melodrama with his companion, The Lady in Red. The lady friend
had tipped off the FBI, who ambushed Dillinger and shot him to death in the
alley next to the theater. This event is recalled in Edith Skom's *The Mark Twain
Murders* as well as in Michael Raleigh's *A Body in Belmont Harbor.*[4]

13.
Steppenwolf Theatre Company
1650 N. Halsted St. 312/335-1650

Steppenwolf Theatre Company, which bills itself as An Actor's Theater, is one of the city's artistic treasures. The group originally began performing in 1974 in a church basement in north suburban Highland Park under the direction of Gary Sinise, Terry Kinney, and Jeff Perry. Today, Steppenwolf's 33 members are committed to the principles of ensemble collaboration and artistic risk. The company has ongoing relationships with established playwrights such as Sam Shepard, Lanford Wilson, and Athol Fugard. In 1988, ensemble member Frank Galati adapted John Steinbeck's Pulitzer Prize-winning novel *The Grapes of Wrath.* Galati and Steppenwolf earned two Tony Awards for Best Play and Best Director after the play opened on Broadway in 1990.

14.
Transitions Bookplace
1000 W. North Ave. 312/951-7323

A peaceful oasis in the rush of the busy Clybourn Avenue shopping corridor, Transitions offers books on spiritual topics, a small coffeeshop, and rushing water from miniature fountains that are sure to put you in a restful mood even if you had to fight traffic to get here.

15.
Clybourn, North, and Halsted area

"Consider the Lilies," a story by Edna Ferber from her 1927 collection *Mother Knows Best,* is set in the Hungarian community of Clybourn, North, and Halsted in the period from 1903 to 1923. The story begins: "Clybourn Avenue has a rather elegant sound. There never was a more inelegant thoroughfare." If you can find any trace left of this neighborhood, you're one up on me.

16.
Green Dolphin Street
Webster Pl. and Ashland Ave. 773/395-0066

This club is perched on the banks of the North Branch of the Chicago River, and those who come by water can tie up their boats outside. The dock is open for sipping drinks and watching pleasure craft and debris go by. The name comes from a street in the novel *Green Dolphin Country* by Elizabeth Goudge (London, Hodder and Stoughton, Ltd., 1944), which is set on a remote island in the English Channel. It was made into a 1947 movie starring Lana Turner, and the title was adopted by jazzmen such as Stan Getz and Miles Davis.

Bookstores

Act I Bookstore, 2540 N. Lincoln Ave. 773/348-6757.

Barnes & Noble Booksellers, 659 W. Diversey Pkwy. 773/871-9004, 1441 W. Webster Ave. 773/871-3610.

Chicago Historical Society bookstore, 1601 N. Clark St. 312/642-4600.

Crown Books, 1714 N. Sheffield Ave. 312/787-4370.

DePaul University Bookstore, 2425 N. Sheffield Ave. 773/325-7700.

Lincoln Park Bookshop, 2423 N. Clark St. 773/477-7087.

Transitions Bookplace, 1000 W. North Ave. 312/951-7323.

Coffeehouses and More

Big Shoulders Café, Chicago Historical Society, 1601 N. Clark St. 312/587-7766.

Bourgeois Pig Café, 738 W. Fullerton Pkwy. 773/883-5282.

Caribou Coffee, 1561 N. Wells St. 773/266-7504.

Coffee & Tea Exchange, 833 W. Armitage Ave. 773/929-6730.

Monterotondo Trattoria Italia, 612 W. Wrightwood Ave. 773/883-7273.

North Pond Café, 2610 N. Cannon Dr. 773/477-5845.

Seattle's Best Coffee, 1700 N. Wells St. 312/649-1620.

Other Places of Interest

Couch Mausoleum, just north of the Chicago Historical Society building and the Abraham Lincoln statue.
The only family tomb remaining from the graveyard that once occupied the park.

DePaul University, Lincoln Park Campus, 2135 N. Kenmore Ave.

Lincoln Park Conservatory, Fullerton Pkwy. and Stockton Dr. 312/742-7736.

Moody Memorial Church, 1609 N. LaSalle Dr.
A Byzantine and Romanesque structure on Clark Street across from the Chicago Historical Society, built in 1925.

Peggy Notebaert Nature Museum, 2430 N. Cannon Dr. 773/871-2668.

Second City Theatre, 1616 N. Wells St. 312/337-3992.

NORTH SIDE

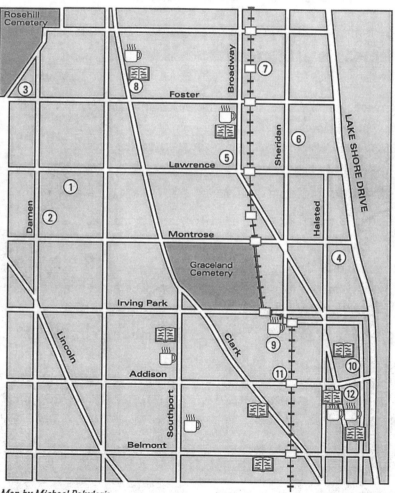

Map by Michael Polydoris.

North Side/ Carl Sandburg Country

By Jeff Hall.

L. Frank Baum

V. I. Warshawski, the heroine of Sara Paretsky's mystery novels, might do much of her detecting work in the Loop or on the far South Side, but the North Side is where she hangs her fedora each night (unless, of course, she's been dumped in Dead Stick Pond by some would-be murderers or put in the hospital after another encounter with some other bad guys). Newspaper columnist Mike Royko chose to live in a condo along the lakefront where he could be close to the softball fields where he loved to play. Studs Terkel and his late wife Ida lived in a home on the North Side; Carl Sandburg lived on North Hermitage with his wife Lilian and their first daughter.

The combination of good housing and the proximity to green spaces and the lakefront has long attracted literary figures to the North Side of Chicago, which stretches from (appropriately) North Avenue all the way to Howard Street on the city's northern boundary with Evanston. This area encompasses lots of trendy neighborhoods such as Lakeview, Lincoln Square, Andersonville, and Rogers Park.

Today, the North Side attracts poets, playwrights, novelists, journalists, technical writers, book collectors—there's something for everyone up here. During the course of my research for this book, I was told that a good number of writers live in the residential streets around the Sulzer Regional Library at

Lincoln and Sunnyside Avenues. Some of the faculty at Lane Tech High School at Addison Street and Western Avenue are published writers as well.

Many of the qualities that make the North Side an outstanding place for lovers of literature to live and work can be traced back to classic Chicago novels of the so-called Golden Age in the early twentieth century. For instance, one place to make money in real estate is this area. It was that way at the turn of the century, too. One of the main characters in Henry Blake Fuller's novel *With the Procession* is a character named McDowell who is regarded as Chicago's finest poet—and who also happens to be a real estate speculator.

The North Side, like downtown, is also a central location for the city's theater scene. The dreams of aspiring actors who come to Chicago are not new, either. In Dreiser's 1900 novel *Sister Carrie,* Carrie Meeber first realizes success upon the stage when she comes to Chicago from a small town in Wisconsin.

A character named Elizabeth in *Mr. Salt,* a 1903 novel by Chicago writer Will Payne, expresses a desire to achieve fame as a great actress: "What power! What triumph!" she thinks. "To seize this slow, voiceless multitude in her spell, lifting them up for once to the passion for which they yearned, fusing them into one exalted heart." She isn't just acting: she is thinking about the power of art to get past walls of privilege and money, to tear down barriers, to provide a refuge from the harsh world.

Because the sites in this section are spread over such a wide area, I have tried to make things more manageable by doing two things. First, I am only suggesting a driving tour of the area rather than walking tours. You can easily go to a particular location, such as Wrigley Field or Carl Sandburg's house, and walk around the surrounding neighborhood on your own, however. Second, I'm breaking this section into three separate tours. The first is the area where Carl Sandburg lived when he achieved his first success as a poet, the second is the Wrigleyville neighborhood, and the third is Rogers Park.

How to Get There

If driving, take Clark Street or Ashland Avenue, two main north-south streets that run through or near the North Side neighborhoods mentioned in this chapter. If you prefer public transportation, take the Ravenswood elevated line (the Brown Line) to the Montrose stop for the Carl Sandburg area. The Addison stop on the Red Line is a good starting point for the Wrigleyville area, and the Loyola University stop on the Red Line (or any of the other stops to the north, such as Morse Avenue or Pratt Avenue) is a good initial destination for Rogers Park.

Driving Tour #1: Ravenswood, Andersonville, Uptown

1.
Carl Sandburg residence
4646 N. Hermitage Ave.

Photo by Greg Holden.

Carl Sandburg's house.

Carl Sandburg made his first three-day visit to Chicago in 1896. He was excited by the "roar of the streets, the trolley cars, the teamsters, the drays, buggies, surreys, and phaetons."[1] When Sandburg moved to Chicago from Milwaukee in 1912, he took a second-floor apartment in this house with his wife and baby daughter. At the time, he was a struggling young reporter with the *Chicago Evening World,* and later with a small-format daily newspaper called *The Day Book,* which had offices at 500 S. Peoria. He also worked for a short time at *Systems* magazine, a business management magazine that employed another writer,

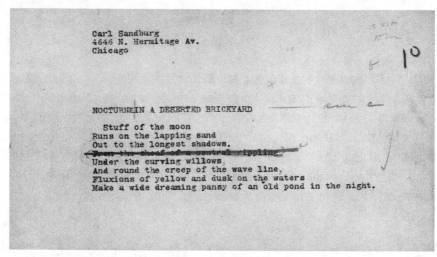

Carl Sandburg
4646 N. Hermitage Av.
Chicago

NOCTURNE IN A DESERTED BRICKYARD

Stuff of the moon
Runs on the lapping sand
Out to the longest shadows.
Under the curving willows,
And round the creep of the wave line,
Fluxions of yellow and dusk on the waters
Make a wide dreaming pansy of an old pond in the night.

Courtesy of the University of Chicago Archives, Joseph Regenstein Library.

Typescript of one of Sandburg's poems.

Edgar Rice Burroughs, who was about to achieve his first great success with a book called *Tarzan of the Apes.*[2] While covering the poet William Butler Yeats's visit to Chicago in 1914, Sandburg heard the famous poet quote his father, saying: "What can be explained is not poetry."[3]

Sandburg came home to these streets every night when he wasn't hanging out at places like the Dil Pickle Club with literary figures like Sherwood Anderson and Ben Hecht. This quiet residential street is far from the stockyards and skyscrapers young Carl immortalized in "Chicago," which was just one of the *Chicago Poems* he wrote in this house and sent to Harriet Monroe's *Poetry* magazine for publication. "Chicago" appeared in *Poetry* in 1914, and it's the one Sandburg poem that everybody knows:

> Hog Butcher for the World,
>
> Tool Maker, Stacker of Wheat,
>
> Player with Railroads and the Nation's Freight Handler;
>
> Stormy, husky, brawling,
>
> City of the Big Shoulders . . .

Alice Corbin, an editor at *Poetry,* urged Alfred Harcourt at Henry Holt and Company to publish *Chicago Poems.* The book came out in 1916 and Sandburg's career as a poet was established. The Sandburgs lived on North Hermitage for about three years, after which they moved to the suburbs—Maywood and later Elmhurst.

Ben Hecht, who worked with Sandburg at the *Chicago Daily News,* told the following story about Sandburg (and about which Hecht's biographer William MacAdams expresses some skepticism): to puncture the poet's seriousness Hecht hired "an out-of work actor, had him dress himself like Lincoln, then wait for Sandburg on a street corner the poet passed on his way home from the *News.* When Sandburg appeared, Lincoln walked toward him, tipped his hat and remarked, 'Evening, Mr. Sandburg.'"

The poet Lisel Mueller writes of being inspired to become a poet herself by reading his work: "Sandburg's unadorned, muscular, straightforward diction lured me as the painted women under the streetlamps lured the farm boys in a city named Chicago."[4]

2.
Zephyr Restaurant
1777 W. Wilson Ave. 773/728-6070

If the Zephyr had been around when Carl Sandburg lived on Hermitage, he would undoubtedly have walked his young daughter there for an ice cream treat. Be sure to ask for the Hemingway Baked Soup, an Italian minestrone with garlic bread and melted cheese which is presumably named after Ernest Hemingway.

Zephyr Restaurant.
Photo by Greg Holden.

3.

Bowmanville Road

South border of Rosehill Cemetery, east of Western Ave.

Rosehill Cemetery and Mausoleum was established in 1859. Spread over 350 acres, it is Chicago's largest cemetery. Rosehill might not be as well known as Graceland Cemetery (see p. 163), but it features Civil War graves as well as the final resting places of Charles Gates Dawes, vice-president of the United States, and such industrial leaders as Oscar Mayer, A. Montgomery Ward, John G. Shedd, and Richard Sears.

Bowmanville Road is a short diagonal street that runs along the south edge of the cemetery only a few blocks from Carl Sandburg's house on Hermitage. "Onion Days," one of the verses collected in *Chicago Poems,* describes a woman named Mrs. Gabrielle Giovanetti, who: "Works ten hours a day, sometimes twelve, picking onions for Jasper on the Bowmanville Road."

Jasper, in the poem, is a Chicago produce seller who also has a connection to Sandburg's neighborhood:

Jasper belongs to an Episcopal church in Ravenswood and on certain Sundays

He enjoys chanting the Nicene creed with his daughters on each side of him joining their voices with his.

It's likely Sandburg was referring to All Saints Episcopal Church at Wilson and Hermitage, a fine example of the "Carpenter's Gothic" style of architecture that dates back to the 1880s and where Sandburg possibly worshipped himself.

Photo by Greg Holden.

All Saints Episcopal Church.

4.
Site of Eugene Field's house
4240 N. Clarendon Ave.

The house where the poet Eugene Field lived for a short period was in Buena Park, still a suburb of Chicago in the 1890s. Field died suddenly in 1895, at the height of his fame as a wit, "children's poet," and columnist whose "Sharps and Flats" ran in the *Chicago Daily News* and inspired Theodore Dreiser and other aspiring writers. Field might well have been a victim of rehabbing stress—he died while enlarging and remodeling the house, which he called the "Sabine Farm." The building was torn down in the 1920s.

Field supposedly liked to work in "open backed bedroom slippers" around the office. He called himself the "Chicago Dante,"

... the bard

Of pork and lard

Field was initially buried in Graceland Cemetery (see pp. 163-164). Years later, his body was moved to more upscale surroundings at the Church of the Holy Comforter, 222 Kenilworth, 847/251-6120, in north suburban Kenilworth. Although his headstone describes him as "The Children's Poet," he himself had said, "I have no particular desire to shine as a writer for small children."

5.
The Green Mill Cocktail Lounge
4802 N. Broadway Ave. 773/878-5552

Chicago novelist Ana Castillo has called the Green Mill one of her favorite nightspots. The lounge frequently presents traditional jazz that fits in perfectly with décor that dates back to the era of Prohibition.

The Green Mill is just as well known for another, very different type of literary event—the Poetry Slam, which you can check out every Sunday night at 7 P.M.

The Poetry Slam is fast becoming a Chicago institution, like July heat waves and Cubs' losing seasons. The Slam is certainly popular: even on a cold Sunday night in midwinter, spectators are likely to be standing four deep at the old oak bar. If you want a seat with a good view of the performers, get to the Green Mill well in advance. Even during the open mic program that starts out the evening's festivities, the spectators crowd the aisles.

The setting for the Slam is full of atmosphere, too. During breaks, be sure to notice the permanently tobacco-stained ceiling and the grotesque woodcarving behind the bar that bears its own poem about "Big Al" Capone and Machine Gun Jack McGurn.

The national version of the Poetry Slam, which is held every year at a large concert hall, features top-notch performers. In contrast, the weekly slams and open mics are sort of like a Cubs game for poetry fans. Most of the crowd comes from other neighborhoods, and even from out of town, to watch participants compete for a $10 prize. The events are hosted by poet Marc Smith, who proclaims: "The more you drink, the more you understand this stuff." I personally agree with a magazine article I once read with the headline: "Open Mike, Insert Foot," but I encourage you to try it out for yourself at least once.

6.
Coffee Chicago open mic
5256 N. Broadway. 773/784-1305

David Hernandez and the other Chicago poets who frequently read from their work at local venues consider the Friday night open mic at Coffee Chicago to be one of the best in the city. The event is hosted by poet John Starrs.

7.
Women and Children First bookstore
5233 N. Clark St. 773/769-9299

At a time when small, independent bookstores have been driven out of business by the big chains, this place has been thriving not just as a retail outlet but as a resource and a center for a community on the city's North Side. If you are

Photo courtesy of Women and Children First.

Women and Children First co-owners Linda Bubon (left) and
Ann Christophersen with photographer Annie Liebovitz.

looking for feminist or children's books, videos, posters, or cards, this is the
place to go.

Women and Children First is one of the country's premier independent
booksellers. Its mission in a nutshell is to specialize in fiction, poetry, and art
books by women; non-fiction books on women's issues; gay/lesbian literature;
and books for children. And the way it goes about conducting its business
embodies everything that makes Chicago's independent bookstores special.

First, there's the community of writers, book lovers, and feminists that
frequents the store. They come for the selection of merchandise as well as for
the readings and book discussions. (The store had 60 programs scheduled in
May 2000 alone.) What is likely to be the frosting on the cake is the chance to
simply visit with one another. New writers are frequently featured readers in
the store as are such famous voices as Sandra Cisneros, Margaret Atwood,
Gloria Steinem, Alice Walker, Hillary Rodham Clinton, Adrienne Rich, and
others.

Then, there's the individual attention given to customers and visiting writers alike by owners Linda Bubon and Ann Christophersen and their staff. This personal touch draws people to the store not only from its own North Side Andersonville neighborhood, but more distant locales around northern Illinois and even farther afield.

For instance, when British mystery writer P. D. James promoted one of her books on a tour of America, she scheduled stops at only six bookstores in the U.S. One of them was at Women and Children First.

"Writers feel they don't get personal attention at the larger chain stores," says Bubon. At Women and Children First, however, there are always auto- graphed books from writers on the table. Many of the books she points out are from Chicago authors; some are former employees of the store.

Sometimes a boost comes from an unexpected place. Writers used to go to the East Coast and West Coast to promote their books, but now Oprah brings more writers to Chicago.

Photo courtesy of Women and Children First.

Children's storytime at Women and Children First.

"Every time we have had a celebration we have seen it as a good opportunity to bring attention to writers who have been important to the growth of the store," Bubon says. And how do the writers respond? It couldn't have been the need for recognition that induced Nicole Hollander and Sara Paretsky—two of the 50 writers who came to the store for its twentieth anniversary party in November 1999—to dress up and put on a skit.

Always ready to move forward with the times, Bubon and Christophersen are working through the American Booksellers Association to create a stronger Internet presence for the Women and Children First Web site, www.womenandchildrenfirst.com. They also don't hide from a fight. They have joined with the ABA and 25 other independent booksellers to file suit against Barnes & Noble and Borders for allegedly working with publishers to drive independent booksellers out of business.

What's the bottom line as far as they are concerned? "Independent stores like ours are keeping Chicago a book town," Bubon says proudly.

8.
Kopi Travelers Café
5317 N. Clark St. 773/989-5674

The din of Clark Street traffic recedes upon stepping into this peaceful, travel-centered oasis. A wall of clocks gives the current times around the world, and travel books and international gifts are sold in the back of the shop. Sitting on the pillows in the front window with espresso and a book, watching the traffic go by, is highly recommended.

9.
Margaret Anderson's apartment
837 W. Ainslie St.

Margaret Anderson, who founded the literary magazine *The Little Review* in Chicago in 1914 and edited it until 1924, was the first person to publish James Joyce's *Ulysses* in America. The book appeared in serial form in *The Little Review* from 1918 to 1920, after Anderson and her co-editor, Jane Heap, had

Chicago: City of Nicknames

How would you describe Chicago? Leave it to writers to come up with creative answers to this question to spice up either their written or spoken comments. Chicago, it turns out, has as many names as it has neighborhoods. See if you can match the nicknames in the first list below with the person who uttered them:

1. City of Boundless Prairies
2. City of the Big Shoulders
3. City on the Make
4. City Without Cobwebs
5. The Jazz Baby
6. Literary Capital of America
7. National Capital of the Essentially American Spirit
8. San-Fran-York on the Lake
9. The Second City
10. That Toddlin' Town

A. Nelson Algren
B. Fred Fisher
C. Ben Hecht
D. A. J. Liebling
E. H. L. Mencken
F. Mike Royko
G. Carl Sandburg
H. Robert Shackleton
I. George Putnam Upton
J. Frank Lloyd Wright

Answers: 1. (I); 2. (G); 3. (A); 4. (H); 5. (C); 6. (E); 7. (J); 8. (F); 9. (D); 10. (B)

Photo by Greg Holden.

Margaret Anderson's apartment.

moved to New York. Anderson and Heap fought to prevent suppression of Joyce's work and continued to print episodes of *Ulysses* even though the U.S. Postal Service confiscated and subsequently burned the January 1919 and January 1920 issues of the magazine on grounds of obscenity and immorality. The New York Society for the Prevention of Vice filed a complaint against Anderson and Heap. The two were eventually found guilty of publishing obscenity in the Court of Special Sessions, fined $50 each, and restrained by court order from any further printing of *Ulysses.*

Anderson was quite an independent and colorful character. In 1915, when funding for *The Little Review* fell through, she decided to save money by living in a tent on the Lake Michigan shore and commuting to her office in the Fine Arts Building downtown (see pp. 252-253). For Anderson, the place to be in Chicago was as close to the water as possible. In her memoirs she says she later took an apartment on the lake "three feet from the water's edge" at 837 W. Ainslie, a place where "the lake filled every window." She reports that she spent most of her time there bathing—in the bathtub, that is, not the lake:

> For me there was a room and bath like a dream of spring—pale green walls, wisteria hangings, a pink rug, a large yellow lamp, a blue lake . . . It was widely separated from the rest of the apartment. If one locked door didn't insulate me I could entrench myself behind two, in the bathroom. I could spend my home life bathing.[5]

After the death of her father, she and her mother had a fight, and her mother took almost all the furniture in the apartment. All that was left were two beds, two knives, two forks, two spoons. Anderson and her longtime ion Jane Heap decided this made the apartment "marvelous nude as the day it was built. Nothing but the lake and the stars in the windows." But one thing was missing: she rented a Mason and Hamlin piano in exchange for an ad in *The Little Review:* "We spent the afternoon pacing the empty apartment in order to burst suddenly into the living room and be startled by it standing there against the windows and the lake."[6]

Today, the expansion of Lincoln Park and construction of Lake Shore Drive has pushed Anderson's apartment considerably farther than three feet from the lake. But it's a safe bet there's still a bathtub up there.

Driving Tour #2: Wrigleyville

The neighborhoods around Belmont Avenue, Addison Street, and Irving Park Road, about a mile in from the lakefront, are dominated by Wrigley Field, the home of the Chicago Cubs National League baseball team. The area is bisected by the Red Line elevated train. These two landmarks frequently find their way into Chicago novels and poems.

A vivid description of the lake occurs in Saul Bellow's 1982 novel *The Dean's December.* The "he" in the following quote refers to the college dean, Albert Corde:

> But at home he sat usually with his back to the decayed city view. From his corner window he could see the Loop and its famous towers, but he looked directly downward at the working of the water on bright days a clear green, easing its mass onto the beaches, white. The waters bathing the waters in sun, and every drop having its own corpuscle of light, the light meantime resembling the splash of heavy raindrops on paved surfaces—the whole sky clear, clear but tense. On days of heavy weather you felt the shock of the waves and heard their concussion through the building. Under low clouds you might have been looking at Hudson's Bay and when the floes came close you wouldn't have been surprised to see polar bear. Only you didn't smell brine, you smelled pungent ozone, the inland-water raw-potato odor. But there was

plenty of emptiness, as much as you need to define yourself against, as American souls seem to do.[7]

10.
Wrigley Field
1060 W. Addison St., 773/338-1100

The ups and downs (mostly downs) that the Chicago Cubs have endured in most decades of the twentieth century reads like a bad novel—a sort of Horatio Alger story in reverse. Aside from the poetry recited by Cubs legend Ernie Banks, the most famous Cubs poem in print first appeared in the *New York Evening Mail* in July 1910. Written by newspaperman-poet Franklin P. Adams, it was inspired by their double-play combination of shortstop Joe Tinker, second baseman Johnny Evers, and first baseman Frank Chance.

> Trio of bear Cubs, and fleeter than birds,
> Tinker to Evers to Chance.
> Thoughtlessly pricking our gonfalon bubble,
> Making a great hit into a double,
> Words that are weighty with nothing but trouble,
> Tinker to Evers to Chance.

11.
Emerald City Coffee Shop
3928 N. Sheridan Rd. 773/525-7847

This little spot near the Sheridan El stop is one of the author's favorite coffeeshops—not too busy, with a good mix of people and a relaxed feel. It's great for people-watching either before or after Cubs games. The reference to the Wizard of Oz books doesn't hurt, either.

Samuel Eberly Gross and *Cyrano de Bergerac*

It takes imagination to be a real estate developer. Where most people see an empty plot of land, the developer envisions houses, streets, a neighborhood. Chicago developer Samuel Eberly Gross had enough imagination to build 10,000 houses, sell 40,000 lots, and build 21 suburbs, and author a romantic comedy called *The Merchant Prince of Cornville* in 1896.

tured a character with a prominent nose. Both works also contained a scene in which the "nosy" protagonist stood under a balcony impersonating a less witty but more physically attractive lover.[8]

Like any man of property, Gross was protective of his territory. He not only charged that Coquelin had aided Rostand in stealing the most essential aspects of *The Merchant Prince,* he threatened to file a court injunction seeking to block any American performance of *Cyrano.* He hired W. J. Sutherland, a Chicago detective, to

> ## "There are big noses everywhere in the world."

Gross published only 250 copies of his work for private circulation. He had submitted his play, however, to the Porte St. Martin Theater in Paris, which held the work for a while and then returned it. The actor-manager of the theater, Constant Coquelin, was a friend of the French playwright Edmond Rostand. When Rostand's masterpiece *Cyrano de Bergerac* appeared, Gross was outraged. Both his play and Rostand's fea-

go to France and seek out evidence of the alleged plagiarism. Sutherland managed to return with an affidavit from an English-speaking servant of Rostand's who contradicted the playwright's assertion that *Cyrano* had been written before *The Merchant Prince* was copyrighted in 1896. This was no small accomplishment, because Rostand was living in a chateau shielded by a 12-foot fence and protected by dogs and guardsmen.

When *Cyrano* came to Chicago with Sarah Bernhardt and the same Coquelin in the principal roles, it was not known whether Chicagoans would get to see the play. Depositions in the case featured a protest from Rostand himself, who argued that "there are big noses everywhere in the world."[9] Gross decided not to file his injunction. He professed to be as eager to see *Cyrano* as anyone in the theatergoing public. In May 1902, Judge Christian C. Kohlsaat issued an injunction in U.S. District Court declaring Gross to be the "the author of Cyrano's being." Gross was awarded nominal damages of $1, and waived all rights to royalties.

It was generally accepted, however, that if Rostand had stolen some of Gross's work, it was a case of a master creating something beautiful out of an amateur's inferior product. Gross's main character is named Ideal, a poet who speaks in blank verse and seeks the hand of the fair Violet with proclamations such as:

> What pure mysterious alchemy
> Doth beauty chaste as thine persuade
> To sublimate its crude degree
> In sweetest herbs of earth displayed!

British biographer and critic Lytton Strachey, in a scathing review of Gross's play in the July 1902 issue of *The Bookman,* called *The Merchant Prince of Cornville* "monstrously absurd," and concluded:

> The only reason, aye, the only excuse for publishing any criticism whatever of this—this thing—is to make as widely known as possible the nature of the stuff claimed to have been stolen by the finest poet of the day from the worst.[10]

12.
Graceland Cemetery
4001 N. Clark St.

Graceland Cemetery was outside the city limits when it was established in 1860. Carl Sandburg's poem "Graceland" describes the elaborate monuments that the city's barons of commerce and industry built for themselves. He portrayed Graceland as

> Place of the dead where they spend every year
>
> The usury of twenty-five thousand dollars
>
> For upkeep and flowers.

Graceland also includes the final resting places of architects Daniel Burnham, author of the *Plan of Chicago;* Louis Sullivan, who wrote *The Autobiography of an Idea;* and the architect Ludwig Mies van der Rohe.

13.
North Side El stops

In "Pet Milk," a story by Stuart Dybek, the narrator and a girl make love on the El train during an express run of the Red Line from the Loop to the Howard Avenue stop. At the time the story was written, the express ran all the way to Howard from the Loop without making a stop. These days, the express train stops at Belmont and other North Side stations, so such activities are even less ... practical.

14.
The Gallery Bookstore Limited
923 W. Belmont Ave. 773/975-8200

This tiny store epitomizes everything the big chain stores can't provide: it's cramped; it's full of quirky hard-to-find titles; and owner William C. Fiedler calls everyone "My Friend" and takes the time to engage you in conversation about your interests (if you're in a talkative mood). Upstairs, on weekends, a completely different store opens up that's a hidden gem for mystery book lovers: the Florence Hanley Memorial Wing, named after the former owner of a Chicago mystery bookstore.

15.
Mike Royko's condo
3300 N. Lake Shore Dr.

Because he was scornful of the Chicago Cubs in many of his columns for the *Daily News, Sun-Times,* and *Tribune,* it's surprising to realize that from 1981 Mike Royko lived less than a mile from the ballpark in a luxurious condo overlooking Lake Michigan. It was a far cry from the West Division Street neighborhood where he grew up (see pp. 119, 121, and 126). Royko was criticized by his rival and one of his favorite targets, the television news anchor Walter Jacobson, for moving into such an upscale abode, but Royko responded with a hilarious column in which he said it was part of an anthropological research into living in all parts of the city.

16.
Broadway stores
Broadway between Diversey Ave. and Addison St.

North Broadway is taking over from Clark and Lincoln as a center for bookstores on the North Side. You'll find the mammoth **Borders Books Music & Café**, 2817 N. Clark, holding down the Diversey-Broadway-Clark intersection. Only a couple of blocks north, there's **Bookleggers Used Books**, 2907 N. Broadway, 773/404-8780, and **Bookman's Corner**, 2959 N. Clark, 773/929-8298. **The Coffee & Tea Exchange**, 3300 N. Broadway, 773/528-2272, is one of Chicago's treasures, providing very fresh coffee blends that they roast themselves, as well as lots of kinds of exotic tea. **Unabridged Bookstore**, 3251 N. Broadway, 773/883-9119, is an excellent neighborhood bookstore that specializes in gay and lesbian literature. Finally, there's **Selected Works Bookstore**, 3510 N. Broadway, 773/975-0002, which also sells old sheet music.

17.
Belmont and Racine Aves.
Belmont (3200 North) and Racine (1200 West)

Imagine V. I. Warshawski coming out of her house with her dog Peppy, which she shares with her downstairs neighbor Mr. Contreras, and jogging down Belmont to the lake. Sara Paretsky's private investigator regularly runs five miles along the lake, accompanied by Peppy.

Driving Tour #3: Rogers Park

Rogers Park was named for one of its early settlers, Phillip Rogers, a major local real estate developer in the mid-nineteenth century. When the elevated train was extended to the far northern reaches of the city in the early twentieth century, people flocked to this neighborhood. The area has had a heavy Jewish population since the 1920s, though today only West Rogers Park is Jewish. Because Rogers Park is so close to the Lake, to the North Shore, and to public transportation leading to the Loop, it has always been popular. Loyola University is a major cultural and educational institution here, as is Mundelein College (which is now part of Loyola). The following isn't so much a tour as a selection of Chicago literary sites located in Rogers Park.

In "Farwell," one of the stories in Stuart Dybek's 1991 collection *The Coast of Chicago,* the narrator visits a now-departed friend who lives in the last apartment building on the block where Farwell Avenue dead ends at the lake. As the story points out, Farwell is only a letter away from farewell, "a street whose name sounded almost like saying goodbye."

"Transport," a surreal prose poem also in Dybek's collection, follows a kiss across the city as it "travels along streets named for coasts—North Shore, Lakeside, Waveland, Surf—that echo as if paved with wet tile."

The narrator in William Maxwell's beautifully written short novel *So Long, See You Tomorrow,* recalls growing up in a small town but moving to Rogers Park. A critical event occurs in a neighborhood school when the young man sees—but snubs—an old friend from his home town:

> In the evening the boys used to cluster on the sidewalk with their bicycles and
> I would walk by them with a dry mouth and my eyes focused on something

farther down the street. I usually ended up at the Lake, where I sat on the rock pile looking out over the water.[11]

Burr Tillstrom, who lived at 1407 W. Sherwin, created Kukla, Fran, and Ollie, a wonderful puppet show that aired during the Golden Age of television. Tillstrom recalled acting in a play in 1935 performed around the city and sponsored by the Works Progress Administration Federal Theater and the Chicago Park District:

> Thornton Wilder, who was teaching at the University of Chicago at the time, directed us in a play Gertrude Stein had written for puppets. It was called *Identity or I am Because My Little Dog Knows Me.* I'll never forget his advice: "Don't worry about the meaning of the words, just think how beautiful they are."[12]

If you venture a mile or so west on Devon, you'll pass lots of different ethnic enclaves. Two bookstores of interest to specific ethnic groups are **Rosenblum's World of Judaica Inc.**, 2906 W. Devon, 773/262-1700, and the **Russian American Book Store**, 2746 W. Devon, 773/761-3233.

Bookstores

Armadillos Pillow, 6753 N. Sheridan Rd. 773/761-2558.

Barnes & Noble Booksellers, 659 W. Diversey Ave. 773/871-9004.

Beck's Book Store, 4522 N. Broadway. 773/784-7963,
   Northeastern Illinois University, 5500 N. St. Louis Ave. 773/588-2770.

Bookleggers Used Books, 2907 N. Broadway. 773/404-8780.

Bookman's Corner, 2959 N. Clark St. 773/929-8298.

Bookworks, 3444 N. Clark St. 773/871-5318.

Borders Books Music & Café, 2817 N. Clark St. 773/935-3909.

Chicago Comics, 3244 N. Clark St. 773/528-1983.

City Newsstand, 4018 N. Cicero Ave. 773/545-7377.

Gallery Bookstore Limited, 923 W. Belmont Ave. 773/975-8200.

Healing Earth Resources, 3111 N. Ashland Ave. 773/EART-HLY.

Heritage Books, 1135 N. Granville Ave. 773/262-1566.

Hit the Road Travel Store, 3758 N. Southport Ave. 773/388-8338.

Lincoln Park Book Shop, 2423 N. Clark St. 773/477-7087.

Mustard Seed Christian Bookstore, 1143 W. Sheridan Rd. 773/973-7055.

Pathfinders Book Store, 1925 W. Thome Ave. 773/262-3888.

Powell's Bookstore, 2850 N. Lincoln Ave. 773/248-1444.

Revolution Books, 3449 N. Sheffield Ave. 773/528-5353.

Rosenblum's World of Judaica Inc., 2906 W. Devon Ave. 773/262-1700.

Russian American Book Store, 2746 W. Devon Ave. 773/761-3233.

Selected Works Bookstore, 3510 N. Broadway. 773/975-0002.

Shake, Rattle and Read Book Box, 4812 N. Broadway. 773/334-5311.

Tres Americas Books Inc., 4336 N. Pulaski Rd. 773/481-9090.

Turtle Island Books, 7001 N. Glenwood Ave. 773/465-7212.

Unabridged Bookstore, 3251 N. Broadway. 773/883-9119.

Women and Children First, 5233 N. Clark St. 773/769-9299.

Coffeehouses

Café Aloha, 2156 W. Montrose Ave. 773/907-9356.

Café Selmarie, 4729 N. Lincoln Ave. 773/989-5595.

Caribou Coffee, 2453 N. Clark St. 773/327-9923,
    3300 N. Broadway. 773/477-3695,
    3025 N. Clark St. 773/529-6366,
    3424 N. Southport Ave. 773/529-4902.

Coffee Chicago, 5256 N. Broadway. 773/784-1305.

Coffee & Tea Exchange, 3300 N. Broadway. 773/528-2272.

Coffee Tree & Tea Leaves Co., 3752 N. Broadway. 773/871-7818.

Emerald City Coffee, 3928 N. Sheridan Rd. 773/525-7847.

Heartland Café, 7000 N. Glenwood Ave. 773/465-8005.

Higher Ground, 2022 W. Roscoe St. 773/868-0075.

Intelligentsia Coffee Roasters & Tea Blenders, 3123 N. Broadway.
    773/348-8058.

Katerina's, 1920 W. Irving Park Rd. 773/348-7592.

Kopi Travelers Café, 5317 N. Clark St. 773/989-5674.

Rainbow Café, 1826 W. Wilson Ave. 773/271-3940.

SuVan's Café and Bake Shop, 3405 N. Paulina St. 773/281-0120.

Viva Java, 1147 W. Granville Ave. 773/274-8040.

Other Places of Interest

Affy Tapple, 7110 N. Clark St. 773/338-1100.

Martin D'Arcy Museum of Art, Cudahy Library, 6525 N. Sheridan Rd.
    773/508-2679.

Loyola University, 6525 N. Sheridan Rd. 773/274-3000.

Mundelein College, 6363 N. Sheridan Rd. 773/262-8100.

Swedish American Museum Association of Chicago, 5211 N. Clark St. 773/728-8111.

Wrigley Field, 1060 W. Addison St. 773/338-1100.

HYDE PARK

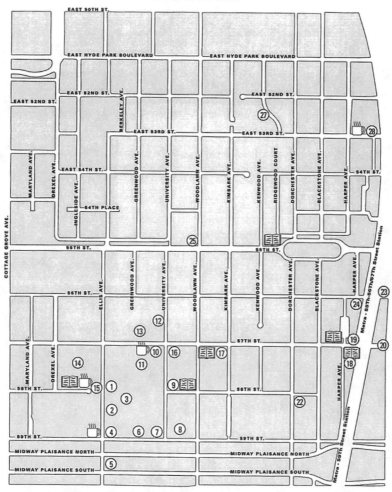

Map by Michael Polydoris.

Hyde Park

Although Hyde Park gets its name from London's famous park, it has neither a Marble Arch nor a Speakers' Corner. This primarily residential neighborhood on Chicago's South Side lakefront has, however, inherited some of its namesake's qualities: its

By Jeff Hall.

Saul Bellow

tradition of outspoken liberal politics and its setting as an island of beauty (not to mention great coffee, bookstores, and libraries) in the middle of a city.

Hyde Park was one of Chicago's first suburbs and was annexed to the city in 1889. It was founded in 1853 as a 48-acre town and was incorporated in 1861. Early residents included prominent business and professional people such as R. R. Donnelley; Julius Rosenwald of Sears; and Gustavus F. Swift, the meat packing magnate. Like other neighborhoods outside the congested center of the city, it grew dramatically after the Chicago Fire of 1871—from 3,644 inhabitants in 1870 to more than 15,000 by 1880. The present-day neighborhood is called Hyde Park-Kenwood, and is bounded by 47th Street on the north, 59th Street on the south, Cottage Grove Avenue on the west, and Lake Michigan on the east. The Kenwood area is located between Hyde Park Boulevard (51st Street) and 47th Street.

Two early events contributed significantly to Hyde Park's literary heritage. The World's Columbian Exposition of 1893 was held here, bringing a multitude of writers to see the sights and attend conferences. Remnants of the event include the Museum of Science and Industry, the Midway Plaisance, the Wooded Island, and Jackson Park. Second, since 1892 the area has been home to the University of Chicago, drawing creative writers as well as the more academic variety. For better or for worse, the University is intertwined with its neighborhood. Faced with deteriorating living structures and businesses, rising crime, and gang activity, the University (which was rumored at one point to be considering a move to the suburbs) led racially integrated urban renewal efforts that dramatically changed the area in the 1950s. While critics claimed that the efforts to clean up the neighborhood robbed it of some of its former spirit, the planners believed they had saved the community. Today the main shopping districts are along 51st, 53rd, 55th, and 57th Streets.

Self-expression of all sorts flourishes in Hyde Park, making it a great place to raise children and a setting for many cultural activities like art fairs and folk festivals. Obviously, Hyde Park is a convenient place to live if your employer is the University of Chicago. But Hyde Park is also home to many others who choose to commute to and from the Loop or other parts of the city. Hyde Park is the residence of writers such as poet Elizabeth Alexander, novelists Richard Stern and Rosellen Brown, and mystery writers Sara Paretsky and Alzina Stone Dale. Saul Bellow attended college here in the 1930s and subsequently taught in the University's Committee on Social Thought before leaving for Boston University in 1993.

The study of literature as well as other areas of the liberal arts was revolutionized by Mortimer Adler, a philosopher, University faculty member, and leader of the "Great Books" movement; and by faculty who founded the Chicago School of Criticism, including Ronald S. Crane. Visiting professors have included T. S. Eliot; students have included Philip Roth, Susan Sontag, James T. Farrell, and Susan Fromberg Schaffer. The Great Books movement is mentioned in the 1974 bestseller *Zen and the Art of Motorcycle Maintenance: An Inquiry Into Values,* by Robert M. Persig, in which a character named Phaedrus applies, unsuccessfully, to take courses in the University's Committee on Analysis of Ideas and the Study of Methods.

I worked at the University for 12 years and still regularly make the trek from the North Side to participate in writing, musical, birdwatching, and other groups in the neighborhood. Hyde Park is a great place to buy books, explore libraries, study literature, and trace the footsteps of writers and their characters.

How to Get There

Public transportation options to Hyde Park include the Metra train, which stops at 47th, 51st, 53rd, and 59th Streets; and the Jeffery Express #6 bus that runs between the Loop and Hyde Park. You can also reach Hyde Park by driving south on Lake Shore Drive, north on Stony Island, or east on Garfield Boulevard.

One of the nicest ways to enter Hyde Park is via the Midway Plaisance, which was once the site of attractions for the World's Columbian Exposition of 1893 such as the Ferris wheel. You should pause to take in the impressive view of the University's facade along 59th Street, keeping an eye out for errant soccer balls, footballs, softballs, and Frisbees. If taking the Dan Ryan Expressway, exit at Garfield Boulevard-55th Street and head east. At Martin Luther King Drive, look for the signs for the University of Chicago Medical Center and follow the bend in the road to the right. Go around the park and, when you get to 59th Street, you'll see Lorado Taft's *Fountain of Time* sculpture and the Midway. Turn left (east) on the Midway to get to the U of C. If coming from Lake Shore Drive, go around Cornell Drive and turn west on 59th Street, just south of the Museum of Science and Industry.

If you're extremely lucky, you'll find a free parking space along the Midway. Otherwise, go to a parking garage. There's one across from the university's Bernard Mitchell Hospital, 5815 S. Maryland; and another just south of 55th between Ellis and Greenwood.

Walking Tour

1.
Administration Building
5801 S. Ellis Ave.
The logical place to start is the University's Administration Building. Maps of

the campus are distributed here, and students lead guided tours of campus every day at noon.

The "Ad Building" is among the most boring architectural designs on campus, but the events within its walls—in truth and in fiction—have been anything but plain and simple. In Saul Bellow's 1982 novel *The Dean's December,* you find a complex and multilayered use of the University of Chicago as not only a setting but as an integral element in a novelistic examination of Chicago. The protagonist, Albert Corde, is a newspaperman who returns to Chicago to be a professor of journalism and dean of students at the University. Corde faces two crises: the murder of a student and the imminent death of his mother. This book contains vivid descriptions of not only the South Side, but of many parts of the city, as Corde questions the responsibility of the University in relation to the bleak and cruel neighborhoods that surround it.

Corde had written a series of articles about institutions such as Cook County Jail, Cook County Hospital, and Robert Taylor public housing. He is seen by the students, however, not as a sympathetic observer but as a racist. The trial of the underprivileged youths who are accused of murder compels Corde to conclude that you have to look at your contemporary surroundings to understand the essential loneliness of the human heart.

In Bellow's novel, the Provost of the University is described not as a typical nerd retreating into an ivy covered tower, but "a rough Chicago man; his neck, his chest, told you that, not big but brutal, definitely—charging linebacker's strength packed into those muscles."

2.
Cobb Lecture Hall
5811 S. Ellis Ave.

Head down the stairs and go into the Main Quadrangle. Turn right (south) and walk to the next building, Cobb Lecture Hall, where many of the undergraduate classes are held. The building was designed by Henry Ives Cobb in 1892, but it's named for the man who donated the money to build it, Silas B. Cobb.

Directly across from Cobb Hall, sits the "C" Bench, a gift of the Class of 1903.

Photo by Thayer Lindner.

Cobb Lecture Hall and "C" Bench.

Until the 1960s it could be occupied only by varsity lettermen and their dates, but it's now okay for you to sit and rest your feet.

In Philip Roth's novel *Letting Go,* the main character is a teacher at the University: "I walked to the University through the crackling weather and the virgin snows, and arrived at Cobb Hall feeling as righteous, as American, as inner-directed as a young Abe Lincoln." Later:

> It was nearly six, and the white tennis courts had a simple geometric grace under the dark sky. The Gothic archways attested to the serious purpose of the place and made me want to believe that we were all better people than one would suppose from the argument we had just had.

Another literary figure who attends classes in Cobb Hall is Eddie Ryan, the main character in James T. Farrell's *The Silence of History* (1963). He finds the University of Chicago an "escape for a young mind."

Just outside Cobb (probably on the student bulletin board that has been there as long as the building itself) another character, Danny O'Neill, reads a note from a famous University professor that changes his life: he discovers that he has been admitted to the professor's creative writing course.[1] O'Neill (who was Farrell's alter ego) now realizes that being a writer is what he was born to do.

Richard Stern, the most distinguished writer on campus and author of *Golk, Other Men's Daughters,* and many other works, often teaches classes in Cobb Hall. Stern once described the University as a "cave, in part of which there is the necessary isolation, in the other part of which are the woes and sweetness of mid-century institutional life."[2]

3.
Swift Hall
1025 E. 58th St.

The building immediately east of the "C" Bench is Swift Hall, home of the University's Divinity School. Swift is the site of a wonderful used book sale held every spring. In the basement, you'll find one of those tucked away coffee shops that are popular with students, faculty, and staff. Swift Coffee Shop is known as the place "Where God drinks coffee" but has also been called the Swift Kick.

4.
Classics Coffee Shop
1010 E. 59th St., 773/702-0177

From the entrance to Cobb Hall walk south along the path nearest the buildings to the Classics Building. Go inside and up the stairs to find one of the prettiest coffee shops on campus. Follow your nose or, if that fails, don't be shy about asking a student or professor for directions.

5.
The Midway Plaisance

Once you have refreshed your body with a snack and your soul with a view of the wood paneling and stained glass windows at Classics Coffee Shop, return to the Quadrangles and head east down the path and through the tunnel, which leads you to the Midway Plaisance. Walk across 59th (watch out for traffic) and follow the paths worn by countless students heading across the Midway to one of the Burton-Judson Courts residence halls, the Law School, or the School of Social Service Administration. When you get to the Midway itself (technically, this is 60th Street), don't go across, but look west to see one of the best-known sculptures by Lorado Taft, who was a member of Harriet Monroe's group The Little Room and had a studio in the Fine Arts Building (see pp. 29-30). Taft also founded Midway Studios, which is a National Historic Landmark located on 60th Street and Ingleside Avenue.

The Midway, of course, was the site of the World's Columbian Exposition of 1893. Some sense of what the Midway was like before that momentous event is suggested in an obscure novel by Clara Louise Burnham called *Sweet Clover: A Romance of the White City:*

> They had sped down Grand Boulevard, through Washington Park, and now entered the Midway Plaisance.
>
> What that name suggested to Chicagoans up to a short time ago was the loneliest, most rural drive of their park system. It even wound through the woods at one point, making the refreshing variety of a curve in the city of straight lines . . . Grassy fields stretched away in level, tranquil monotony in all directions. It was the Midway Plaisance; but with no . . . shadowing forth of the scenes in the near future, when this unknown plot of ground should become the rendezvous and rallying place of the civilized, half-civilized, and savage nations of the earth.[3]

Walk west on the Midway until you get to the statue of Linné, the Swedish botanist; then go back into the Quadrangles through the Harper Memorial Library building.

Photo by Thayer Lindner.

Harper Memorial Library.

6.
Harper Memorial Library
1616 E. 59th St. 773/702-7960

Harper Memorial Library is probably the most beautiful library on campus. You can get to the Main Reading Room on the second floor via elevator or stairs, but do find your way there somehow. It is nothing short of spectacular. The corbels supporting the arches of the Main Reading Room bear printer's marks, which are supposed to represent the transmission of knowledge. There's a whole section of books devoted to Saul Bellow in the North Reading Room. He reportedly enjoyed "the stacks of Harper Library, where we had access to anything we wished to read," when he was a student.[4] (Tread softly when you visit the reading rooms; awakened students are very grumpy.)

It would be bad manners to not greet the huge and imposing bust of American poet Walt Whitman on your way down the main staircase.

Exit Harper on the Quadrangles side and continue east down the path.

(Before you is Stuart Hall, the home of the Graduate School of Business. It has yet another basement that contains yet another good student coffee shop in case you haven't had a sufficient java fix or you're looking for something a little more substantial to eat.)

7.
Social Sciences building
1126 E. 59th St.

The building immediately to the east of Harper is the Social Sciences building. Go to the end of the path, enter the building, and climb the stairs. On the second floor there is a charming wood-paneled space called the Social Sciences Tea Room. Saul Bellow said that when he was an undergraduate at the University he and his literary friends "gathered to talk about poetry, the novel, the theater."[5] Bellow's office was in Room 502 of the Social Sciences building.

Courtesy of the University of Chicago Archives, Joseph Regenstein Library.

Saul Bellow.

One of the more unconventional and colorful members of the University faculty, Thorstein Ve-

Photo by Thayer Lindner.

Rockefeller Chapel.

blen, had his offices in this building. He was known for muttering his lectures in tones that students could barely hear and for erratically giving out grades. Veblen wrote his influential book *The Theory of the Leisure Class* here and drew upon his experiences at the University for his comments on sports and the academic life.

8.
Rockefeller Chapel
59th St. and Woodlawn Ave.

On the exterior of the door of Rockefeller Chapel that leads to the east aisle (on the east side of the building), you'll find busts of English poet John Milton (on the right), and the Italian author of *The Divine Comedy,* Dante Alighieri (on the left).

The chapel was big enough to contain the emotions associated with an important moment in writer Harry Mark Petrakis's career. After ten years of sending submissions to magazines, his story "Pericles on 31st Street" was finally accepted by the *Atlantic Monthly*—but it was too late for his father, who had died, to realize that his son would be a success. On his way to his job as a Hyde Park real estate salesman, Petrakis stopped at

Photo by Thayer Lindner.

John Milton.

at the chapel and sat in the back row, where he cried "wild and grateful tears
. . . tears for the redeeming of my life; for like Lazarus, the miracle of being
reborn once again."[6]

9.
Seminary Co-Op Bookstore
5757 S. University Ave. 773/752-4381

Bookstore aficionados can't miss this one. It's without doubt one of the largest
in Chicago. As if the mazes of twisting and turning aisles and hidden rooms full
of books aren't enough, the Seminary Co-Op is located in a picturesque place.
It's in the basement of the Chicago Theological Seminary, which is marked by
the big red bell tower at 58th and University. Seminary sells new books; the
used bookstores are on 57th Street. But if you are looking for any type of
scholarly book, this is the place to go.

10.
Reynolds Club
57th St. and University Ave.

The Reynolds Club is a place for student clubs and organizations; it contains
lounges, a dining hall called Hutchinson Commons that is modeled after one at
Oxford University in England, a bell tower where medieval-style "change ring-
ing" regularly peals out over the campus, a student radio station, and much
more.

The C-Shop is the coffee shop adjacent to Hutchinson Commons. Try to get
a table by one of the narrow Gothic windows that overlook Hutchinson Court
and do some student-watching.

The third floor of the Reynolds Club has a small 126-seat theater where, on
January 14, 1904, Irish poet W. B. Yeats attended a performance of his play *The
Land of Heart's Desire* given by the University of Chicago Dramatic Club.
Student plays are still performed there regularly.

Exit through the C-Shop and walk immediately to the right past the picnic
tables. A series of plays is held here every summer. Walk through the wooden

archway that separates the Reynolds Club from the adjacent Zoology Building. On the other side, shaded by old ginkgo trees, you find Botany Pond.

11.
Botany Pond
Adjacent to Zoology Building
and Cobb Gate

Botany Pond, which is stocked with goldfish in summer, wasn't quite as neat and tidy as when James T. Farrell was a student in the College. But it was here by the banks of the pond that he conceived his great Chicago trilogy *Studs Lonigan.*

Courtesy of the University of Chicago Archives, Joseph Regenstein Library.

Botany Pond.

Farrell used to walk across Washington Park to the University to take classes in Cobb Hall or hang out at the C-Shop. He wrote the story "Studs" for an Advanced Composition class taught by James Weber Linn (who taught English at the University for more than 40 years and himself wrote the novels *Winds Over the Campus* and *This Was Life).* After getting an enthusiastic response from Linn, another faculty member, Robert Morse Lovett (who taught English at the University from 1909 to 1936 and coauthored *A History of English Literature* with William Vaughn Moody), encouraged him to develop the story in greater detail. Farrell later called Linn and Lovett "the spiritual godfathers of Studs Lonigan."[7]

One day in the late 1920s, Farrell sat with a friend named Mary Hunter on the grass near Botany Pond and he made the first outline of the book. "In a sense,

Studs Lonigan was born that afternoon," he later recalled.[8]

Walk north through the impressive Cobb Gate and cross 57th. Turn right (east) and walk down 57th to University; turn left (north) on University and go toward Bartlett Commons.

12.
Bartlett Commons
5640 S. University Ave.

As this book is being written, this building is being converted from a gymnasium into a dining hall. Its distinctive architectural elements, however, will remain. Over the front doorway is a stained glass mural by Edward Sperry, an associate of Louis Comfort Tiffany. The 15,000 pieces of glass that comprise this wonder depict a scene from Sir Walter Scott's novel *Ivanhoe:* Rowena crowns Ivanhoe at the tournament of Ashby de la Zouche. To the left, are Prince John and his entourage; to the right, Cedric and his friends.

Pause for a moment in front of the apartment building on the southeast corner of 57th and University. An Indian poet named A. K. Ramanujan lived here in the early 1990s; his poem *Chicago Zen* contains some Koan-like riddles. One of them gains new meaning when you take a walking tour down 57th:

> Watch your step. Sight may strike you
>
> blind in unexpected places.
>
> The traffic light turns orange
>
> on 57th and Dorchester, and you stumble,
>
> you fall into a vision of forest fires,
>
> enter a frothing Himalayan river,
>
> rapid, silent.
>
> On the 14th floor,
>
> Lake Michigan crawls and crawls
>
> in the window...[9]

As you can see, there isn't anything remotely resembling a stoplight at 57th and Dorchester. But then, there aren't any forest fires or Himalayan rivers, either. Not the last time I looked, at least.

Retrace your steps down University and west on 57th to the monolithic structure on the right, which is the University's Regenstein Library, affectionately known to students as the Reg. The students themselves are affectionately known as Reg Rats.

13.
Regenstein Library
1100 E. 57th St.

Unfortunately, the Regenstein Library "stacks"—in other words, the general holdings—are not open to the public. But visitors can request a pass to use the Library's Special Collections holdings. These are a gold mine for anyone doing research or writing papers about particular literary figures: The archives of *Poetry* magazine are here, which include manuscripts of poems by Carl Sandburg, Wallace Stevens, and many others; so are the papers of James T. Farrell, Thornton Wilder, Frank O'Hara, Harriet Monroe, Clarence Darrow, Eugene Field, and André Gide. Thanks to the Internet, you don't even have to be on campus to start your treasure hunt. After browsing through the catalog of holdings in the Special Collections area of the University's Web site www.lib.uchicago.edu/e/spcl), call 773/702-8705 to get more information. Obtain a day pass at the Privileges Office near the front entrance.

Walk west on 57th and cross Ellis. Turn left (south) and cross 57th. Walk half a block south on Ellis until reaching the entrance for the University's Science Quadrangle. The building immediately facing you is John Crerar Library.

14.
John Crerar Library
5730 S. Ellis Ave. 773/702-7720

If biological, medical, and physical sciences are your game, this is your lucky day. The Crerar Library, one of the most extensive science libraries in the world, is open to the public.

The lobby of Crerar Library contains a striking sculpture by John David Mooney called *Crystara*. In the mystery novel *Angel Fire* by Andrew M. Greeley, biologist and Nobel laureate Sean S. Desmond encounters his guardian angel here. Desmond is a faculty member at the University, and his daughter attends the University Laboratory Schools. He and his two daughters live in the Cloisters, an apartment building at 58th and Dorchester. Greeley isn't always very positive about the neighborhood around the University. "Only a dummy would walk five blocks through this neighborhood at night," he remarks.

Chapter 7 of *Angel Fire* opens with the following vision:

> In search of an angel, the week after his award was announced, Sean Desmond had wandered into the new John Crerar Library in the med school/ biology quad. On the northeast corner of the campus . . . someone had remarked at lunch that a Chicago writer had compared the sculpture in the atrium of the library to an angel.[10]

Desmond muses on the sculpture: "Long, graceful, rounded aluminum struts bound together by solid bars of Waterford crystal—think of how many bottles of Black Bush or Jameson's Special Reserve that much crystal might hold."

When you're ready to leave Crerar, go right (south) to 58th, then turn left (east) on 58th and walk about a block to Ellis.

15.
University Bookstore
970 E. 58th St. 773/702-8729

The beautiful old brick building on the corner of 58th and Ellis is the University Bookstore building. Today it actually houses two bookstores. Students buy their academic texts on the second floor. On the first floor is a small branch of Barnes & Noble, as well as a Starbucks, where you can fortify yourself for seeing the rest of Hyde Park.

Driving Tour

Hyde Park is certainly small enough to walk around, particularly on a fine spring or fall day, but if you want to save your strength for carrying home new books, you can drive to some of these sites around the neighborhood as well.

Courtesy of the University of Chicago Archives, Joseph Regenstein Library.

James Weber Linn.

16.
Quadrangle Club
1155 E. 57th St. 773/493-8601

In *Winds Over the Campus* (1936) by James Weber Linn, the protagonist, Professor Grant, drops by the Faculty Club (which is actually called the Quadrangle Club), gives an address, and sits at the legendary round table where certain faculty sit. Linn knew whereof he spoke, he himself being a professor at the University:

... The big dining room was crowded as usual, but at the particular round table generally occupied by men in one or another of the departments on the science side, there was a vacant seat, and Grant took it at once. In his forty years at the University he had seen the scientists, physical, natural and pseudo (as he called the sociologists and the economists) crowd the classicists, the teachers of language, the historians and the philosophers into a corner, and themselves not only assume the center of the stage but take over most of the University dialogue, and for a long time he had resented this, naturally; but of late he had come to take the educational pre-eminence of science more or less for granted, and he found the shoptalk of the anatomists, the physicists, the geologists vigorous and agreeable. But today there was no shoptalk. [11]

17.
57th Street bookstores and restaurants
Between Kimbark and Harper Aves.

The stretch of 57th between Kimbark and Harper is a book lover's paradise. At one of the stores, pick up a map published by the Hyde Park Booksellers Association that lists 12 local establishments that sell books. Three of the best bookstores in the city are here as well as yet more coffeeshops and other stores and restaurants.

57th Street Books, 1301 E. 57th, 773/84-1300, has a terrific children's section and frequently holds readings by writers.

Medici, 1327 E. 57th, 773/667-7394, is the classic Hyde Park coffeehouse and restaurant.

O'Gara & Wilson, 773/363-0993, moved to 1311 E. 57th a few years ago from what was considered to be the oldest bookstore location in the city a few blocks west.

Caffé Florian, 1450 E. 57th, 773/752-4100, is known for its desserts as well as coffee and lots more good food.

Photo by Greg Holden.

57th Street Books.

Powell's Books is a huge resource at 57th and Harper, 773/955-7780.

18.
5700 block of Harper

Sue Miller's *Family Pictures* spans 40 years of a single family. The father was in psychiatric residency at the University so the kids grew up in Hyde Park; one child goes to the 1968 Democratic Convention in Chicago with college friends; another attends the University of Chicago. There is a description of a group of (relatively) inexpensive houses in a small square on Harper Avenue that apparently refers to the group of houses immediately south of Powell's Books at 57th and Harper:

> Children of the street playing wildly, unsupervised, on the worn grass, until the rectangle of light above them, like a window to the sky, darkened and adult voices from up the street, pitched high and set rhythmically to carry over distance and the squall of the children's games, began to call them in. Houses were cheaper because the train tracks ran right behind it.[12]

19.
Illinois Central Railroad

The Illinois Central (I.C.) (now called the Metra) was the train line created when developer Paul Cornell sold the land to the city; he gave the city back 60 acres of land in exchange for a train station. Since then the electric train has been one of the main connections that link Hyde Park to downtown Chicago to the north and to suburbs such as Flossmoor to the south.

In *So Big*, Edna Ferber calls the University of Chicago "Midwest University." But, aside from the coal smoke, her description is still pretty accurate:

> You heard such wonderful things about Midwest University, in Chicago. On the south side. It was new, yes. But those Gothic buildings gave an effect, somehow, of age and permanence—the smoke and cinders from the Illinois Central suburban trains were largely responsible for that, as well as the soft coal from a thousand neighboring chimneys. And there actually was ivy. Undeniable ivy, and mullioned windows.[13]

20.
Jeffery Express bus

The #6 Jeffery Express bus runs from State St. in the Loop to Hyde Park; one of its stops is at 57th St. and Stony Island Ave.

The protagonist of Bette Howland's title story in her collection *Blue in Chicago* is a graduate student at the University of Chicago, living "in a small studio on top of a high rise." She takes the local bus downtown rather than the Jeffery Express or the Illinois Central train. She studies on the bus, not yet aware that she is the only white occupant: "The thing I'd forgotten was how the bus kept turning. Up Fifty-first Street to Drexel; down Drexel to Forty-seventh; up Forty-seventh to Martin Luther King Drive; down King to Forty-third . . . Every few blocks it nosed onward, plunging deeper and deeper into the black ghetto." A key sentence: "Race is a prominent fact of life in Chicago, a partitioned city, walled and wired." She can't help but react with suspicion when a black passenger asks for a match. (Don't expect to smoke on a CTA bus these days, by

Photo by Thayer Lindner.

Jackson Park near 57th and Stony Island, with the
Museum of Science and Industry in the background.

the way.)

Maurice Browne had his Little Theater troupe rehearse in the studio of a scene designer named Bror Nordfeldt, who lived at 57th and Stony Island. In his excellent book *Chicago Renaissance: The Literary Life in the Midwest,* Dale Kramer describes the actresses in the female Greek chorus in the Little Theatre's production of Euripedes' *The Trojan Women.* They practiced outdoors in Jackson Park near 57th but passersby, used to the strange goings-on in the artists' colony in the neighborhood, were unruffled by the sight of the women chanting:

> And I — never again
>
> Shall I sway to the shuttle's song,
>
> Weaving wool spun from a home-bred fleece!
>
> Instead, one last, last look at the face of my dead sons,
>
> Then go to meet yet worse—
>
> Forced, maybe, to the bed of some lustful Greek—
>
> Listen, gods to my curse
>
> On the night that hides such wrong!

21.
Edna Ferber residence
1642 E. 56th St.

The author of *So Big* and *Show Boat* regularly lived with her mother Julia in Hyde Park. In a letter she alluded to the beauty that erupts every spring after a grim Chicago winter, as well as less pleasant aspects of urban life:

> The lake's going on as usual, and things are green (you don't know what that means after six months of brownstone fronts) and burglars tried to break in last night, and it's the same old Chicago.[14]

(Ferber's biographer Julie Goldsmith Gilbert lists 5414 E. View Park as her address in Hyde Park; the city of Chicago gives it as 1642 E. 56th.)

22.
Saul Bellow residence
5805 S. Dorchester Ave.

Saul Bellow studied sociology at the University of Chicago but is not an alum. He came back in later years, however, to teach in the Committee on Social Thought program. A 1973 directory lists his address as 5805 S. Dorchester. The likely location is the Cloisters, an apartment building whose address today is 5801-11 S. Dorchester.

Nearby are the University of Chicago Laboratory Schools, 1362 E. 59th, founded by John Dewey. Poet Langston Hughes, whose poems dealt with the tribulations and joys of American blacks, once taught there.

23.
Bret Harte School
56th St. and Stony Island Ave. 773/535-0870

Named after the nineteenth-century humorist, short story writer, and poet who wrote about the American West.

24.
Site of Sherwood Anderson residence
5654 Rosalie Ct. (now Harper Ave.)

Anderson, the novelist and short story writer, lived in Hyde Park with his first wife Cornelia Lane. He was a copywriter at the time. The house has long since vanished and been replaced with more modern structures.

25.
Jimmy's Woodlawn Tap
1172 E. 55th St. 773/643-5516

For many decades, this humble-looking bar on 55th just west of Woodlawn has been a gathering place for University of Chicago faculty, staff, and students as well as workers and residents from across the South Side. Mike Nichols and Elaine May, who were students at the University in the 1950s, used to meet at

Jimmy's to discuss their routines with the Compass Players (which began in the Compass Tavern, further west on 55th), a legendary improvisational comedy troupe that eventually became the Second City company.

In *Search the Shadows,* a mystery novel by Barbara Michaels, the narrator Haskell Maloney goes to the University's Oriental Institute Museum for a job interview. Her prospective employer takes her to a restaurant that is "slightly more pretentious than your average hamburger-and-fries short-order house; there were plastic tablecloths on the tables, and a bar. It was apparently a favorite hangout for students and faculty alike . . . " Jimmy's isn't mentioned by name, but it's obvious what hangout she's describing. (Michaels, by the way, is the pseudonym of Barbara Mertz, a University of Chicago graduate who also writes mysteries under the name of Elizabeth Peters.)

Photo by Greg Holden.

Ben Hecht's house.

26.
Edgar Lee Masters
4853 S. Kenwood Ave.

The beautiful homes in this area of north Hyde Park befit Masters's station in the 1910s as a successful lawyer and partner in the legal firm of Clarence Darrow. Like the present-day lawyer/novelist Scott Turow, Masters labored in his spare time on the poetry that would make him famous. His poems were eventually collected under the title *Spoon River Anthology.*

27.
Ben Hecht's house
5210 S. Kenwood Ave.

This fine residence was the home of Chicago journalist, playwright, novelist, and screenwriter Ben Hecht. He lived here in the early 1920s, around the time he was publishing the *Chicago*

Literary Times and *Erik Dorn,* what is generally agreed to be his best novel.

28.
Valois "See Your Food" Restaurant
1518 E. 53rd St. 773/667-0647

I'm not kidding about the "See Your Food" part. Just look at the sign above the restaurant's front entrance. This neighborhood institution, a cafeteria-style no-frills eatery, was immortalized in *Slim's Table,* a 1992 book by a young sociologist. Mitchell Duneier did four years of research, examining the lives of a group of working-class black men who met regularly for lunch at Valois. The book shows how the men care for one another and maintain their dignity despite their poverty.

In *Endless Love,* the 1979 novel by Scott Spencer, the narrator is a student at Hyde Park High School who sets fire to the Blackstone Avenue home of Jade Butterfield, the girl he loves obsessively. The Butterfield home is described as "a New England frame house in the middle of Chicago." The boy's lawyer takes him to a "working class cafeteria on 53rd St." that is almost certainly Valois.

Bookstores

Ex Libris Theological Books, 1340 E. 55th St. 773/955-3456.

57th Street Books, 1301 E. 57th St. 773/684-1300.

O'Gara & Wilson, Ltd., 1311 E. 57th St. 773/363-0993.

Powell's Book Store, 1501 E. 57th St. 773/955-7780.

Scholar's Books, 1379 E. 53rd St. 773/288-6565.

Seminary Co-op Bookstore, 5757 S. University Ave. 773/752-4381.

University of Chicago Bookstore, 970 E. 58th St. 773/702-8729.
Run by Barnes & Noble with a café selling Starbucks coffee, it's still the University of Chicago bookstore.

Coffeehouses and More

If you can't find good coffee in Hyde Park, you must not be looking! The University and immediate neighborhood have some of the most picturesque coffee shops and most interesting restaurants in Chicago.

Bonjour Café Bakery, 1550 E. 55th St. 773/241-5300.

C-Shop, 5706 S. University Ave.
Located in the Reynolds Club and overlooking Hutchinson Commons.

Café Siena, 1617 E. 55th St. 773/363-7742.

Caffé Florian, 1450 E. 55th St. 773/752-4100.

Classics Coffee Shop, 1010 E. 59th St., Room 20.

Cox Lounge, Stuart Hall (the Graduate School of Business) basement, 5835 S. Greenwood Ave.

Ex Libris, Regenstein Library, A-Level.
A convenient place to take a break from work at the Reg. Go down the stairs near the front entrance on 57th St.

Jimmy's Woodlawn Tap, 1172 E. 55th St. 773/643-5516.

Medici on 57th, 1327 E. 57th St. 773/667-7394.

Piccolo Mondo, 1642 E. 56th St. 773/643-1106.

Social Sciences Tea Room, 1126 E. 59th St., Room 201.

Stay Up 4 Ever, 1329 E. 57th St. 773/684-3532.

Swift Coffee Shop, Swift Hall basement, 1025-35 E. 58th St.

Valois Restaurant, 1518 E. 53rd St. 773/667-0647.

Other Sites of Interest

Bergman Gallery of the Renaissance Society, Cobb Hall, Room 418,
5811 S. Ellis Ave. 773/702-8670.
Closed Mon. Open Tues.-Fri. 10 A.M.-5 P.M., Sat.-Sun., 12 P.M.-5 P.M.
Admission is free; a donation is suggested.

Court Theatre, 5535 S. Ellis Ave. 773/753-4472.

Du Sable Museum of African-American History, 740 E. 56th Pl.
773/947-0600.
Open Mon.-Sat. 10 A.M.-4 P.M., Sun. 12 P.M.-4 P.M..
Adults $3, students and seniors $2, children under 13 $1. Free on Thurs.

Hyde Park Art Center, 1701 E. 53rd St. 773/324-5520.
Open Mon.-Sat. 10 A.M.-5 P.M.

Oriental Institute Museum, 1155 E. 58th St. 773/702-9520.
www.oi.uchicago.edu.
Closed Mon. Free, though a donation is suggested.

Robie House, 4747 S. Woodlawn Ave. 708/848-1976.
Tours are organized by the Frank Lloyd Wright Home and Studio Foundation
daily at 11 A.M., 1 P.M., and 3 P.M.

David and Alfred Smart Museum of Art, 5550 S. Greenwood Ave.
773/702-0200.
Open Tues., Wed., and Fri. 10 A.M.-4 P.M. Thurs. 10 A.M.-9 P.M., Sat.-Sun.
12 P.M.-6 P.M. Closed Mon. and holidays. Café and bookstore are open
seven days a week.

University Theater, 1131 E. 57th St. 773/702-3414.

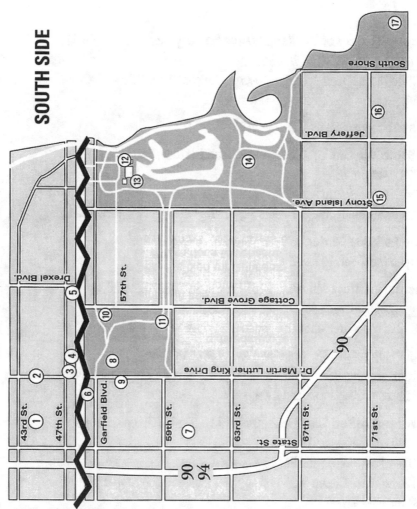

SOUTH SIDE

Map by Michael Polydoris.

South Side

The term "South Side" is a catch-all I'm using to encompass a huge chunk of Chicago real estate. Most tour buses bypass this area (with the glaring exception of the campus of the University of Chicago, which is a world unto itself) but "real" Chicago books have always mined the South Side for literary gold.

By Jeff Hall.

Richard Wright

I'm talking not about the tomes put out by Messrs. Frommer or Fodor, but about works such as Richard Wright's *Native Son,* Saul Bellow's *The Adventures of Augie March,* James T. Farrell's *Studs Lonigan* trilogy, Gwendolyn Brooks's *Maud Martha,* and many of the stories and novels of writers as diverse as Sara Paretsky, Richard Stern, and Steve Tesich . . . the list goes on and on.

Like virtually all parts of Chicago, the South Side has undergone dramatic changes since the so-called Golden Age of Chicago literature in the 1920s. The area that was home to James T. Farrell, Edna Ferber, Ben Hecht, Richard Wright, and, more recently, Harry Mark Petrakis, bears little resemblance to the part of Chicago they actually knew. For that matter, the "real" neighborhood is just a starting point for writers. Leon Forrest's complex 1000-plus-page novel *Divine Days* takes place in a sort of "South Side of the mind" called Forest County. There are resemblances to the South Side but the book's location is far more magical and fantastic than the area ever was in reality.

Sara Paretsky, who makes ample use of the South Side in her bestselling mystery novels, isn't speaking specifically of this area, but she could be, when she says:

> The eye with which I see Chicago is always half cocked for alienation and despair, because for me the city is a dangerous place where both states are only just below the surface.

In the spirit of full disclosure, I must admit that for several generations now my family has resided on the North Side. That said, I must also tell you that—even though when we are sitting in our back yard we can hear the roar of the crowd from the Friendly Confines of Wrigley Field—we are White Sox fans.

From another perspective, South Sider Petrakis writes that his family "knew there was a North Side (home of the ritzy Cub fans) and a West Side, but for all the relevance these sections had for us, they might have been cities in Europe."[1]

How long-time Chicagoans define their allegiance depends on a variety of factors, only one of which is what side of the Loop they happen to live. Even though a single neighborhood that can be considered "classic Chicago" doesn't really exist, you will find many characteristics on the South Side that feel such a "real" Chicago.

When touring this area expect to be surprised. The beauty of Jackson or Washington Park can fill you with wonder. The Pullman and Calumet City areas can feel like another world. Following in the footsteps of Sara Paretsky through the Lake Calumet area is like discovering another country. You may not meet many tourists with cameras hanging from their necks but, with a little planning and luck, you'll find scenic and historic spots as well as good and affordable restaurants.

You can't go too far wrong, after all, when you follow good writing. Chicago novels are the keys to the South Side neighborhoods you are seeing—unlocking the doors to what's behind the scenes, how things used to be, how people really tick.

How to Get There

A car is the best way to see the South Side; for areas like Lake Calumet or Pullman, you need your own wheels. If Jackson Park and the lakefront is all you have time for, the Metra train will deposit you in Hyde Park or the #6 Jeffery Express bus will take you from State Street in the Loop to the Museum of Science and Industry.

Driving Tour #1: South King Drive

The big wide thoroughfares in this area, such as King Drive and Drexel Boulevard, are lined with beautiful old stone houses that proclaim affluence. Poverty, however, is also no stranger to the area. Saul Bellow, who studied and worked at the University of Chicago just a mile away, wrote frequently about this part of the city. In his classic story "Looking for Mr. Green," a man wanders the Black Belt, where half of the city's African-American population once lived, trying to hand out relief checks to people who haven't bothered to pick them up:

> There were large numbers of newcomers in this terrific, blight-ridden portion of the city between Cottage Grove and Ashland, wandering from house to house and room to room. When you saw them, how could you know them? They didn't carry bundles on their backs or look picturesque. You only saw a man, a Negro, walking in the street or riding in the car, like everyone else, with his thumb closed on a transfer.[2]

It's vitally important for Bellow's protagonist George Grebe to know that Tulliver Green, the man he is seeking, *is* a real person with a face and a history, not an anonymous name on a piece of paper.

1.
Daniel Burnham's house
4300 S. King Dr.

Though he wasn't a novelist or poet, the man who uttered the phrase "Make no little plans, they have no magic to stir men's blood" was definitely a visionary. In 1909 Daniel Hudson Burnham (1846-1912) wrote one of the most influential books in Chicago history: *The Plan of Chicago.* Don't expect to find Burnham's house here; it was torn down long ago—an event that was probably not part of the great architect's master plan.

2.
The Marx Brothers' house
4512 S. King Dr.

Photo by Thayer Lindner.

The Marx Brothers lived in this house on King Drive.

The Marx Brothers' house, on the other hand, is still standing and does deserve a look-see. The Marx Brothers are known, of course, for their cinematic rather than their literary output. But Adolph Marx (otherwise known as Harpo) *was* the author of *Harpo Speaks,* and his brother Julius wrote an autobiography called *Groucho and Me.*

"When I was in my late teens our family moved to Chicago," Groucho recalls in Chapter 9 of *Groucho and Me.* "Pop had exhausted the possibilities of his misfit tailoring on the Eastern seaboard, and was all set to conquer new and unsuspecting worlds on the shores of Lake Michigan." He says his mother purchased this handsome house for eight thousand dollars: "She had paid a thousand dollars down, and the landlord was under the delusion that he would eventually get the balance."[3]

Elsewhere, Groucho talks about buying his first car in Chicago when he and his brother Gummo grew tired of taking "the clattering El train" to visit their girlfriends on the North Side. One time Zeppo tricked them into thinking the car had broken down by removing part of the ignition. After his brothers boarded the train to meet their girlfriends, Zeppo reattached the part and drove off to see his own girlfriend. Groucho had bad luck with transportation in Chicago; he describes losing the push rods from another auto on Michigan Avenue and causing a traffic jam while he retrieved them from the pavement.

3.
Robert S. Abbott home
4742 S. King Dr.

Robert S. Abott, founder and publisher of the *Chicago Defender,* lived here. The *Defender,* 2400 S. Michigan, 312/225-2400, was a trend-setting and highly influential publication that has been credited with encouraging the migration of southern blacks to the city after the First World War. Founded in 1905, the paper had a weekly circulation of 230,000 at its peak of popularity around 1915.[4] It now has a daily circulation around 30,000.

4.
Site of Regal Theater
4719 S. South Park (now Martin Luther King Dr.)

The original Regal Theater was where Bigger Thomas and a friend went to see a movie near the beginning of Richard Wright's 1940 masterpiece *Native Son.* In the film, a "wild man" throws a bomb into a room where rich white people are having a party, and they scream, "He's a Communist!" Bigger and his friend try to figure out what a Communist is. Bigger is inspired to do something big, and is filled with excitement about taking a job as a chauffeur for the white Dalton family that lives on Drexel Boulevard.

The heroine of Gwendolyn Brooks's novel *Maud Martha* also attends the Regal Theatre. She was not impressed with the show, and after the applause dies down she realizes that the audience of poor blacks has enjoyed an all-too-brief respite from its troubles: "For a half-hour it had put that light gauze across its little miseries and monotonies, but now here they were again, ungauzed, self-assertive, cancerous as ever. The audience had gotten a fairy gold."[5]

Gwendolyn Brooks (1917-2000) herself grew up at 4334 S. Champlain, but her house no longer stands—in fact, that block is almost vacant. One of the most famous and popular of all Chicago writers, Brooks was named Poet Laureate for the state of Illinois in 1968. She received an Academy of Arts and Letters award, two Guggenheim Foundation fellowships, a National Endowment for the Arts award, and the Shelley Memorial Award.

Profile: Sterling Plumpp

Chicago does not automatically welcome its poets and writers with open arms—and that is precisely why writer and "Blues poet" Sterling Plumpp has chosen to live here since 1962. "Chicago did me a favor by not embracing me," explains Plumpp, who is a professor and associate head of the department of African-American Studies at the University of Illinois at Chicago. "The value of Chicago to me is its ruthlessness: the forces of life and death and survival compete openly on these mean streets. And beyond this ruthlessness is an anonymity which allows one—to paraphrase Richard Wright—"to wring meaning from meaningless suffering."

Plumpp was born in 1940 in Clinton, Mississippi, and was raised by grandparents who were sharecroppers on a cotton plantation. After he joined other family members in Chicago, his sense of the rhythm and soul of his plantation roots only grew more acute—thanks to the "motley crew of Blues singers who moaned, groaned, bellowed and shouted at shrines up and down Roosevelt Road, Madison Street, Lake Street, and 16th Street." These Blues singers, he says, were the poets who caught the spirit of what he himself wanted to write.

The longer I stayed in Chicago, the more Mississippi in me grew. Therefore, Chicago is that oasis in a desert of searching where I discovered my roots as a southern writer. The iconography and sounds of its Blues and jazz became the foundation of my poetic language. What I have always longed for was a personal space to define myself and invent a life for myself. And, furthermore, I knew the tenets of writing as espoused by James Baldwin and Richard Wright. Baldwin had found that space in exile in Europe and Wright had found it in the Windy City. In many ways, in leaving Mississippi I was following the path of Wright who had left in 1927 though he remained in Memphis two years before arriving here...

Photo by Roberta Dupuis-Devlin. Courtesy of UIC Photographic Services.

Sterling Plumpp.

His first Chicago job was as a postal worker, but he enrolled at Roosevelt University while "jotting, scribbling, and making attempts at writing poetry." He graduated in 1968, continuing with graduate work until 1971. He found important parts of his education, however, outside the classroom.

Initially, Chicago was an excellent laboratory for me. I perused books for hours at a store on Wabash near Monroe and I spent hours in Powell's Book Store. Powell's is still my favorite bookstore. I could see Howlin' Wolf at Sylvio's on Lake and Kedzie on Friday nights, catch Wynton Kelly, Kenny Dorham, and Philly Joe Jones at McKie's on Cottage Grove near Sixty-Fifth on Saturday night, or visit the Opera House to be spellbound by Black Nativity with the incredible Marian Williams screaming jubilations.

Not all of the sights and sounds of Chicago are pretty, but all are grist for Plumpp's literary mill. "Chicago is a chaotic landscape I shape into poems about the life I know. It is a tough tale and a tough tale is what my experiences portend. Chicago is the place where I found the space to begin my lifelong search for self and purpose," he says.

Plumpp's 1998 poetry collection *Ornate with Smoke* (Third World Press) takes readers on a poetic journey through the musical landscape of jazz. He has written 14 books and his work has been published in literary magazines around the world. Honors include the Richard Wright Literary Excellence Award, given annually to writers from Mississippi, as well as the Carl Sandburg Prize for poetry (1993) and the DuSable Prize for literary excellence (1983).

Driving Tour #2: Studs Lonigan's Neighborhood

The "Studs Lonigan Neighborhood" is where author James T. Farrell grew up just west of Washington Park across from the tennis courts on South Park Avenue (now Martin Luther King Drive). Sadly, scenes like the one at the opening of Chapter 3 of *The Young Manhood of Studs Lonigan* are still all too common:

> Aloof and alone, his stomach like a lump of lead, Studs stood on the sidewalk by the vacant lot near Fifty-eighth and Indiana.[6]

Farrell's own family church was Corpus Christi—still there at 4920 S. King Dr. The neighborhood where Studs lived and went to school, and where Farrell himself lived, is just south of here, around 57th and 58th Streets.

After he revisited the neighborhood in 1954, Farrell said in an article entitled "Farrell Revisits Studs Lonigan's Neighborhood": "The Old Studs Loni-

gan neighborhood is a corner of America where many of my memories hide as
though in blocks of stone and along dull and commonplace looking streets." For
him it "throbbed with significances of a personal past."[7]

Farrell lived in Chicago for his first 27 years, from 1904 to 1931. Farrell's
hero Danny O'Neill lived in a building on the corner of 57th and Indiana, and
that is where Farrell himself lived, too. It's important to remember that Farrell
always bristled at the notion that the neighborhood where he had grown up
was a slum.

5.
The Dalton home (Native Son)
4605 S. Drexel Blvd.

Bigger Thomas, the poor black hero of *Native Son*, feels afraid that he had to
walk to a white neighborhood to see about a job at the Dalton family home, so
he takes along his knife and gun. The area seems to Bigger "a cold and distant
world; a world of white secrets carefully guarded." He inadvertently kills Mary
Dalton by smothering her with a pillow, then stuffs her body in the furnace in
the basement.

Today, there is no home at 4605 S. Drexel. If you use your imagination,
however, the house at the northeast corner of 48th Street and Drexel will serve
as a nice stand-in for the Dalton house.

6.
Lorraine Hansberry house
5330 S. Calumet Ave.

Playwright Hansberry lived here from 1930 to 1938. In 1938, her family
attempted to move to a new house in the predominantly white Washington
Park neighborhood, but was evicted by the Illinois courts on the grounds that
existing racial codes were being violated.

Hansberry's most famous play, *A Raisin in the Sun* (1959), is set on the
South Side. The story describes a conflict between a mother who wants to buy a
house with $10,000 she has received from her dead husband's life insurance

policy and her son who wants to invest in a liquor store. In 1969 *A Raisin in the Sun* won the Drama Critics Circle Award, later becoming a film that starred Sidney Poitier.

7.
Studs Lonigan's home and William W. Carter School
5740 S. Michigan Ave. 773/535-0860

A two-story building on Wabash just south of 57th Street, on the east side of the street, is supposed to be the home of the Lonigan family. Farrell's biographer Edgar M. Branch places it "next to the fence marking the boundary of the Carter Public School playground."[8] This home was reportedly the residence of a friend of Farrell's who served as the model for Studs Lonigan, William "Studs" Cunningham. Both the real and fictional Studs used to play in the William W. Carter Public School playground, which you can still see at 5740 S. Michigan.

In *Stelmark: A Family Recollection,* Chicago writer Harry Mark Petrakis also recalls growing up in the neighborhood around 61st and Michigan. His father was the parish priest at St. Constantine and Helen Church for 28 years. He writes: "I seem to remember streets of matching brick three-story apartment buildings, all with cramped-as-kangaroo pouch entrances, and the windows veiled by flimsy gossamer curtains."[9]

8.
Washington Park
Bounded by Cottage Grove Ave., 60th St., Martin Luther King Dr., and 51st St.

Washington Park, designed by Frederick Law Olmsted and opened in 1873 when the area was still outside the city limits, was long considered the jewel of Chicago's park system, along with Jackson Park and the Midway Plaisance that joins the two. During the warm weather, you are likely to find athletes in action, just as James T. Farrell himself played baseball in the park in 1915 and 1916.[10] Edgar M. Branch identifies the "Lily Pool" as the little pool just east of King Drive, on the south side of Garfield Boulevard, after the swimming pool.

9.
Site of James T. Farrell's house
5700 block of S. King Dr.

In an essay entitled "My Beginnings as a Writer," Farrell remembers a rainy afternoon when he was in 8th grade:

> I sat by our parlor window in the apartment on South Park Avenue looking out at the wet trees and the dying greenness of Washington Park. It was Saturday and I wanted to be out playing . . . But I didn't go out. I didn't go searching for any of the boys. I sat with a five-cent composition book and my cathedral's *History of the United States* before me, and I looked out at the wet damp park and at the dark and dreary sky which hung over it in a leaden gloom. I heard my grandmother puttering about in the back of the apartment. I wrote. Swept along, I filled page after page of my composition book.[11]

Much of the action in Cyrus Colter's *The Rivers of Eros* (1972) takes place on South Park Avenue just west of the park. Zack works hard in his garage on 51st Street. Tortured by thoughts of his wife's infidelity, he goes to a bar called Trent's at 55th and South Park and to another called the Oasis on 51st. Drinking, however, is unable to derail his train of thought that his wife has made him "the laughing stock of every tavern and pool room on the Southside."[12]

10.
DuSable Museum Sculpture Garden
Outside DuSable Museum of African American History, 740 E. 56th Pl.

This is the probable site of the "Bug Club" mentioned in the Studs Lonigan novels, where radicals went to speak out against the evils of capitalist society.

There is a sculpture of German dramatist and critic Gotthold Lessing by Albin Polasek in the garden.

Lorado Taft and *The Fountain of Time.*

11.
The Fountain of Time
Midway Plaisance and Cottage Grove Ave.

At the south edge of Washington Park and at the western end of the Midway Plaisance, stands this monumental sculpture. It took Lorado Taft 14 years to complete *The Fountain of Time,* and it is generally considered to be his masterpiece. *Time* stands across a pool of water gazing at a wave of humanity that includes 100 separate figures representing birth, love, family, life, religion, and other themes. Time has taken its toll on Taft's handiwork, too. Despite several renovations in the 1990s, the figures have decayed due to the weather and the exhaust fumes released by the often heavy traffic heading through the park.

Driving Tour #3: Jackson Park
World's Fair Visions

Frederick Law Olmsted designed Jackson Park, which is on the lakefront east of the University of Chicago, as well as Central Park in New York City. He

Courtesy of the University of Chicago Archives, Joseph Regenstein Library.

The Ferris wheel and the Midway at the World's Columbian Exposition of 1893.

originally envisioned the Midway Plaisance, which connects Jackson and Washington Parks, as a canal that would help drain the marshes in the area.

After the Chicago Fire, another architect named H. W. S. Cleveland simplified the plans and nixed the idea of turning the Midway into the canal. Olmsted returned to the city when Jackson Park was chosen as the site of the World's Columbian Exposition of 1893.

In *Sweet Clover: A Romance of the White City* by Clara Louise Burnham (1894), the following view is presented of the construction of the fair:

But Chicago, which had formed a habit of making stepping-stones of obstacles, now said "I will" with greater doggedness of purpose than ever before, and sending steam dredges to invade the wilderness, began the patient, laborious grabbing, which was necessary to excavate in one place, and fill in another. Meanwhile the oldest inhabitant wandered about, looking on, wondering and fascinated. The maiden, going in advance of the feller of trees, caught with her kodak a farewell glimpse of the wood-road, that had furnished a foothold amid the sand for the spring violets of her childhood. The small boy looked longingly at the sloughs, which had been first to freeze in autumn, and thought it a thousand pities that Chicago had been so brave as to deserve the Fair.[13]

As poet and journalist Eugene Field wrote in his "Sharps and Flats" column in the *Chicago Daily News:*

Come, boys, let's away to the Midway Plaisance, there are visions of loveliness there to behold!

The Columbian Exposition, popularly called the "White City," attracted millions of visitors to the city.

After the fair, Jackson Park was converted back to expanses of green. Today the park is so big that it accommodates a golf course and driving range, along with a lagoon, island, and world-class museum.

12.
Museum of Science and Industry
57th St. and Lake Shore Dr. 773/684-1414

The museum is housed in one of the few structures preserved from the Columbian Exposition. Designed by Charles B. Atwood, it originally served as the Palace of Fine Arts. After the fair, the structure housed the Field Museum of Natural History until it moved to its present location at Lake Shore Drive and Roosevelt Road.

The Chicago poet and lawyer Edgar Lee Masters, who visited the fair as a young man, rhapsodized in later years that the Palace of Fine Arts building was a "miracle," and "one of the genuine glories of Chicago," pointing out that the building was of "pure Greek classic style in the Ionic order." He added:

Between the white columns of the peristyle the blue Lake flashed and dreamed all that summer before the entrance gaze of the many thousands who paused in their walk about the Court to contemplate the beauty of the scene.[14]

A novel called *Samantha at the World's Fair,* published in 1893 by "Josiah Allen's Wife" (Marietta Holley), tells the story of two simple country folks who journey in their horse-drawn cart from the hamlet of Jonesburg to Chicago to see the Exposition. Like much of nineteenth-century humor, the book is written in dialect. At a boarding house Samantha and Josiah Allen meet a character named Mr. Bolster who introduces them to the city. His description shows the idealistic terms in which the earliest writers viewed the city:

> Chicago has the most energetic and progressive people in the world. It hain't made up, like an Eastern village, of folks that stay to home and set round in butter-tubs in grocery stores, talkin' about hens. No, it is made up of people who dared—who wuz too energetic, progressive, and ambitious, to settle down and be content with what their fathers had. And they struck out new paths for themselves, as the Pilgrim Fathers did.[15]

Time and again, Chicago is seen as the center of the United States, the fair as a sign of a new age of "Freedom, and Justice, and Perfect Rights for man and woman, Love, Joy, Peace."[16]

In contrast, there's Robert Herrick's view of the Fair. Herrick, a scholar lured to the University of Chicago at the time of its opening in 1892, wrote about two dozen novels. He never warmed to the city and his novels are gloomy, many of them directly concerning Chicago life. Herrick's *The Web of Life* (1900) was set shortly after the fair closed, and mentions the "rotting buildings of the play-city" as a setting.

Open Mon.-Fri. 9:30 A.M.-4 P.M., Sat.-Sun. 9:30 A.M.-5:30 P.M. Adults $7, seniors $6, children 3-11 $3.50.

Courtesy of the University of Chicago Archives, Joseph Regenstein Library.

Robert Herrick.

Photo by Thayer Lindner.

Clarence Darrow Bridge.

13.
Clarence Darrow Bridge

Directly south of the museum, across from the lagoon

Clarence Darrow, the famous lawyer who defended Loeb and Leopold and argued for evolution in the Scopes Monkey trial, lived on 60th Street just across

the park. (His house has long since been demolished.) He liked to walk on this bridge, and after his death it was named the Clarence Darrow Bridge in his honor. Every March, a group meets on the bridge on the anniversary of his death to throw a wreath into the Jackson Park lagoon.

Just west of this bridge, a walking path leads south to another bridge that crosses the lagoon to the Wooded Island. This was the location of a Japanese garden and temple during the Exposition, and a tea garden was added after it closed. The tea garden was renamed the Osaka Garden after it and the bridge underwent substantial renovation on the 100th anniversary of the Exposition in 1993.

Courtesy of the Chicago Public Library.

Clarence Darrow.

Harriet Monroe was a reporter for a while at the *Chicago Tribune* and, of course, founded *Poetry* magazine in 1912. She wrote a poem, "Columbian Ode," for the dedication of the Columbian Exposition, which is perhaps her best. She and her sisters had slept in a cottage on Wooded Island the night before the dedication, and then watched the sun rise over the "White City." It was a time when the dreams of citizens were sure to come true as Chicago came into its own as a world-class city. She wrote:

> And at night, when the palaces were hung with lights that trailed gold fringes in the water, when the boats drifted in and out of shadows, and iridescent domes and towers faded off into darkness—then was a passion of great beauty evoked out of dust and fire; for a moment all unreal things were real, and dreams had the hardihood of marble. [17]

Photo by Thayer Lindner.

The *Republic.*

14.
The *Republic*
Richards and Hayes Drs., Jackson Park

This 24-foot-tall statue is impressive, especially when it's glowing in the afternoon sun. But it's actually only a small-scale replica of the 65-foot original created by Daniel Chester French that occupied a central spot in the Court of Honor at the Columbian Exposition. Legend has it that this smaller version once served as the final hole in a miniature golf course in Jackson Park.

The *Republic* is described with memorable detail in *Samantha at the World's Fair.* Samantha herself nearly glows with admiration as she goes on for several pages about her delight in finding a symbol of the new status of her sex (she uses the word "sect"):

THE MINUTE WE PASSED THE GATE WE WUZ OVERWHELMED WITH TH[E] ONSPEAKABLE ASPECT OF THE BUILDIN'S.
—See page 206

From Marietta Holley's Samantha at the World's Fair.

Samantha and her husband look in wonder at the fair.

A female, most sixty-five feet tall! Why, as I looked on her, my emotions riz me up so, and seemed to expand my own size so, that I felt as if I, too, towered up so high that I could lock arms with her, and walk off with her arm in arm, and look around and enjoy what wuz bein' done in the great To-Day for her sect, and me; and what that sect wuz a-branchin' out and doin' for herself.[18]

As Samantha thinks these uplifting thoughts, two women join her. One comments on how good the figure of the *Republic* would look in ruffled skirts and a dress with sleeves and high-heeled shoes.

Marge Piercy has an entirely different take on the statue, which she refers to as Columbia, in *Going Down Fast,* a novel about the urban renewal that dramatically changed the area around the University of Chicago in the 1950s:

> Columbia stood in Jackson Park near a missile installation, an enormous figure bearing aloft a large bushy cross and an eagle perched with its claws dug into the world. She wore voluminous robes and had a small head. In the sun she flashed and blinded, visible for blocks and though labeled the Republic, obviously a goddess of Empire.[19]

In Piercy's book, a young "pimply-faced hood" beats up

" How sweet she would look !"

From Marietta Holley's Samantha at the World's Fair.

The *Republic* as envisioned by Samantha.

an old man at the feet of the goddess, a symbol of the poverty and violence that take place in the shadow of the powerful forces.

Driving Tour #4: South Shore

Immediately south of Jackson Park is the pleasant residential community of South Shore. South and west of this you'll find areas that are commercial to industrial and boring to fascinating.

In its heyday, the area was populated by the rich, who frequented the South Shore Country Club for golf and social events. Today as then, residents enjoy living in beautiful homes in close proximity to the lake.

15. & 16.
James T. Farrell residences
7136 S. East End Ave.
7046 S. Euclid Ave.
2023 E. 72nd St.

Farrell told Branch that he moved out of the old neighborhood where he worked on his Studs Lonigan trilogy. Among addresses where he hung his hat were 7136 S. East End and 7046 S. Euclid, and in 1920 he occupied a five-room flat on the second floor of the three-story building at 2023 E. 72nd. One notable gathering place for the mostly affluent Irish Catholics who lived in the area at that time was the Church of St. Philip Neri at 72nd and Merrill. With a style reminiscent of English cathedrals, it was completed in 1926.

17.
South Shore Country Club
7059 S. South Shore Dr.

"The white paint was peeling and the gates sagging at the old South Shore Country Club, once a symbol of that area's wealth and exclusivity. As a child I

used to imagine I would grow up to ride a horse along its private bridle paths."
Sara Paretsky obviously wrote this description in *Blood Shot* (1989) before the
current owners, the Chicago Park District, finished an extensive rehab of the
building in 1983. The restored, spacious facility, formerly the South Shore
Country Club, is a magnificent jewel of the city. Its amenities include a nine-
hole golf course, lighted tennis courts, a beautiful beachfront and picnic area, an
art gallery and adjoining solarium, a ballroom, and a theater.

Driving Tour #5: Pullman

In the late 1870s, George M. Pullman selected a site near the depot of the
Illinois Central Railroad at 111th Street for his Pullman railroad car factory and
a company town. Several buildings have been damaged by fire, including the
Administration Building at 111th and South Cottage Grove Avenue. A variety of
housing designed for workers still stands as do horse stables at 11201 S. Cottage
Grove. You can also visit the Hotel Florence at 11111 S. Forrestville, where
Pullman's guests stayed; and his place of worship, Greenstone Church at 112th
South St. Lawrence. Paretsky's V. I. Warshawski also gives us a quick tour of the
Pullman neighborhood:

> It's been over a century since the Army Corps of Engineers and George
> Pullman decided to turn the sprawling marshes between Lake Calumet and
> Lake Michigan into an industrial center. It wasn't just Pullman, of course—
> Andrew Carnegie, Judge Gary, and a host of lesser barons all played a part,
> working on it for sixty or seventy years.

Driving Tour #6: Beverly

This integrated, affluent neighborhood of fine Victorian homes is bounded by

87th Street on the north, Western Avenue on the west, 119th Street on the south, and (roughly) Ashland Avenue on the east. Beverly is the setting for *St. Valentine's Night* by Andrew M. Greeley—a "magic neighborhood." The protagonist, Neal Connor, comes home to Beverly, and is surprised to find the area still flourishing, full of pricey, well-maintained homes:

> The dowager homes on the ridge above Longwood Drive still looked down superciliously on the small park next to the Rock Island station, conscious no doubt that they stood on the highest point in Cook County and that the drive was the historic Vincennes Trail.
>
> The Ravine, a gully cut through sand dunes thousands of years ago, was still picturesque, virtually the only wooded hills in Chicago; its homes clung to the sides of the ancient dunes as if they were in a Swiss village.

Gwendolyn Brooks's poem "Beverly Hills, Chicago" looks at the neighborhood from the perspective of poor black outsiders driving by the beautiful houses they cannot own:

> The dry brown coughing beneath their feet,
>
> (Only a while, for the handyman is on his way)
>
> These people walk their golden gardens.
>
> We say ourselves fortunate to be driving by today.
>
> . . . Even the leaves fall down in lovelier patterns here.
>
> And the refuse, the refuse is a neat brilliancy.

In her novel *i left my back door open,* April Sinclair's protagonist Dee Dee Joy recalls growing up in Morgan Park, the neighborhood south of Beverly between 107th and 119th Streets. Her school was "filled with graffiti and stopped-up toilets and kids looking for fights . . . you had to be tough in order to be respected. Otherwise you were a target . . . your reputation was everything.[20]

18.
Carter G. Woodson Regional Library
9525 S. Halsted St. 312/747-6900

One of the largest public library collections in the country is housed in this facility: the Vivian G. Harsh Collection of Afro-American History and Literature. Available only to researchers, the collection features Afro-American periodicals, manuscripts of Richard Wright and Langston Hughes, and a wealth of reference materials related to Afro-American history.

Driving Tour #7: The East Side

Sara Paretsky, in the introduction to *Windy City Blues* entitled "A Walk on the Wild Side: Touring Chicago with V. I. Warshawski," remarks:

> Of all Chicago neighborhoods the most interesting to me are those on the far southeast side, where Dead Stick Pond fights for survival beneath the rusting sheds of the old steel mills. The whole history of the city is contained in four small neighborhoods there—South Chicago, South Deering, Pullman, and the East Side.

Photo by Greg Holden.

A view through the chain link fence that surrounds "Dead Stick Pond."

Later, she provides you with her own detailed directions for a mini-driving tour of the South Side areas she knows well, culminating in the ghostly body of water she calls Dead Stick Pond, where her character V. I. Warshawski was dumped and left for dead:

Sara Paretsky.

"Despite warning signs, on a good day you can find anything from a pair of boots to a bedstead dumped in Dead Stick Pond."

As you pass the homes that cower in the shadows of the Chicago Skyway bridge, think of Saul Bellow's description, in *The Dean's December,* of "ancient Chicago, open back stairs and porches clapped together of gray lumber, held up by crude cross-trusses."

19.
The East Side

In *Blood Shot* (1988), our friend and tour guide V. I. Warshawski talks about a little-known neighborhood called the East Side. Where, exactly, do you find the East Side?

> I had forgotten the trick to getting into the East Side and had to double back to Ninety-fifth Street, where an old-fashioned drawbridge crosses the Calumet River . . . Five bridges form the neighborhood's only link to the rest of the city. Its members live in a stubborn isolation, trying to recreate the Eastern Euro-

pean villages of their grandparents.

Jimbo Marino, the Chicago cop and hero of Eugene Izzi's novel *Bad Guys*, occupies a rundown apartment in this area:

> The apartment he was living in was a dive, in a neighborhood once thriving and vibrant, two blocks from the lake. Now it was in decay as the mills closed and the sharks bought the houses for the price of unpaid taxes. The homes wound up gutted, renovated, the single-family dwellings cut into four apartment units—each unit housing more people than used to live in the place when it was family owned.[21]

The Roseland neighborhood on the far South Side (also called New Holland or High Prairie) was a Dutch farming community at one time. Edna Ferber captured its essence so well in *So Big* that the novel won the Pulitzer Prize in 1924. It tells the story of Selina Peake who moved to the Pleistocene Beach Ridge area to teach at High Prairie School. When her husband dies she takes over the family truck farm and markets her produce in the city.

Peake probably travelled back and forth on Thornton Road, which was lined with the small frame houses of the Dutch vegetable and dairy farmers. The *Local Community Fact Book of Chicago* reports that High Prairie was located between 103rd and 111th, between Cottage Grove and Halsted.[22]

Bookstores

African American Images Inc., 1909 W. 95th St. 773/445-0322.

Beverly Books, 9915 S. Walden Pkwy. 773/239-7760.

Black Expression Book Source, 9500 S. Western Ave., Evergreen Park. 708/424-4338.

Bookies Paperbacks & More, 2419 W. 103rd St. 773/239-1110.

Borders Books Music & Café, 2210 W. 95th St. 773/445-5471.

John Rybski Books, 2319 W. 47th Pl. 773/847-5082.

Anne W. Leonard, 1935 W. 95th St. 773/239-7768.

Moody Bookstores, 112 W. 87th St. 773/994-0633.

Reading on Walden Bookstore, 9913 S. Walden Pkwy. 773/233-7633.

Student Book Store, Ford City Mall East. 773/582-4375.

Underground Bookstore, 2056 E. 71st St. 773/955-1797,
1727 E. 87th St. 773/768-8869.

Coffeehouses

Beverly Bean Co., 2734 W. 111th St: 773/239-6688.

Café Simone, 10307 S. Hale Ave. 773/238-0650.

Java Express, 10701 S. Hale Ave. 773/233-8557.

Some Like It Black Coffee Club & Gallery, 4500 S. Michigan Ave.
773/373-8834.

Other Places of Interest

Beverly Art Center, 2153 W. 111th St. 773/445-3838.

Drury Lane South Theater, 2500 W. 95th St., Evergreen Park.
708/422-0404.

ETA Creative Arts Foundation, 7558 S. South Chicago Ave.
773/752-3955.

Florence Hotel, 11111 S. Forrestville Ave. 773/745-8900
Named for George M. Pullman's favorite granddaughter, this restaurant fea-

tures daily specials served in charming Victorian surroundings.

Oak Woods Cemetery, 1035 E. 67th St.
Features a monument called Lincoln the Orator.

OAK PARK

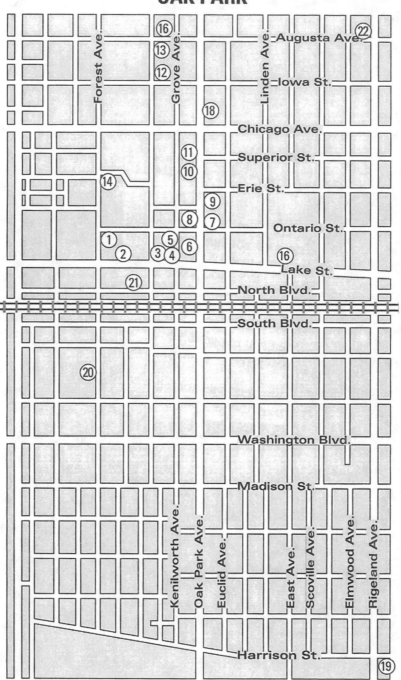

Map by Michael Polydoris.

Oak Park

> "I had a wonderful novel to write about Oak Park and would never
> do it because I did not want to hurt living people."[1]

—Ernest Hemingway

Since the turn of the century, Oak Park has attracted artists, writers, educators, and lovers of art and literature. What is it about this affluent suburb that has provided such fertile literary ground? Perhaps its location is the key. Oak Park is nestled between the western city limits of Chicago and the even more upscale town of River Forest just to its west. Residents can enjoy a lifestyle that has a distinctly urban fla-

By Jeff Hall.

Ernest Hemingway

vor while reaping the benefits of living in a suburb; they can breathe a heady mixture of city smog and suburban greenery and benefit from both stimulation and relaxation. (It's said that Ernest Hemingway, Oak Park's most famous literary son, used to go hiking along the Des Plaines River and through Thatcher Woods just west of nearby River Forest.[2]) The city is known for excellent public schools, architecturally rich housing options, and liberal politics.

Maybe you're trying to find a Hemingway-like "clean well-lighted place." Or perhaps you want to swing like Tarzan out of the urban jungle. Whatever your motivation, Oak Park makes a great destination for city dwellers who are eager to take a day trip but don't want to go too far afield. The city is a book lover's delight, with plenty of trendy shops, architectural gems, and cultural attractions also thrown into the mix.

Oak Park was once home to the Potawatomi, Sac, and Fox Indians. White settlers first arrived in the 1830s. One of the early families had the picturesque name of Kettlestrings. After emigrating from England, the Kettlestrings ran a tavern near what is now Harlem Avenue and Lake Street. Fifty cents was the charge for supper, bed, and breakfast. Oak Park had only 500 residents before 1871, but by 1890 the number had increased to 4,500. The large number of churches within its boundaries gave the town its original nickname of "Saints' Rest." Members of those congregations kept dry liquor laws on the books for nearly 100 years.

Oak Park boasts a large percentage of houses that are old but well-preserved. Many of the more architecturally significant (including 13 designed by Frank Lloyd Wright) are located within the Oak Park National Historic District, an area roughly bounded by Harlem Avenue on the west, Augusta Boulevard on the north, Ridgeland Avenue on the east, and Madison Street on the south. Oak Park has at least four commercial districts as well. The two northern shopping areas are found along North Avenue and Chicago Avenue. The central business area, "The Avenue," is centered on Lake Street and Oak Park Avenue. The "Harrison East" business district contains arts meccas such as galleries and theaters, as well as coffeeshops.

Oak Park was home to two very successful (and very different) twentieth-century writers: Ernest Hemingway and Edgar Rice Burroughs, the author of the Tarzan novels. It's well worth visiting the sites with connections to these literary lights—particularly when combined with a visit to the Home and Studio of Oak Park's other famous resident, Frank Lloyd Wright. It's remarkable how many homes and other sites associated with these illustrious figures have been preserved, in contrast to Chicago, where writers' homes are bulldozed to make way for condos, apartment buildings, parking lots, etc., without a second thought.

Successful children's book author Harriette Gillem Robinet, author of *Washington City Is Burning* and *The Twins, the Pirates, and the Battle of New Orleans,* calls Oak Park home today; so does novelist Alex Kotlowitz, journalist and author of *There Are No Children Here* and *The Other Side of the River,* and winner of the 1998 Heartland Prize for fiction. Another Heartland Prize winner, Jane Hamilton, grew up in Oak Park and now lives in Wisconsin. Her novel *The Short History of a Prince* contains some Oak Park settings, though the story refers to the town as Oak Ridge.

How to Get There

Oak Park is located about ten miles due west of the Chicago Loop. The city's proximity to transportation is one of its assets. You can easily get there via the Metra train or the CTA's Green Line. Or, exit the Eisenhower Expressway at either Austin or Harlem heading north.

Walking Tour

The Oak Park Historic District is a pleasant place to walk on a sunny afternoon, and you can cover a good number of literary sites along with your choice of Frank Lloyd Wright houses.

1.
Oak Park Visitors Center
158 N. Forest Ave. 708/848-1500

Start your tour by parking in the garage at Lake and Kenilworth. Walk a half-block east, turn north on Forest, and go to the Oak Park Visitors Center. Pick up a map and purchase tickets here for attractions such as the Frank Lloyd Wright Home and Studio and the Ernest Hemingway Museum and birthplace.

I'm not sure how Hemingway would have felt about all the attention his home town devoted to him during the centennial of his birth (July 21, 1899) and after. After graduating from Oak Park-River Forest High School and going to work as a reporter for the *Kansas City Star,* he spent as little time as possible here. Anthony Burgess, in *Ernest Hemingway and His World,* says Hemingway was happy to break free of the constraint of "happy but stuffy Oak Park."[3] Hemingway's own description of Oak Park as a place of "wide lawns and small minds" is well known.

He did, however, spend his first two decades or so in Oak Park and his childhood teachers taught him much about writing. He left Oak Park to go to war as a volunteer ambulance driver and came back a wounded hero. His early history can be traced in a single afternoon's walk.

2.
Afri-Ware Inc.
948 Lake St. 708/524-8398

Return to Lake and walk east. First, you'll pass Afri-Ware, a store that sells African books and artifacts and is the site of a monthly Afrikan Perspective Book Club. Continue east on Lake.

3.
First United Church of Oak Park
848 Lake St.

The church where Ernest Hemingway was baptized in 1899 is at Kenilworth Avenue.

4.
Oak Park Public Library
834 Lake St. 708/383-8200

In their haste to head for the birthplace, devotees of Hemingway should not overlook this exciting resource. Go to the Information Services desk and ask the librarian for access to the Hemingway Collection. You'll be led to a special room in the back that contains a big bookcase full of books about the author and his family. Of particular interest are five black binders containing original photos donated by Hemingway's friends, and lots of articles about his years in school and his other connections to the town. Other Oak Park sons and daughters are not overlooked by the library, which also maintains a Local Authors Collection of books written by local writers.

5.
Site of Hemingway's interim home
161 N. Grove Ave.

Behind the library you find . . . nothing. Actually, this is the location where Hemingway lived for one year (1905-1906). The home, originally at 161 N. Grove, was moved to Chicago and Elmwood late in 1999.

Photo by Thayer Lindner.

Ernest Hemingway as a young boy.

6.
Scoville Park
Lake St. and Oak Park Ave.

Walk across Grove and visit Scoville Park. Hemingway and his sister Marcelline went sledding here when they were children. Climb to the top of the hill where the War Memorial bears Hemingway's name among those of other veterans. A tree just north of the memorial was planted in the writer's honor when he died.

Scoville Park War Memorial.

Photo by Thayer Lindner.

Photo by Thayer Lindner.

Ernest Hemingway Museum.

7.
Ernest Hemingway Museum
200 N. Oak Park Ave. 708/848-2222

Walk northeast across the park and down the hill to the corner of Oak Park and Ontario. The imposing building with the four columns is the Oak Park Arts Center, which houses the Hemingway Museum. The fee that you pay either here or at the Visitors Center admits you to both this facility and Hemingway's birthplace. Guests can view a video on young Ernest's high school years, inspect first edition book jackets of his works, and look at rare photos and artifacts from his life. A bookstore on the premises sells the inevitable Hemingway Museum hat and T-shirt. The museum sponsors a special celebration each year on Boxing Day, December 26.

One of the most interesting pieces in the museum, which is on permanent display, is the original "Dear Ernest" letter sent to Hemingway by Agnes von Kurowsky, the nurse he fell in love with when he was recuperating in a hospital in France after being wounded during World War I.

In *A Farewell to Arms,* Hemingway's 1929 novel about his love affair with Agnes, he comments about the war: " . . . I had seen nothing sacred, and the things that were glorious had no glory and the sacrifices were like the stockyards at Chicago if nothing was done with the meat except to bury it."[4]

8.
The Write Inn
211 N. Oak Park Ave.
708/383-4800

Leave the museum, turn right, and walk north on Oak Park Avenue. Across the street is this 65-room hotel, which was built in the 1920s. Many writers stayed here while working on their books, particularly during the 1930s and 1940s.

Photo by Thayer Lindner.

The Write Inn.

9.
Dr. William E. Barton home
228 N. Oak Park Ave.

Barton, author of a two-volume *Life of Abraham Lincoln,* was the foremost Lincoln scholar before Carl Sandburg took his crown. His son Bruce Barton became more famous than his father. He was a successful advertising man and for many years was chairman of the advertising agency Batten, Barton, Durstine, & Osborne (BBDO) and served two terms in the U.S. Congress in the 1930s. He was the Barton of the famous FDR diatribe against conservative Republicans: "Martin, Barton, and Fish." Bruce Barton used his advertising experience to write *The Man Nobody Knows,* a book heavily influenced by the stock market and business enthusiasm of the 1920s, that describes Jesus Christ as "the world's greatest organization man." This was followed by *The Book Nobody Knows,* his book about the Bible.

10.
Site of Edgar Rice Burroughs's Oak Park homes
325 N. Oak Park Ave., 1918-1919
821 S. Scoville Ave., 1910-1911 (a rented home)
414 Augusta St., 1914-1917
700 Linden Ave., 1917-1918

Continue walking north and cross the street. 325 N. Oak Park is the site of one of several homes that were owned by Oak Park's second best-known novelist, Edgar Rice Burroughs. This home, which Burroughs purchased after he had achieved considerable success, featured a third-floor ballroom.

Burroughs moved frequently, both in Oak Park and Chicago. His Oak Park houses were within spitting distance of Ernest Hemingway's birthplace and a few blocks from Hemingway's childhood home. It's interesting to speculate whether Hemingway, as a student at Oak Park-River Forest High School, was inspired to pursue his own future career by the presence of a successful writer in his neighborhood.

Burroughs's most famous work, *Tarzan of the Apes,* was published shortly after he moved to the home at 414 Augusta in 1914. While living on Augusta, Burroughs turned out at least ten more books and many stories for *All-Story* and other pulp fiction magazines.

Photo by Thayer Lindner.

Edgar Rice Burroughs's house at 414 Augusta.

Edgar Rice Burroughs

Edgar Rice Burroughs.

Edgar Rice Burroughs had plenty of other chapters in his life before becoming a writer. Born on West Washington Boulevard in Chicago in 1875, he worked at a number of failed businesses before turning to pulp fiction. He sold lead pencil sharpeners from an office at Market and Monroe; he was a gold miner; and he was a railroad policeman, among other things.

Burroughs became seriously interested in writing adventure and fantasy stories when he was required to inspect the ads his pencil sharpener company had placed in pulp fiction magazines. He

wrote *Tarzan of the Apes* not in Oak Park but in his *System* magazine office in the Chicago Loop, 5 N. Wabash. He also became well-known for his "John Carter of Mars" series of books.

Burroughs will probably always be destined to take a back seat to Oak Park's more illustrious son. The creator of Tarzan, however, achieved success on his own terms, and is highly revered by an intense group of followers who devote lavish attention to his life and work. You'll find tons of information about Burroughs on a Web site created by Bill Hillman (http://home.westman.wave.ca/

> Long before George Lucas pushed *Star Wars* merchandise, Edgar Rice Burroughs created the modern multimedia marketing company with his ERB, Inc. to promote Tarzan and related products.

%7Ehillmans/erblinxx.html). The last word on this writing and marketing genius, however, has to be Irwin Porges's monumental book *Edgar Rice Burroughs: The Man Who Created Tarzan,* which weighs in at 800 large-format pages.

One of Burroughs's greatest achievements was the modern multimedia marketing company, ERB Inc., which he created to promote Tarzan and related products many years before George Lucas pushed the *Star Wars* lines of merchandise. The history of Burroughs and Tarzan was captured in the exhibit "Tarzan, Mars and the Fertile Mind of Edgar Rice Burroughs" that was shown in early 2000 at the Historical Society of Oak Park and River Forest. Some parts of the exhibit will be displayed on a permanent basis at the Society.

Burroughs moved around quite a bit, gradually purchasing bigger and bigger houses as his success grew and grew.

11.
Hemingway birthplace
339 N. Oak Park Ave. 708/848-2222

Continue walking north to visit the Ernest Hemingway birthplace, a fine Victorian home at 339 N. Oak Park (when Hemingway was born, the street

Hemingway's birthplace.

Photo by Thayer Lindner.

Photo by Greg Holden.

Hemingway's boyhood home on Kenilworth Avenue.

number was actually 439).

Hemingway was born in the second-floor bedroom with his father (an obstetrician) attending. He lived here from 1899 to 1905. Take a tour and see how the house is being meticulously restored by the Ernest Hemingway Foundation of Oak Park. Little, if any, original furnishings remain, but the foundation is working from old photographs to make the home look pretty much as it did in 1900.

12.
Hemingway's boyhood home
600 N. Kenilworth Ave.

Walk north on Oak Park a few blocks to Iowa Street. Turn left (or west) to see the house where Hemingway actually spent the bulk of his elementary school and high school years, 1906-1919. The home is a private residence, but the Hemingway Foundation hopes to purchase it one day. Hemingway's bedroom

Classic Chicago Books

In my humble opinion (I admit, I'm not an impartial observer) Chicago literary works reveal a lot more about the city than do travel guides. Good Chicago novels also guide readers to areas of the city that they wouldn't get to otherwise. In case you're looking for a few especially good books to take on vacation or use in a term paper, here are some suggestions:

Chicago: City on the Make, Nelson Algren

> It isn't hard to love a town for its broad and bending boulevards, its lamplit parks and its endowed opera. But you can never truly love a place til you love it for its alleys, too. For the horse-and-wagon, cat-and-ash-can alleys below the thousand-girded El.

The Man With the Golden Arm, Nelson Algren

Dawn, Theodore Dreiser

Chapter 29 of *Dawn,* Theodore Dreiser's two-volume autobiography, contains one of the best descriptions of this city ever written . . . and one of the most ecstatic and overblown as well. Much is made of the long quote that begins: "Hail Chicago! First of the daughters of the new world!" Keep in mind, though, that elsewhere in *Dawn* he says "Those first days in Evansville!" Dreiser also describes Chicago as the City of Rats and goes into great detail on the size and ferocity of the city's vermin. With that in mind, here's the rest of Dreiser's fevered peroration about the city:

> Would that I were able to suggest in prose the throb and urge and sting of my first days in Chicago! A veritable miracle of pleasing sensations and astounding and fascinating scenes. The spirit of Chicago flowed into me and made me ecstatic. Its personality was different from anything I had ever known; it was a compound of hope and joy in existence, intense hope and intense joy. Cities, like individuals, can flare up with a great flare of hope. They have that miracle, personality, which as in the case of the individual is

always so fascinating and so arresting.

The Dean's December, Saul Bellow

The Adventures of Augie March, Saul Bellow

Sister Carrie, Theodore Dreiser

The Coast of Chicago, Stuart Dybek

Young Lonigan, A Boyhood in the Streets, James T. Farrell
Published in 1932, this is the first volume of Farrell's Chicago trilogy. His
hero Studs Lonigan inspired Studs Terkel's nickname.

Show Boat, Edna Ferber
Edna Ferber, author of *Show Boat* and *So Big,* isn't primarily known as a
Chicago writer, but many of her short stories are set here, as well as a good
deal of her 1926 novel *Show Boat* itself.

The Cliff-Dwellers (1893), Henry Blake Fuller
Great writing by a writer who's almost forgotten today and who was an early
practitioner of the art of making literary hay by attacking one's own home
town.

1001 Afternoons in Chicago, Ben Hecht

The Great Wheel (1957), Robert Lawson
A writer and illustrator of children's books relates how a boy named Conn
came from Ireland to America and helped George Washington Ferris build
the great Ferris wheel at the World's Columbian Exposition of 1893.

Blood Shot, Sara Paretsky

Tunnel Vision, Sara Paretsky

The Jungle, Upton Sinclair
Who among us did not have to read in high school about Jurgis Rudkus's
awful bloody existence? What we forget, now that the stockyards are long
gone, is that this novel was a sensation in its time and brought about
important labor reforms.

was in the middle of the three dormer windows on the second floor. In 1928, his father, depressed and suffering from diabetes, shot and killed himself in a bedroom on the second floor. When Hemingway returned for the funeral, it was his last visit ever to his home town.

13.
Oliver Wendell Holmes Elementary School
508 N. Kenilworth Ave.

Walk a block south on Kenilworth, passing Holmes Elementary School, where Hemingway was a student from 1905 to 1913. Think about how close the school is to Hemingway's home, and recall the last sentence of his story "Soldier's Home," when the spiritually wounded soldier rejects his parents and thinks about his sister: "He would go over to the schoolyard and watch Helen play indoor baseball." This is probably the schoolyard he was referring to.

14.
Frank Lloyd Wright Home and Studio
and Charles MacArthur residence
951 Chicago Ave. 708/848-1976

Turn west on Chicago and head to the Frank Lloyd Wright Home and Studio. Wright, of course, is best known as the founder of the Prairie School of architecture. But he was also the author of books such as his *Autobiography* and *The Natural House.* You'll find these works and more at The Gingko Tree Book Shop, which is part of the Wright Home and Studio.

It's not well-known, but another famous person lived at 951 Chicago after Frank Lloyd Wright: playwright Charles MacArthur, best-known as the co-author with Ben Hecht of *The Front Page.* MacArthur and Hecht also co-wrote the screenplay for *Wuthering Heights,* the 1939 version starring Lawrence Olivier and Merle Oberon. The film was nominated for an Academy Award for Best Screenplay.

Wright abandoned his wife Catherine and their five children in 1910 when he ran off to Europe with Mamah Borthwick Cherney, the wife of a client. At that time the house was broken into apartments. His wife and children used the income from the apartments on upper floors to maintain an apartment on the main floor. Local historians agree that MacArthur was one of the tenants, though it's not known exactly how long he lived there.

15.
Lake Street businesses
Forest Ave. and Lake St.

Walk west on Chicago to Forest, and go back south to Lake. You can get a cup of coffee and a bite to eat at **The Daily Grind Café**, 119 N. Marion. 708/524-5282. At the corner of Forest and Lake, be sure to visit **Barbara's Bookstore**, 1100 Lake, 708/848-9140, a link in a small "independent" chain that holds frequent author events.

Driving Tour

Oak Park has lots of other attractions, especially those related to Edgar Rice Burroughs, but they're more widely distributed around town and best seen with a car:

16.
Oak Park and River Forest High School
Lake St. and Scoville Ave. 708/383-0700

There's a Hemingway Remembrance Garden at the Scoville entrance to the local high school. The light fixtures are original—the same ones Hemingway and his sisters walked past as students. Fannie Biggs, one of Hemingway's teachers while he was here, influenced him strongly. Young Ernest edited the student newspaper, *The Trapeze,* and gave a speech on the "class prophecy" at his graduation in 1917.

"I liked him very well in grammar school," a childhood friend was quoted as saying in a *Chicago Sun-Times* article published at the author's death in 1961. "But toward the end of senior year I didn't like him so well any more. He became very egotistical. He had a bad case of 'I' trouble."

Another graduate of Oak Park-River Forest High School, Barbara Mertz, graduated with a doctorate in Egyptian studies from the University of Chicago's Oriental Institute. She now writes mystery novels under two pseudonyms: Barbara Michaels and Elizabeth Peters.

Photo by Thayer Lindner.

Hemingway's high school yearbook photo.

17.
River Oak Arts
255 Augusta St. 708/524-8725

This flourishing local arts group has offices inside the Dole Library. It frequently holds writing workshops, round table discussions, and other events.

18.
Carl Rogers residence
547 N. Euclid Ave.

The famous psychotherapist, developer of client-centered therapy and author of *On Becoming a Person,* lived here.

19.
Buzz Café
208 S. Lombard Ave. 708/524-2899

Buzz Café holds poetry readings every first and fourth Wednesday of the month. It's part of the growing Harrison Street arts community, which includes the **Harrison Street Cooperative**, 208 W. Harrison, 708/386-7019, a performing and fine arts center.

20.
Historical Society of Oak Park and River Forest
217 S. Home Ave. 708/848-6755

The Historical Society of Oak Park and River Forest, located in the magnificent Farson-Mills House at Pleasant and Home, has copies of books written by authors who called Oak Park home, including Bernice Clifton, who wrote the novel *None So Blind,* and Janet Lewis, author of *The Wife of Martin Guerre.* You'll also find photos and artifacts left over from the society's extensive exhibit on Edgar Rice Burroughs, which took place in early 2000.

21.
Edgar Rice Burroughs's office
1020 North Ave.

Edgar Rice Burroughs supported himself and his family not only through his writing but through the marketing of Tarzan and other merchandise. His company, Edgar Rice Burroughs, Inc., had its office at this address. He successfully marketed action toys, dolls, games, and other items related to Tarzan and his other characters years before *Star Wars* lunch boxes. Burroughs also used this office to recruit for the Illinois Reserve Militia in 1918. He was a major in command of the First Battalion, Second Infantry.

Two individuals who also played important roles in the marketing of Tarzan had Chicago connections. Actor Johnny Weissmuller, widely considered to have been the definitive Tarzan, grew up in Chicago after his family moved here from Romania in 1909. James Allen St. John, an illustrator for McClurg Publishing who created covers for many of the original Tarzan books, lived in the Tree Studios artists' colony on West Ontario (see pp. 67-68).

James Park Sloan

James Park Sloan is Professor of English at the University of Illinois at Chicago. A widely published short story writer and literary critic, he is the author of *Jerzy Kosinski: A Biography.* (Dutton, 1997). He has also written a number of novels, including *The Last Cold-War Cowboy* and *The Case History of Comrade V.* His first novel, *War Games,* draws upon his experience as a paratrooper in Vietnam. This book won the New Writers Award from the Great Lakes College Prize Committee.

Photo courtesy of UIC Photographic Services.

I came to Chicago accidentally because my then-wife's family lived here, but I have stayed because I like it. A lot of the people who know me do not know me as a writer, or at least do not think of me as a writer. This serves to prevent me from getting wrapped into a writer's persona from which I cannot see the world clearly.

There is not a large literary community here, but it is enough. Most of my writer friends are colleagues and former students such as Jim McManus and Sharon Solwitz. I met Algren a few times before he left Chicago, but our interests about the city were different. He was all for the underdog. So am I, except that I think we are all underdogs. Chicago is the underdog city, and it is a good place for an underdog to live. Chicago is an easy city. That's a strange compliment, I guess, but it is meant as a compliment. Chicago is a city where you can hold on to yourself. You can ignore it in the way that you cannot ignore New York.

I actually live (again) in River Forest, after living on the lake shore for about ten years. I spend time at the libraries in Oak Park and River Forest and sometimes in Forest Park. I shop at Barbara's Book Store. I work in the basement of my house beneath a single light bulb and a tiny window—Dostoevski's underground fellow, maybe, except that the little boy of the house, who is seven, often plays soldiers a few feet away. He doesn't know that writing is not supposed to be interrupted, and I am a sucker for stopping to orate on things like the charge up San Juan Hill.

Bookstores

Afri-Ware Inc., 948 Lake St. 708/524-8398.

Barbara's Bookstore, 1100 Lake St. 708/848-9140.

Centuries & Sleuths Bookstore, 7419 Madison St., Forest Park. 708/771-7243.

Crown Books, 2340 Harlem Ave. 708/447-7939.

Left Bank Bookstall Used & Rare Books, P.O. Box 3516. 708/383-4700 or 800/287-2665.

Magic Tree Bookstore, 141 N. Oak Park Ave. 708/848-0770.

Persistence of Memory Booksearch, 1016 North Blvd. 708/660-0122.

Coffeehouses

Buzz Café, 208 S. Lombard St. 708/524-2899.

Caribou Coffee Company, 423 N. Harlem Ave. 708/358-1212.

Daily Grind Cyber Café, 119 N. Marion St. 708/524-5282.

Other Places of Interest

Brookfield Zoo, 31st St. and First Ave., Brookfield. 708/485-2200.
Located just a few minutes from Oak Park to the south, this 216-acre zoo is
home to more than 2,600 animals. Open daily at 10 A.M.; closing times vary
throughout the year. Admission $7 for adults, $3.50 for children/seniors.

Cernan Earth and Space Center, 2000 Fifth Ave., River Grove.
708/456-0300, x. 3372.
This facility, operated by Triton Junior College and located just a few
minutes west of Oak Park, offers earth and sky shows, space exhibits, and
popular weekend laser shows set to rock music.

Ernest Hemingway birthplace, 339 N. Oak Park Ave. 708/848-2222.
Open Thurs., Fri., and Sun. 1 P.M.-5 P.M., Sat. 10 A.M.-5 P.M. Admission to
both the birthplace and Hemingway Museum is $6 for adults, and $4.50 for
youths 18 or younger and seniors 65 and over.

Ernest Hemingway Museum, 200 N. Oak Park Ave. 708/848-2222.
Open Thurs., Fri., and Sun. 1 P.M.-5 P.M., Sat. 10 A.M.-5 P.M. Admission to
both the birthplace and Hemingway Museum is $6 for adults, and $4.50 for
youths 18 or younger and seniors 65 and over.

Festival Theatre, Forest Ave. just north of Lake St. 708/524-2050.
An ensemble that performs Shakespeare outdoors in Austin Gardens each
summer.

Frank Lloyd Wright Home and Studio Foundation, 951 Chicago Ave.
708/848-1976.
Open daily 10 A.M.-5 P.M. Tours Mon.-Fri. 11 A.M., 1 P.M., and 3 P.M.; Sat.-Sun.
11 A.M. and 3:30 P.M. Admission is $8 for adults, $6 for youths 18 or younger
and seniors 65 and over, and free for children 6 and under. A combination
ticket for the Home and Studio and a guided walking tour is $14 for adults,
and $10 for youths 18 or younger or seniors 65 or over.

Historical Society of Oak Park and River Forest/Historic Pleasant Home, 217 S. Home Ave. 708/848-6755.

The local historical society is located in the Pleasant Home, an opulent 30-room mansion designed by Prairie School architect George W. Maher in 1897. Tours held 12:30 P.M., 1:30 P.M., and 2:30 P.M. Thur.-Sun. until Dec. 1; winter tours Dec. 1 - Feb. 28 12:30 P.M. and 1:30 P.M. Admission is $5 for adults and $3 for youths 18 or younger.

Oak Park Conservatory, 615 Garfield St. 708/386-4700.

Enjoy special floral displays and walk through tropical, fern, and desert greenhouses year-round.

Oak Park Visitors Center, 158 N. Forest Ave. 708/848-1500.

Under the Gingko Tree Bed & Breakfast, 300 N. Kenilworth. 708/524-2327.

Stay in a Queen Anne home with a wraparound front porch, built around 1890.

Unity Temple, 875 Lake St. 708/383-8873.

A National Historic Landmark, this concrete building was designed by Frank Lloyd Wright in 1905 for the Oak Park Universalists. It's the site of a popular performance series, the Unity Temple Concerts.

Write Inn, 211 N. Oak Park Ave. 708/383-4800.

Wright's Cheney House Bed & Breakfast, 520 N. East Ave. 708/524-2067.

Stay in a prairie style house designed by Frank Lloyd Wright in 1904.

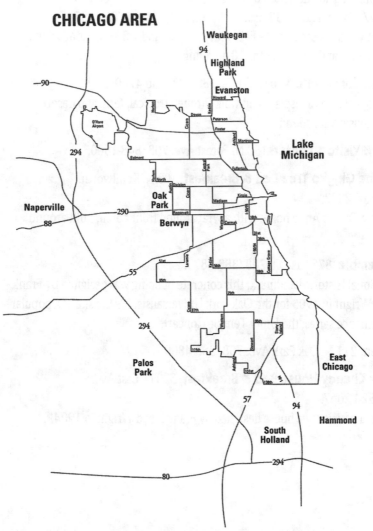

CHICAGO AREA

Waukegan

94

Highland Park

Evanston

Howard

O'Hare Airport

Devon
Kedzie
Peterson

Foster

Ashland
Montrose

Lake Michigan

Nagle

Cicero

Belmont

294

Central Park

Fullerton

Harlem
North
Division

Oak Park

Cicero

Kinzie

Madison

Naperville

290

Roosevelt

I-90/94

Berwyn

88

Weston
Cermak

12th

121st

I-90/94

51st

Laramie

Kedzie

59th

Cottage Grove

55

63rd
Kedzie
63rd
95th

75th

294

Cicero
87th

119th

99th

Stony Island

115th

Stewart

103rd
Ashland

131st

East Chicago

Palos Park

138th

57

94

Hammond

South Holland

294

80

294

Map by Michael Polydoris.

Literary Sites Near Chicago

When the city seems to be closing in on you (like a sentence jumbled with parenthetical statements, lists, and similes—like this one, in other words), you've got to get away and breathe some fresh air. New York writers can escape to Cape Cod. Londoners can dip their toes in *By Jeff Hall.* the ocean at Brighton. If you live in Chicago, you have your choice of a plethora of destinations that offer a change of scenery and satisfaction of book-related cravings.

Ray Bradbury

As opposed to a modern day-tripper watching the skyline grow smaller and smaller in the rear view mirror, a literary figure is likely to view the scene from the window of a train racing across the prairie toward the big city and adventure. In the early days of the twentieth century, Chicago writers depicted this perspective over and over because the movement from agrarian to urban surroundings was, in many cases, a defining transition in their own younger and more vulnerable years. Think about the following passages as you're heading to the city on I-55 from the south, I-94 from the north, or I-80 from the west:

In *Moon-Calf* (1921), a novel by Floyd Dell, who was originally from Kentland, Indiana, a young writer turns his back on small-town Illinois and yearns for the promise of the big city:

He saw again in his mind's eye . . . a picture of the map on the wall of the railway station—the map with a picture of iron roads from all over the Middle West centering on a dark blotch in the corner.

> "Chicago!" he said to himself . . . the rhythm of [the] word . . . said itself over and over in his mind: "Chicago! Chicago!"

For a classic perspective, you can't beat Theodore Dreiser's opening chapter of *Sister Carrie,* in which the heroine enters Chicago on the train:

> They were nearing Chicago. Signs were everywhere numerous. Trains flashed by them. Across wide stretches of flat open prairie they could see lines of telegraph poles stalking across the fields toward the great city. Far away were indications of suburban towns, some big smoke-stacks towering high in the air. . . .
>
> "This is Northwest Chicago," said Drouet. "This is the Chicago River," and he pointed to a little muddy creek, crowded with the huge masted wanderers from far-off waters nosing the black-posted banks. With a puff, a clang, and a clatter of rails it was gone. "Chicago is getting to be a great one," he went on. "It's a wonder. You'll find lots to see here."[1]

Carl Sandburg's father worked for the railroad, as did many of the Scandinavians in his hometown of Galesburg, and he spent many defining moments viewing America from a railroad car. In the following passage of "Mamie," Sandburg's heroine sees the train as the means to transport her to the land of dreams:

> Mamie beat her head against the bars of a little Indiana town and dreamed of romance and big things off somewhere the way the railroad trains all ran.
>
> She could see the smoke of the engines get lost down where the streaks of steel flashed in the sun and when the newspapers came in on the morning mail she knew there was a big Chicago far off, where all the trains ran.

Sometimes, of course, the reality was different than the fantasy, as presented bluntly by Upton Sinclair in *The Jungle:*

> Every minute, as the train sped on, the colors of things became dingier; the fields were grown parched and yellow, the landscape hideous and bare.

Our current mayor, Richard M. Daley, a consummate tree hugger, is doing his best to enhance neon lights with natural beauty. But, as Ray Bradbury said about his Waukegan childhood, it's not your surroundings so much as the people you are with, the experiences you have, and how you give them life through your own imagination and love. This chapter offers a few suggestions of suburban locations where you can let your imagination roam.

Driving Tour

1.
Northwestern University
633 Clark St., Evanston. 847/491-3741

Located just north of the Chicago city limits, Evanston is a desirable habitat for writers because it maintains both a city flair and suburban comfort. Being the home of Northwestern University and plenty of bookstores, it also draws culture vultures.

The town is easily reached by public transportation via Metra or CTA (at Howard Street switch from the Red Line to the purple Evanston Express). Of course if you're going by car, the view from Chicago to Evanston as you cruise up Lake Shore Drive makes getting there half the fun.

If the weather is good, visit the Shakespeare Gardens, which are just east of Sheridan Road and north of Howes Chapel on the grounds of Garrett Theological Seminary. Challenge yourself to relate the garden's flowers and herbs to literary references from the bard's plays.

The late Leon Forrest, who was born in Chicago, was the author of *There Is a Tree More Ancient Than Eden* (1973), *Two Wings to Veil My Face* (1984), and *Divine Days* (1992). Before his death in 1997 he was Professor of English and Chair of African-American Studies at Northwestern. Novelist and short story writer Cyrus Colter is Professor Emeritus in English here. Garry Wills, the author of many fiction books including *Cincinnatus, Bare Ruined Choirs,* and *Nixon Agonistes,* is presently at Northwestern.

2.
Evanston Booksellers

Some of Evanston's independent bookstores, such as the fondly-remembered Chandler's, have gone out of business under pressure from the two big downtown booksellers, Borders Books Music and Café and Barnes & Noble, which get a lot of attention. But if you're looking for used, rare, or specialty books, a little searching around can yield great rewards or, at the very least, provide a delightful way to while away an afternoon.

Something Wicked, 810 Church St., 847/328-1300; is the largest bookstore specializing in mystery, horror, and true crime books in the Chicago area. The shop carries a complete selection of Chicago mystery writer Eugene Izzi's books, most of which are hard to find elsewhere. **Bookman's Alley**, run by Roger Carlson, is in the rear of. 1712 Sherman Ave., 847/869-6999. Sue E. Holbert runs **Booklady Used and Rare Books**, 400 Main St., 2C, but call ahead for an appointment at 847/869-1385 or 888/863-1385. If you're into science fiction, chart a course for **The Stars Our Destination**, 705 Main St., 847/570-5925, www.sfbooks.com, which regularly holds author signings and has extensive collections of used paperbacks as well as rare books and collectibles. **Phyllis Tholin Books**, 847/475-1174, specializes in Chicago and women's history. **Paul Rohe and Sons, Booksellers**, 2339 Hastings Ave., 847/491-9132, is open by appointment only. Former *Chicago Tribune* reporter and Chicago history writer Kenan Heise runs **Chicago Historical Bookworks**, 831 Main St., 847/869-6410. If you want to talk about the city's past, he's your man. Heise's store is open Thurs. 11 A.M.-8 P.M., Sat. 11 A.M.-6 P.M., Sun. 11 A.M.-5 P.M., and by appointment. And don't forget the scholarly slant of **Great Expectations Book Store**, 911 Foster St., 847/864-3881, a long-time favorite of Evanston readers.

3.
Ravinia/Margaret Anderson on the Beach
Highland Park

Margaret Anderson, editor of the literary magazine *The Little Review,* wrote a wonderful reminiscence called *My Thirty Years' War.* She recounts meeting virtually all the literary stars in the city early in the 1900s, plus goodies such as having lunch with Toscanini and arranging a lecture by anarchist Emma Goldman.

She knew that she had to eat and also to cover operating expenses for her magazine. So around 1915, she did what seemed (to her, at least) to be the most logical thing: she decided to save money on housing by finding a most unusual new place to live:

> I left the train at Ravinia, walked east and south along the shore toward Braeside. Between the bluff and the water's edge there was a wider strip of beach and no summer colony on the heights at Lake Bluff.

She erected several large tents, complete with wood floors and Oriental rugs. For six months, she lived "a North Shore gypsy life." She commuted to Chicago to work on *The Little Review* and lived by the water's edge until November when she moved into an apartment. Her lifestyle did not preclude entertaining. She reports that Ben Hecht and Maxwell Bodenheim walked to the camp from Chicago and left poems pinned on the tent. Sherwood Anderson visited and told stories around the campfire.

Wardrobe and laundry costs were also minimal. She had only one blouse, one hat, and one tailored suit. Each evening after coming home from work, she washed the blouse in the lake.

I don't necessarily recommend camping without a permit today. But you can probably enjoy an economical afternoon at the lake shore with only a few necessities such as a picnic lunch and a book purchased at one of the Highland Park bookstores. **Titles Inc.**, owned by Florence Shay, sells rare and fine books at 1931 N. Sheridan Rd., 847/432-3690. It's open Mon.-Sat. 10:30 A.M.-5 P.M. **George Ritzlin Maps & Books**, 473 Roger Williams Ave., 847/433-2627, specializes in maps and atlases from the sixteenth to nineteenth centuries and is open Wed.-Fri. 10 A.M.-5 P.M. and Sat. 10 A.M.-4 P.M.

Outta Here:
Writers Who Got Out vs. Those Who Came Home

One of the trends among Chicago writers is leaving. Like actors and other artists, they find New York and Hollywood more practical places to make a living. Chicagoans turn leaving the city into art. Much of *Ain't Gonna Be the Same Fool Twice,* April Sinclair's second novel, takes place in San Francisco. But the story is full of references to Chicago, as the main character accustoms herself to a radically different environment and people from different backgrounds. "Chicago is a nice place to be *from,* " Stevie's friend tells her. She faces the native Chicagoan's eternal struggle—whether to stay here or move to the coast. Lately, though, the trend has reversed: writers (like artists, like rock stars) come here from elsewhere to live. Here are just a few examples:

OUT

- **Ben Hecht**, went to Hollywood to write movies

- **Nelson Algren**, off to New Jersey to drink

- **Saul Bellow**, off to Boston

- **Carl Sandburg**, bought a goat farm in Flat Rock, North Carolina

- **Ernest Hemingway**, off to Paris with the Lost Generation

IN

- **Sara Paretsky**, came here from Lawrence, Kansas

- **Cris Mazza**, came here from California

- **Scott Turow**, went to Harvard, came back home to Chicago

- **Ana Castillo**, lived in California, later moved back to Chicago

4.
North Shore Suburbs

The affluent Cook County lakefront towns north of Evanston—Wilmette, Kenilworth, Winnetka, and Glencoe—provide a fertile setting for crime stories and tales of family divisiveness. The most notable example is *Ordinary People,* the novel that Robert Redford made into a movie and that was filmed in part on the North Shore.

Mystery writer Scott Turow, who was born in Chicago, now makes his home on the North Shore. He could easily support himself by writing full-time, but chooses to continue his job as a lawyer in the Loop. Most of his books, like *Presumed Innocent,* take place in a fictitious location called Kindle County.

In Glencoe, check out **Writers' Theatre Chicago**, a group that meets in the **Books on Vernon** bookstore, 664 Vernon Ave., 847/835-5398. This theater, dedicated to dramatizing the writer's voice, has offered looks at such literary giants as William Blake, Oscar Wilde, the World War I poet-lovers Siegfried Sassoon and Wilfred Owen, and Shakespeare.

5.
Ray Bradbury
Waukegan

Ray Bradbury, the author of the autobiographical book *Dandelion Wine* and science fiction classics *The Martian Chronicles* and *Fahrenheit 451,* was born in Waukegan on August 22, 1920. He grew up in a duplex at 11 S. St. James that is currently a private home (and that, at this writing, was painted bright lavender). Bradbury's grandparents lived nearby at 619 Washington; this is the home the writer remembers so fondly, especially picking dandelions there for homemade wine. The author lived in Waukegan on and off until 1934, when the family moved to Los Angeles, California.

Bradbury wrote that the roots of his most famous novel, *Fahrenheit 451,* stretched back to days spent exploring the public library: "From the time I was nine on up through my teens I spent at least two nights a week in the town library in Waukegan, Illinois. In the summer months, there was hardly a day I could not be found lurking about the stacks, smelling the books like imported spices, drunk on them even before I read them."[2]

In the introduction to his beautifully crafted autobiographical novel *Dandelion Wine,* Bradbury recalls a critic's surprise "that I should have been born and raised in Waukegan, which I renamed Green Town for my novel, and not noticed how ugly the harbor was and how depressing the coal docks and railyards down below the town." He adds that, in addition to visiting circuses and his grandfather's house, Waukegan offered many places of wonder and imagination for a five-year-old boy. He spoke eloquently about his Waukegan childhood through much of his writing, including the following poem about his home town:

> Byzantium, I come not from
>
> But from another time and place
>
> Whose race was simple, tried and true
>
> As boy
>
> I dropped me forth in Illinois
>
> A name with neither love nor grace
>
> Was Waukegan, there I came from
>
> And not, good friends, Byzantium
>
> And yet in looking back I see
>
> From topmost part of farthest tree
>
> A land as bright, beloved and blue
>
> As any Yeats found to be true.[3]

The **Waukegan Public Library**, 128 N. County St., 847/623-2041, has a mini-collection of Bradbury's books and newspaper articles, as well as other information about him. The WPL is open Mon.-Thurs. 9 A.M.-9 P.M., Fri. 9 A.M.-6 P.M., Sat. 9 A.M.-5 P.M., and Sun. 1 P.M.-5 P.M. This is not the library Bradbury would have gone to as a child. The old library building still stands a few blocks from the present one, but it is being converted into a high-tech communications center.

Cris Mazza

Cris Mazza is the author of nine books of fiction, including most recently *Dog People*, a novel; and *Former Virgin*, a collection of short fiction. Some of Mazza's other books include *How to Leave a Country*, winner of the PEN/ Nelson Algren Award, and the critically acclaimed *Is It Sexual Harassment Yet?* She also co-edited *Chick-Lit* and *Chick-Lit 2*, anthologies of women's fiction. A native of Southern California, Mazza still spends summers in San Diego, but resides the rest of the year in Elmhurst. She is a recent recipient of an NEA fellowship and teaches in the Program for Writers at the University of Illinois at Chicago.

Mazza had a strong response to the Nelson Algren *Chicago: City on the Make* quote I asked writers to address (see the Introduction, p. 9):

> While it might not have been hackneyed at the time, if anyone attempted to write a "Chicago story" now which offered the wind and a hustler as the two major tokens, I suspect the writer would be accused of not being a Chicagoan but a poseur. This would be akin to someone writing about my native San Diego using palm trees and surfers as symbols of the place's personality, not realizing it's an ecologically delicate semi-arid coastal scrub where coyotes, who live in natural but urban canyons, outnumber surfers. Nelson Algren not only comes from a different era of Chicago history but from a different era of American literature as well—an era, in both cases, dominated by boastful, posturing men. Even the prose style is bombastic and self-aggrandizing. Writers of this sort didn't put forth questions, perceptions, or slices of human nature to ponder, but statements of "truth" and self-assured answers. I'm glad Chicago is no longer anything like this

> **Maybe breaking *free* of its old stock image, created by macho swaggerers for the city to live up to, whether it be windy, mob owned, big shoulders, or city-that-works, was a first step that allowed the now robust, diverse, and vehemently autonomous Chicago literary community to exist in the first place.**

Photo courtesy of UIC Photographic Services.

Author Cris Mazza.

quote suggests, either in the personality of the city the selection aims to describe or in the personality of the writer that the selection puts in-your-face.

Among its actual virtues, Chicago is a fragile last-bastion of business independence, where, for example, non-corporate bookstores still cling—most of them successfully—to existence. The same is true of neighborhood hardware and appliance stores, non-chain bars and restaurants, and even a few pharmacies. Maybe it takes a non-native to notice, but I don't know of many other places where independently owned—not to mention visually funky—hot dog stands and fast food restaurants flourish in the face of corporate chains. What does this have to do with a writing community? It does seem that the community itself, its varied parts, embodies individual identity. Not just writers, but literary magazines like *ACM, Other Voices, TriQuarterly,* and *Fish Stories;* organizations like River Oak Arts, The Guild Complex, and various long-lived writing groups; publishers like Tia Chucha and the university presses; and collegiate writing programs at the Art Institute, UIC, Columbia, and others—each seems, in its own way, particular and standing apart from corporate or national character trends and literary cliques. Maybe breaking *free* of its old stock image, created by macho swaggerers for the city to live up to, whether it be windy, mob owned, big shoulders, or city-that-works, was a first step that allowed the now robust, diverse, and vehemently autonomous Chicago literary community to exist in the first place.

I guess what I'm saying is that the city described in Algren's poem doesn't exist, so it can't claim to either own or not own anyone or anything. Yet did the literary community that developed here *require* Chicago as fodder in order for it to grow and survive? It's people who characterize and form Chicago, not the other way around. But it does seem that Chicago is sort of a self-sufficient island, not relying on nor linked inexorably to New York, London, Paris, Tokyo, or any other "center of the world." That quality it seems, admittedly an un-researched observation from a non-native, has to be significant to Chicago's cultural life, including but not limited to visual art, music, theater, and literature.

Favorite Bookstore in the City

Barbara's or Women and Children First. The people who work there (including managers and owners) do actually *read.* But there are many other independent bookstores I haven't had time to investigate. The same with Anderson's Bookshop in the western suburbs.

Aspiring Writers

An aspiring writer in Chicago is no different than anywhere else. Read and write, read and write, read and write, go to readings, read book reviews, *listen* to the people who talk to you about your writing, and don't waste time and energy hanging around in bars or coffeehouses trying to look like a writer.

Places to Go for Inspiration

I stay home most of the time. If inspiration isn't in me, I'm not going to be able to go anywhere and find it. And some days it's not in me. So I do yard work.

You'll find an extensive file of newspaper clippings about Bradbury among the collections of the **Waukegan Historical Society**, 1911 N. Sheridan Rd., 847/336-1859. The facility is located north of downtown Waukegan on the grounds of the former Hull House summer camp; it's open Wed.-Fri. 10 A.M.-2:30 P.M.

If it's a nice day, cap off your visit to Bradbury country with a trip to **Ray Bradbury Park**, just three blocks west of the public library, between Washington Street on the south and Grand Avenue on the north.

Another bestselling author, John Jakes, lived in Waukegan for ten years and taught English at the local high school. He put food on the table by writing public relations copy before his historical novels, such as *North and South*, became so popular that they were turned into made-for-TV movies. His books *Homeland* and *American Dream* follow the fortunes of the fictional Crown family of Chicago and, in the process, examine the history of the last century.

A current Waukegan resident, Eleanor Taylor Bland, sets her mystery novels in a fictional town that is really Waukegan. Bland eloped with a sailor at the age of 14 and raised two children. In 1972, she was diagnosed with cancer and given two years to live. She decided to achieve two goals: getting a college degree and writing a book. She has since earned degrees in accounting and education. Bland's mystery novels follow the adventures of her character Marti Macalister, including *See No Evil, Dead Time,* and *Slow Burn.*

If there's an empty space on your bookshelf, you can fill it with something other than dust at **Eileen Donohue's Galaxy of Books**, 1908 Sheridan Rd. in Zion, a town north of Waukegan. The store specializes in hunting, fishing, military, natural history, science and comics, among other things. Open Tues.-Fri. 12 P.M.-7 P.M. and Sat. 10 A.M.-5 P.M.; phone 847/872-3313 for Sun. hours.

6.
Jack's Restaurant
5201 W. Touhy Ave., Skokie. 847/674-5532

To get to or from Chicago's environs, the expressway system is inescapable. And, having joined the throng of cars in the throes of gridlock during rush hour, the need to escape will soon become overwhelming.

Anyone who grew up in the suburbs northwest of the city (like the author), is familiar with a refuge that has soothed many a road-weary traveler—an all-night restaurant called Jack's, which is just off the Edens Expressway near Touhy. Roslyn Rosen Lund's 1978 novel *The Sharing* opens with Sophie Mandel driving against commuter traffic down the Edens Expressway, getting off at Touhy, and finding a restaurant with a "U-shaped counter." This is the first place where she can eat after her husband's death. She doesn't mention Jack's by name, but the place has had a U-shaped counter and has been open around the clock for many years.

7.
O'Hare Airport Air Force Base
Mannheim and Higgins Rds.

Chicago newspaper legend Mike Royko got his first job in journalism while stationed at the U.S. Air Force base near O'Hare Airport in the 1950s. He became an editor of the base newspaper, the *O'Hare News,* by lying about previously being a reporter for the *Chicago Daily News.* Of course, years later he became famous (and belatedly truthful) by writing a column for the *Daily News.*

This book's author grew up in Des Plaines, just a mile north of O'Hare, and continued to live there while commuting to college classes at the University of Illinois at Chicago. The author moved to Chicago in 1982.

8.
Miller Beach
Gary, Indiana

If you brave the odor of the steel mills and venture into Gary, Indiana, look for a corner named Miller Beach. If you can find a cottage near the lake, imagine that it is the house where two of the most famous authors of the 1950s, Nelson Algren and Simone de Beauvoir, carried on their love affair. They lived there in the early 1950s while she was preparing to write her best-seller *The Second*

Sex. Algren regarded this as his country house and hoped to make de Beauvoir his wife, but it was not to be. It might, however, have been the place where de Beauvoir learned "what it is to be a woman," as suggested in a November 2, 1999, *Chicago Tribune* article on their relationship.

In his prose poem *Chicago: City on the Make* (1951) Algren wrote memorably of this area:

> Wheeling around the loop of the lake, coming at Chicago from east and south, the land by night lies under a battle-colored sky. Above the half-muffled beat of the monstrous forges between Gary and East Chicago, the ceaseless signal-fires of the great refineries wave an all-night alarm.[4]

9.
Hinsdale

Hinsdale, one of the region's more affluent suburbs, is located southwest of the city. It is described in Sara Paretsky's 1988 novel *Blood Shot:*

> Hinsdale is an old town about twenty miles west of the Loop whose tall oaks and gracious homes were gradually being accreted by urban sprawl. It's not Chicagoland's trendiest address, but there's an aura of established self-assurance about the place . . . . When you go from the city to the north of west suburbs, the first thing you notice is the quiet cleanness. . . "

10.
Naperville

Naperville, the burgeoning western suburb that's now one of the largest cities in the state, shows up in Paretsky's novel *Guardian Angel:*

> Naperville, about thirty miles west of the Loop, is one of Chicago's fastest-growing suburbs. It's ringed by genteel tract houses on sizable lots—home to the middle managers of Chicago, and to a depressing amount of concrete. Mighty tollways crisscross the southwest suburbs, eating up farmland and leaving steep, jagged cols in their wake.
>
> Inside the concrete stilts and the endless succession of malls, fast-food

places, and car dealers sit the remains of the town. A hundred years ago it was a quiet farm community, without much connection to Chicago, beyond a river that carried freight between the city and the Mississippi. A number of people, rich either from the land or the water, built themselves solid Victorian homes there. One of those had belonged to Tiepolo Felitti.

11.
FitzGerald's Rhythm and Rhyme Review

6615 Roosevelt Rd., Berwyn.
708/788-2118 (recording of events), 708/788-6670 (live)
www.fitzgeraldsnightclub.com

To read at FitzGerald's, one of the region's favorite clubs, just show up and sign in. There's a $4 cover for this Tuesday-night open poetry and performance event, but there's no drink minimum. After an 8 P.M. presentation by a featured artist, the mic opens up at about 9:30 P.M. to poets, songwriters, performers, etc.

12.
East Chicago, Indiana

A prosaic town southeast of the city, East Chicago is the setting for Steve Tesich's novels. The area on a hot summer night is beautifully evoked in Tesich's 1982 novel *Summer Crossing*. A recurring image is that of trucks rumbling by on Indianapolis Boulevard: "A Sunrise Oil Company truck roared past me through the light. The cartoon mascot on the back smiled his huge smile. The sun always shines." The protagonist's girlfriend drives him to Whiting Beach off of Indianapolis Boulevard.

> The moonlight shining through a thin cover of clouds made them seem florescent. We walked toward the water, her high heeled boots tapping across the cement and then suddenly becoming silent as they hit the sand. A breeze was blowing from across the lake, warm and humid. Her blouse fluttered. Her hair blew back. I could see the lights of Inland Steel in the distance. The water smelled of industry and jobs.

13.
Carl Sandburg homes
Maywood, Illinois
Elmhurst, Illinois

Carl Sandburg moved from the North Side of Chicago to a small house at 616 S. 8th Ave. in Maywood. Here he wrote the poems collected in *Cornhuskers* and *Smoke and Steel.* In 1919, Sandburg moved to 313 York St. in Elmhurst, where he worked on *Abraham Lincoln: The Prairie Years,* the first book in his great six-volume biography. He also compiled the *American Songbag* and worked on his *Rootabaga Stories* for children. Because of the success he achieved as an author and poet while there, Sandburg called this house "Happiness House." Sandburg's brother-in-law, the photographer Edward Steichen, also lived in Elmhurst, as did his friend Eugene Debs, the labor organizer and socialist leader. The house where Sandburg and his family lived until 1930 has been torn down.

Discover more about this period of Sandburg's life at the **Elmhurst Historical Museum**, 120 E. Park Ave., 630/833-1457. Artifacts in their Sandburg collection include examples of his correspondence to *Poetry* magazine editor Harriet Monroe from 1915 to 1933, letters from other periods of his life, copies of speeches, and news clippings and magazine articles related to the poet. The museum also includes books by other Elmhurst authors, such as Robert Pruter's *Chicago Soul,* a book about the development of Chicago's soul music scene from the 1950s to the 1970s.

14.
Sherwood Anderson residence
Palos Park

Near the end of his time in Chicago, Anderson spent the winter at an artists' colony in Palos Park. In a November, 1920, letter he calls the place "charming" even though it is only the size of a box. "From my window I look out on oak forests, and they are charming now," he says. He also reports that Theda Bara, the "vamp" of silent movie days, drove out to Palos Park from Chicago to visit him because she admired his work.[5]

To his friend Bab Finley he wrote in September 1920:

I went last week to a place called Palos Park and there got a little 3 room box of
a house at the edge of a forest. I hope to move into it some time next week. It
is about an hour out of Chicago—south and east [*author's note: actually, it's
west, not east*]. Cook County has a forest reserve of some 17,000 acres out
that way and there is poor transportation—but a few trains a day so it is not
suburban. The land rises up there out of the flat bed of what was probably once
the floor of the lake and there are lovely rolling hills and fields—oak forests
with now and then cultivated fields. I am very happy about it and my little
place only costs me 12.50 a month and can be heated by one stove.[6]

Members of the Palos Historical Society know Anderson lived in the area,
but they aren't sure exactly which house he occupied. Carlos Baker, Ernest
Hemingway's biographer, mentions that Anderson invited Hemingway to his
house in Palos around 1920, just before he urged Hemingway to go to Europe.

While in the area, check out **Palos Books Ltd.**, 10303 S. Roberts Rd.,
708/430-5977, which sells general books as well as rare books and first editions. Open Mon.-Fri. 10 A.M.-8 P.M., Sat. 10 A.M.-6 P.M., and Sun. 12 P.M.-5 P.M.

Part II

Literary People & Places

Literary Events

One of the most pleasant ways to mark the seasons of the year is through books. You can trace the progression of the calendar (and, accordingly, our own progression through the seasons of our lives) through such Chicago works as Campbell McGrath's *Spring Comes to Chicago;* Steve Tesich's *Summer Crossing* and John McCutcheon's famous cartoon "Injun Summer"; Carl Sandburg's poem "Under the Harvest Moon"; and Saul Bellow's *The Dean's December.*

Just as reading such works encourages us to observe and appreciate the seasonal changes in the surroundings we often take for granted, attending book-related events in and around the city can be a productive way to mark the passing of time. Here is a selection of events you can use to whet your literary appetite based on the calendar.

Chicago Black History Month Book Fair and Conference
February
This event is sponsored by Western Union and is held at the Chicago Park District's South Shore Cultural Center, 7059 S. South Shore Dr., 312/747-2474.

African American Read-in Chain
February
An annual African-American Read-in Chain is held at Governors State University, 1 University Pkwy., Park Forest, 708/534-5000, to celebrate Black History Month. It's sponsored by National Council of Teachers of English.

Mystery Conference
February
This three-day event in early February is sponsored by William Rainey Harper Junior College, 1200 W. Algonquin Rd., Palatine, 847/925-6000. On Friday, a welcome dinner is held; on Saturday, mystery writers give lectures and

participate in panel discussions; on Sunday, visitors can take classes and workshops led by writers.

Weekend of Mystery
March
This intriguing annual event takes place at the Newberry Library, 60 W. Walton St., 312/943-9090. It includes a Mystery Dinner Theatre featuring a live Clue game and a two-day "Mysteries (and More!)" book fair.

Midwest Bookhunters Spring Book Fair
Late March
Sponsored by the nonprofit Midwest Bookhunters organization for 25 years, this spring book fair takes place on the campus of Loyola University Chicago, 1052 W. Loyola Ave., 773/508-3444. At this writing the Midwest Bookhunters had 130 members from ten Midwestern states, and the group is steadily growing. Membership is open to booksellers who have been recommended by two current members. This organization also holds a book fair any time from September to November. For more information, call coordinator Joycelyn Merchant at 773/989-2200, visit www.midwestbookhunters.org, or send e-mail to info@midwestbookhunters.org.

Indiana Dunes National Lakeshore Artist-in-Residence Program
March
If you're a writer or other artist and love the great outdoors, this could be the program for you. March 30 is the deadline for participation. Chosen applicants receive free lodging at a house or campsite for two to four weeks, June through September. Call 219/926-7561, x. 225, or write to 1100 N. Mineral Springs Rd.; Porter, IN 46304.

The Antiquarian Book Fair
April
This book fair is held in late April in conjunction with the Chicago International Antiques and Fine Art Fair at the Merchandise Mart, Wells St. between Kinzie St. and the Chicago River. Call 800/677-6278 for more information.

Brandeis Used Book Sale
Late May/Early June
Held at Old Orchard Shopping Center, Old Orchard Rd. and Skokie Blvd., Skokie, this mammoth book sale takes place around Memorial Day under several huge tents in the parking lot just west of the mall. It has been sponsored for many years by the North Shore chapter of the Brandeis University Women's Committee to raise funds for the university library. Opening night is the only time admission is charged. More than 25,000 bibliophiles, including rare book dealers and collectors, are drawn to the event from all over the country. Lines can be long, but at the end of the sale books are sold at bargain rates. Nearly half-million used books are separated into 44 subject areas, including art, photography, music, and history. For more information, call 847/724-9715.

Printers Row Book Fair
Early June
A two-day event started by Bette Cerf Hill, Printers Row is one of the city's major literary events, attracting 70,000 people in 1999. A series of tents is erected on South Dearborn Street between Congress Parkway and Polk Street. New and used books, as well as music and ephemera, are offered by more than 170 booksellers. There are also author readings, open mics, panel discussions, workshops, music acts, food booths, and activities for children. Admission is free. For more information, call 312/987-9896.

Newberry Library Book Fair
July
The Newberry's annual book fair is combined with an oratory festival, the Bughouse Square Debates, and is held late in the month in and near the library, 60 W. Walton St. More than 100,000 books are available for browsing. Admission is free; call 312/255-3510 for more information.

Oz Fest
August
Join Dorothy, the Tin Man, and other characters from the *Wizard of Oz* at this kid-oriented festival held on Cannon Drive, east of Lincoln Park Zoo. The event

includes everything to make a festival festive, plus costume contests in categories such as Scarecrow, Cowardly Lion, and Flying Monkey. Call 773/929-TOTO to learn more.

57th Street Children's Book Fair
September
The 57th Street Children's Book Fair is an ordinary name for an extraordinary event where culture reigns. Kids who know the Harry Potter books, and those who haven't read them yet, can join in a parade of faculty members from the book's Hogswarts School of Witchcraft and Wizardy. Youngsters, and parents too, can dress up as any literary character that strikes their fancy and join an opening parade along 57th Street between Dorchester and Kimbark Avenues. Call 773/536-8103 to learn more.

Chicago Book Week
October
Subtitled "City of Big Readers," this event was launched in 2000 and is designed to raise awareness about Chicago as a center for writing, books, and publishing. The weeklong celebration of books and writers is sponsored by the City of Chicago and includes workshops, tours, children's programs, and much more. Call 312/747-4300 for more information.

Children's Science Book Fair
October
This book fair is held at an appropriate location sure to provide children with plenty of other diversions: the Museum of Science and Industry, 57th St. and Lake Shore Dr. Call them at 773/684-1414 to find out exact dates and times.

Carl Sandburg Literary Arts Ball
October
Get dressed up and do some literary celebrity-watching at this Chicago Cultural Center ball, 78 E. Washington St. On this occasion, luminaries honor local writers. Find out more at 773/269-2922.

Chicago Humanities Festival

November

Since 1990, the Chicago Humanities Festival has offered sessions related to literature, art, history, and drama at locations throughout the city. Artists and thinkers from around the world participate in readings, panel discussions, and other events organized around a theme. Past festivals have dealt with "Crime and Punishment," "Work and Play," "He and She," and "Old and New." For details call 312/661-1028 or visit www.chfestival.org.

Festival of Children's Books

December

Several dozen Chicago-area children's book illustrators and authors share stories and demonstrate their talents at the Festival of Children's Books, sponsored by the Museum Shop of the Art Institute of Chicago. Other popular features are a coloring corner and raffles. Admission is free; guests are asked to donate a new or used book which, in turn, will be given to local schools. For more information, call 312/443-7263.

Literary Places

Considering the number of bookstores, book sales, book fairs, and writers in this very literary city, it's not surprising that book discussion groups regularly spring up all over the city and the suburbs. Many of these are held by local libraries—check the one in your area and you're likely to find a discussion group where you can exchange ideas about a particular book with other readers.

Some groups are open to the public; others are simply informal gatherings of neighbors who happen to live in the same apartment or condo building. You have to depend on old-fashioned word of mouth to find out about the neighborhood events. Other groups like the Salon 2000 meet in a public place on a regular schedule and publish a list of upcoming topics.

If you're ever excited, irritated, or just plain provoked about a book or book-related issue, you don't have to keep your thoughts to yourself; join one of the following groups or visit one of the venues listed below to share what's on your mind—or just listen to what others have to say.

Book Clubs and Salons

Chicago has always been a meeting place for writers, playwrights, poets, and other artists. The salon—an informal gathering of individuals who talk about books and other literary topics—was a Chicago institution in the golden age of the 1910s and 1920s, but it's just beginning to enjoy a resurgence now. Ben Hecht, Charles MacArthur, and Carl Sandburg used to meet at the home of Fanny Butcher, a literary critic for the *Chicago Tribune.* Hecht and MacArthur worked together at Butcher's home on what was to become their most famous play, *The Front Page.*

Salon 2000
Every first Tuesday of the month at 6:30 P.M., the Women's Theatre Alliance Salon Series 2000 meets at the Red Lion Pub, 2446 N. Lincoln Ave. Organizers Nicole Adelman and Beth Ann Bryant-Richards modeled their group on the nineteenth-century salon: a forum where participants can freely discuss their theories of art and literature. Salon 2000 also provides writers with a place to read from their works, thus putting their ideas into practice. After each meeting an open mic is held. Call 312/408-9910 for more information.

Rare Book Center Discussions
The Chicago Rare Book Center, 56 W. Maple St., 312/988-7246, occasionally conducts discussions on classic books such as *Jane Eyre,* or workshops on general book-related topics such as collecting modern first editions.

Oprah's book club
One of the most popular book discussion groups in the country, if not the world, is located right here in Chicago. It's Oprah Winfrey's book club, which has done much to promote Chicago as a destination for authors, as well as a literary center of activity. Each month or so, Oprah picks a book that she likes especially and invites her viewers and fans to read and discuss it together. Comments and responses can be posted online at Oprah's Web site, www.oprah.com. Past selections have included *Song of Solomon* by Toni Morrison, *Black and Blue* by Anna Quindlen, and *A Map of the World* by Jane Hamilton.

Heartland Literary Society
The Heartland Literary Society is an association of nearly 200 members, cosponsored by the *Chicago Tribune* and the Northern Trust Bank, that is dedicated to furthering the interest and awareness of contemporary literature and poetry in the Chicago area. Luncheons with authors are held about eight times a year at the Northern Trust, 50 S. LaSalle St. In addition to the author's presentation, the event includes a booksigning, questions and answers, and a reception. Nonmembers are welcome to attend, but reservations are required. For more information, call 312/444-3519.

Great Books Foundation

This organization holds reading and discussion groups around the country and recommends books for both children and adults. The Junior Great Books program is a set of books for young readers in grades K-12. The group's Chicago Area Great Books Council conducts theater outings and discussions several times a year and can be reached at 630/961-4120. Or visit the foundation on the Web at www.greatbooks.org.

Chicago Shakespeare Theater Great Books Discussion Groups

Discussion leaders from the Great Books Foundation facilitate discussions about plays in production at that time at the Chicago Shakespeare Theater on Navy Pier, 600 E. Grand. Registrants pay a $5 fee and should call the box office in advance to sign up (312/595-5600). Participants are urged to closely read the play in question prior to the meeting.

Everyone's Welcome Book Club

This book club, which meets at the Borders Books Music & Café, 2210 W. 95th St., 773/445-4571, and discusses primarily works of fiction, especially that which explores diverse cultural backgrounds. Meetings are held the first Wednesday and first Thursday of each month.

Performances

The Guild Complex

The Guild Complex, a nonprofit "literary arts center" holds poetry-related events every Tuesday and Wednesday night at the Chopin Café, 1543 W. Division St. The Complex also holds special events throughout the year such as the $500 Gwendolyn Brooks Open Mike Award, and the Leftover Poetry Awards, a $50 prize. Among the highlights of the center's calendar are its three annual festivals— winter's Musicality of Poetry Festival; the springtime Poetry Video Festival, in which people from all over the country submit home movies of themselves reading poetry; and summer's Zambo Festival featuring performance poetry.

WBEZ's Stories on Stage

Stories on Stage showcases Chicago area actors and other artists who present live dramatic readings of literary works in a theatrical setting. Performances in the year 2000 were held at the Museum of Contemporary Art, 220 E. Chicago Ave. Typically, performances feature three to four published stories; general admission is $13, or $12 for students/seniors. Order tickets by calling 312/397-4010. To find out more, call the Stories on Stage hotline, 312/832-3404, or visit WBEZ's Web site, www.wbez.org.

Open Mics

There is no shortage of poetry open mic activities in the city, but writers can probably also get away with reading excerpts from their journals or letters to or from past lovers. Schedules can change without warning; be sure to call ahead to make sure the event is happening on a particular day or time.

Sundays

Green Mill, 4802 N. Broadway. 773/878-5552.
Uptown Poetry Slam with Marc Smith, 7 P.M., $5.

Mondays

Red Lion Pub, 2446 N. Lincoln Ave. 773/348-2695.
8 P.M., $4 entrance fee (no extra charge to read).

Tuesdays

Café Aloha, 2156 W. Montrose Ave. 773/907-9356.
Open mic, 7 P.M., free.

Chopin Theater, 1543 W. Division St. 773/486-4331.
Open mic presented by the Guild Complex, 9:30 P.M., free.

FitzGerald's, 6615 Roosevelt Rd., Berwyn. 708/788-2118.
  Rhythm and Rhyme Review, 8 P.M. presentation by a featured artist,
  open mic 9:30 P.M. for poets, musicians, and other performers, $4.

Wednesdays

Heartland Café, 7000 N.Glenwood Ave. 773/465-8005.
  10 P.M., 9:30 P.M. signup., $2.

Thursdays

Borders Books & Music, 2210 W. 95th St. 773/445-4571.
  8 P.M., free.

Gallery Cabaret, 2020 N. Oakley Ave. 773/489-5471.
  9 P.M., free.

Fridays

Gourmand Coffeehouse, 728 S. Dearborn St. 312/427-2610.
  8 P.M., free.

Coffee Chicago, 5256 N. Broadway. 773/784-1305.
  7 P.M., $2 suggested donation.

Saturdays

Some Like It Black Coffee Shop & Gallery,
  4500 S. Michigan Ave. 773/373-8834.
  The Universal Show, 10 P.M., call ahead to be put on guest list.

Writing Workshops

Red Fish Studio Writing Workshop
Sandi L. Wisenberg, who has taught writing in the Chicago area for about 14

years, regularly holds writing workshops and is available to coach writers—to help them start, finish, revise, market, or plan fiction and nonfiction projects. Call her at 773/871-5361 or send e-mail to slwisenberg@juno.com.

Clothesline School of Writing

Molly Daniels, who taught poetry and fiction writing through the University of Chicago Continuing Education department for many years, recently moved to Minnesota, but returns to Chicago several times a year to teach workshops at the Fine Arts Building. This book's author was one of her students. Contact her by writing or calling the Fine Arts Building, 410 S. Michigan, 312/939-3700, to find out more.

Literary Street Names

Most of Chicago's street names memorialize such unglamorous but important figures as real estate subdividers. Still, a fair number recognize important writers or fictional characters. Some are well-known; others make you wonder about the artistic tastes of the people who named them—apparently, some of these folks were more well-read than you might at first think.

The primary resource for this material was *Streetwise Chicago: A History of Chicago Street Names,* by Don Hayner and Tom McNamee (Chicago: Loyola University Press, 1988).

Nelson Algren Avenue (1900 block of West Evergreen Avenue)

Carmen Avenue (5100 N from 830 W to 8652 W)
Named after George Bizet's opera *Carmen*.

Dante Avenue (1432 E from 6330 S to 9158 S)
Named after the Italian poet Dante Alighieri.

Draper Street (2540 N from 1200 W to 1258 W)
Remembers Lyman Copeland Draper, a historian and biographer of Daniel Boone.

Dunbar Avenue (246 E from 9200 S to 9254 S)
Named after Paul Lawrence Dunbar (1872-1906), short story writer, novelist, playwright, and first African-American poet to gain national acclaim.

Esmond Street (10920 S at 1800 W to 11180 S at 1900 W)
Possibly named after a farmer, and possibly named after William Makepeace Thackeray's novel *The History of Henry Esmond* (1852).

Franklin Boulevard (500 N from 3020 W to 3558 W)
Named for Benjamin Franklin, statesman, inventor, publisher, and author of *Poor Richard's Almanac,* one of the nation's most famous autobiographies, and many other works.

Gale Street (4926 N from 5358 N 5358 W to 5456 W)
Possibly named for Stephen Francis Gale, who owned one of the city's first bookstores in 1835.

Goethe Street (1300 N from 86 E to 754 W)
Memorializes Johann Wolfgang von Goethe, German poet, novelist, and dramatist (1749-1832).

Hamlet Avenue (1448 W from 11000 S to 11230 S)
No, it's not likely to have been named after Shakespeare's play, but probably after a small village in Morgan Park—in other words, a hamlet.

Hawthorne Place (3442 N from 500 W to 598 W)
Named for American writer Nathaniel Hawthorne (1804-1864), author of *The Scarlet Letter*, among other works.

Hugh Hefner Way (a stretch of West Walton near Michigan)
Named in honor of the *Playboy* magazine founder and onetime Chicago bon vivant.

Hiawatha Avenue (4522 W at 6005 N to 6128 W at 7142 N)
Hiawatha was an Native American who led the organization of the Iroquois in the sixteenth century; the name is more commonly associated with the hero of Henry Wadsworth Longfellow's poem *Hiawatha*. (See **Minnehaha Avenue**, pp. 283-284.) The neighborhood of Forest Glen, in which Hiawatha, Minnehaha, and other Native American street names can be found, was originally

Photo by Greg Holden.

given as land grants to Billy Caldwell, who was half Native American himself.

Homer Street (1948 N from 1530 W to 5174 W)
Named for the Greek epic poet Homer, author of the *Iliad* and the *Odyssey*.

Ibsen Street (6900 N from 7200 W to 7654 W)
Named for Henrik Ibsen, Norwegian playwright (1828-1906).

Irving Park Road (4000 N from 600 W to 8399 W)
This big east-west street was named for American author Washington Irving (1783-1859), who wrote *The Legend of Sleepy Hollow.*

Jefferson Street (600 W from 470 N to 1938 S)
Named for President Thomas Jefferson, author of the *Declaration of Independence* and other important documents.

Latrobe Avenue (5232 W from 5386 N to 6440 S)
Named for Charles Joseph Latrobe, a best selling author of the early nineteenth century who wrote *The Rambler in North America, 1832-1833,* and who visited Chicago in 1833.

McClurg Court (400 E from 530 N to 678 N)
Named for Alexander McClurg, a bookseller who owned one of the city's most popular bookstores in the late nineteenth century.

Medill Avenue (2334 N from 1200 W to 7190 W)
Named for Joseph Medill (1823-1899), friend of Abraham Lincoln and publisher of the *Chicago Tribune.*

Minnehaha Avenue (5400 W from 6300 N to 6558 N)
Named for Minnehaha, the heroine of Henry Wadsworth Longfellow's poem "Hiawatha."

> As unto the bow the cord is,
> So unto the man is woman,
> Though she bends him, she obeys him,
> Though she draws him, yet she follows,
> Useless each without the other!

> Thus the youthful Hiawatha
> said within himself and pondered,
> Much perplexed by various feelings,
> Listless, longing, hoping, fearing,
> Dreaming still of Minnehaha,
> Of the lovely Laughing Water,
> In the land of the Dacotahs.

Natoma Avenue (6600 W from 6558 N to 6258 S)

Another street that immortalizes a literary character, in this case a Native American girl from one of Victor Herbert's operas.

Norwood Street (6032 N from 1200 W to 7756 W)

Named after a fictitious community called Norwood in a novel by the writer Henry Ward Beecher, *Norwood: or Village Life in New England* (1868). Beecher describes Norwood as a place where the "middle class comprised the great body of the people, all dependent upon their skill and activity for a living, and all striving to amass property enough to leave their families at their death in independent circumstances." This pretty accurately describes the Northwest Side of Chicago as well, through which Norwood Street runs.

Poe Street (1013 W from 1864 N to 1890 N)

Named for American poet Edgar Allan Poe (1809-1849).

Sandburg Terrace (118 W from 1530N to 1556 N)

Named for Carl Sandburg (1878-1967), poet, biographer, and journalist.

Schiller Street (1400 N from 72 E to 2158 W)

Named for Johann Christoph Friedrich von Schiller (1759-1805), considered the father of modern German literature.

Shakespeare Avenue (2132 N from 1400 W to 6926 W)

Named for William Shakespeare (1564-1616), English poet and playwright.

Vanderpoel Avenue

Named for John H. Vanderpoel (1857-1911), Dutch immigrant and artist teacher, whose textbook, *The Human Figure* (1909), is used in art classes worldwide.

Walton Place (980 N from 516 W to 532 W)
Named for Isaak Walton (1593-1683), English writer and biographer and author of *The Compleat Angler.*

Wieland Street (224 W from 1400 N to 1556 N)
Named for German poet/philosopher Christoph Martin Wieland (1733-1813).

Great Chicago Literary Put-Downs

Now that you've learned all the uplifting and inspiring aspects of Chicago's literary history, here are a few pithy comments just to balance your perspective of the Windy City:

"Queen and guttersnipe of cities, cynosure and cesspool of the world: Not if I had a hundred tongues, everyone shouting a different language in a different key, could I do justice to her splendid chaos."

—G. W. STEEVENS, ENGLISHMAN,
The Land of the Dollar
(New York: Dodd, Mead & Company, 1897), p. 144.

"I know thy cunning and thy greed / Thy hard high lust and willful deed / And all th' glory loves to tell / Of specious gifts material."

—RUDYARD KIPLING
From Sea to Sea: Letters of Travel, Part Two
(New York: Doubleday, Page & Company, 1914), p. 139.

"To money [Chicago] gives worship . . . but to the writer it gives neglect—the campaign of silence."

—OPIE READ
The Colossus
(N.p.,1893), p. 121.

"For there is no room left for the serious writer to stand up in old seesaw Yahoo Chicago."

—NELSON ALGREN
Chicago: City on the Make
(Chicago: The University of Chicago Press, 1987), p. 95.

"Undisciplined—that is the word for Chicago. It is the word for all the progress of the Victorian time, a scrambling, ill-mannered, undignified, unintelligent development of material resources."

—H. G. WELLS
The Future in America
(New York and London: Harper and Brothers, 1906), pp. 60-61.

"I forget you were a Chicagoan."

"All that clamminess and police corruption," Asher called from the kitchen, "produces baldness early. Either you're perspiring into your hatband or worrying to death."

—PHILIP ROTH
Letting Go
(New York: Random House, 1962), p. 425.

Trivia Quiz

Taking the following quiz will provide you with a few extra credit points about a few of the fascinating characters who wrote in and about Chicago.

1. True or False: Allan Pinkerton, who was Lincoln's bodyguard and founded a security service, also wrote novels.

2. True or False: Noted bank robber Jesse James wrote an account of his one and only visit to the big city called *Jesse James in Chicago*.

3. True or False: The claim of a Chicago real estate developer that he was responsible for the authorship of the famous play *Cyrano de Bergerac* was upheld by a judge.

4. Multiple Choice: Which Chicago mayor wrote not one but two novellas? **a.** Richard M. Daley; **b.** William Hale Thompson; **c.** Carter Harrison II; **d.** Carter Harrison I.

5. Fill in the Blank: Which great Chicago writer was described in the following quotation after he died in Sag Harbor, New York, on May 14, 1981:

> He belonged to Chicago. That city hurt him into art, praised him, damned him, and finally broke his heart . . . _____ talked about Chicago the way some men talk about women they have loved, not wisely, but too well.

6. What vegetable is being described in the following passage from Henry Blake Fuller's *The Cliff-Dwellers?*

> He towered and swayed like a rank plant [the "Chi-ca-gou!"] that has sprung rapidly from the earth and has brought the slime and mold on its sheath and stalk.

7. True or False: Meat packing tycoons Philip Armour and Gustavus Swift offered Upton Sinclair a large sum of money to tone down *The Jungle*, his novel about the horrors of the packing industry.

8. What was the name of the Irish character immortalized by Finley Peter Dunne in *Chicago Herald* columns 100 years ago?

9. In 1910, the manager of the Chicago Cubs wrote a novel with the not-so-subtle title of *The Bride and the Pennant: The Greatest Story in the History of America's National Game, True to Life, Intensely Interesting.* What was his name?

10. True or False: Iceberg Slim is the pseudonym of a former pimp who published several books in the 1960s and 1970s.

11. Ernest Hemingway was born and raised in Oak Park, Illinois, just west of Chicago. What other famous author lived just a few blocks from Hemingway's home?

12. What publishing house tried to back out of publishing Dreiser's *Sister Carrie* for fear of controversy, but only a few years later printed *The Jungle*, which resulted in a presidential investigation that led to passage of the Pure Food and Drug Act and Beef Inspection Act?

Answers

1. True; called *The Burglar's Fate* and *The Detectives,* they were based on a real bank robbery in Geneva, Illinois.

2. False; Jesse never set foot in Chicago. This is a real novel, though, written by W. B. Lawson in 1898.

3. True; his name was Samuel E. Gross.

4. d.; *A Summer's Outing* and *The Old Man's Story,* 1891.

5. Nelson Algren; eulogized by Pete Hamill in a *Minneapolis Tribune* article entitled "Author Dies Shunned by the City He Loved."

6. An onion.

7. False; they died before the book was published.

8. Mr. Dooley.

9. Frank Chance, of "Tinker to Evans to Chance" fame.

10. True; his real name is Robert Beck.

11. Edgar Rice Burroughs, author of the Tarzan books.

12. Doubleday, Page, and Company.

Chicago Authors

A list of the works of the authors contained in this book would be virtually as long as the book itself. The following list, however, is meant to serve as a historical resource to focus briefly on some of the authors who lived in and/or wrote about Chicago. Offering a sample of some of their themes and awards, it may give a sense of how they were affected by the city and how the city was affected by them.

Jane Addams (1860-1935)
Pacifist, suffragette, founder of Hull House; wrote books and articles about social problems, and two autobiographies, including *Twenty Years at Hull House;* Nobel Peace Prize, 1931.

George Ade (1866-1944)
Humorist and playwright; his creation was the "brash but good-hearted Artie."

Mortimer Adler (1902-)
American philosopher and former University of Chicago professor; served as chairman of the board of editors of the *Encyclopaedia Britannica.*

Nelson Algren (1909-1981)
Wrote brutally realistic short stories and novels about life in Chicago slums; affair with Simone de Beauvoir was fictionalized by her in *The Mandarins* (1956).

Michael A. Anania (1939-)
Novelist, poet, and professor at the University of Illinois at Chicago.

Sherwood Anderson (1876-1941)
Wrote short stories and novels about life in the Midwest.

L(yman) Frank Baum (1856-1919)
Journalist, playwright, writer of children's books.

Saul Bellow (1915-)
Novelist, playwright; topics include urban isolation, Jewish tradition, and Chicago corruption; National Book Award, *The Adventure of Augie March;* Pulitzer Prize, 1975, *Humboldt's Gift;* Nobel Prize in Literature, 1976.

Eleanor Taylor Bland (1944-)
Mystery writer, lives in Waukegan, Illinois.

Gwendolyn Brooks (1917-2000)
Poet, novelist; themes included struggles, and dreams of blacks, especially in Chicago; Pulitzer Prize for Poetry, 1950, *Annie Allen.*

Edward Rice Burroughs (1875-1950)
Novelist born in Chicago, lived in Oak Park; wrote about the fantastic and unearthly; most famous for his Tarzan series of novels.

Ana Castillo (1953-)
Writer born in Chicago, lives here with her son; has written novels including *Peel My Love Like an Onion,* the poetry collection *I Ask the Impossible,* and a children's book *My Daughter, My Son, The Eagle, The Dove.*

Willa Cather (1876-1947)
Novelist; portrayed courage of pioneers and wrote about Chicago in her novel *Lucy Gayheart.*

Maxine Chernoff (1952-)
Novelist, short story writer, poet, and graduate of the University of Illinois at Chicago; received the Carl Sandburg Award for her poetry collection *New Faces of 1952;* novels include *A Boy in Winter* and *Plain Grief.*

Sandra Cisneros (1955-)
Novelist born in Chicago, now lives in Texas; American Book Award, 1983, *The House on Mango Street.*

Cyrus Colter (1910-)
Novelist and short story writer; taught at Northwestern University and was a practicing lawyer.

Alzina Stone Dale (1931-)
Author of *Mystery Reader's Walking Guide: Chicago* as well as a similar book for Washington, D.C.; lives in Hyde Park in the house where she grew up.

Clarence (Seward) Darrow (1857-1938)
Lawyer, lecturer, writer, novelist; in addition to anti-capital punishment material and a collection of defense summations, wrote an autobiography; defended Loeb and Leopold, and John T. Scopes.

Charles Dickinson (1951-)
Author of *Crows, With or Without,* and *Waltz in Marathon*; short stories have appeared in *The New Yorker* and other magazines; lives in the northwest suburbs and is a copy editor for the *Chicago Sun-Times.*

John Dos Passos (1896-1980)
Born in Chicago; best-known for his *USA Trilogy* of novels (1937), as well as *Manhattan Transfer* (1925).

Theodore (Herman Albert) Dreiser (1871-1945)
Journalist, novelist; topics included weaknesses and troubles of American artists, naturalism, socialism.

Finley Peter Dunne (1867-1936)
Columnist, essayist; wrote more than 700 essays and columns featuring his character Mr. Dooley.

Stuart Dybek (1942-)
Born in Chicago and lives in Kalamazoo, Michigan; author of several short story collections including *The Coast of Chicago* and *Childhood and Other Neighborhoods;* recipient of a a Guggenheim fellowship and a special citation from PEN/ Hemingway Prize Committee.

James T(homas) Farrell (1904-1979)
Novelist; wrote about lower middle-class Irish-Catholic life in the South Side slums in the *Studs Lonigan* trilogy.

Edna Ferber (1887-1968)
Wrote novels, short stories, plays, musicals, films; socialist who romanticized unsung heroes of the Midwest; Pulitzer Prize, 1924, *So Big.*

Eugene Field (1850-95)
Born in St. Louis; known for his witty newspaper column "Sharps and Flats," as well as such sentimental children's poems as *Little Boy Blue* and *Wynken, Blynken, and Nod.*

Henry Blake Fuller (1857-1929)
Novelist, critic, satirist, and native Chicagoan; author of the novels *The Cliff-Dwellers* and *With the Procession* as well as other works.

Lorraine Hansberry (1930-1965)
Playwright born in Chicago; wrote *Raisin In the Sun;* her works celebrated individuals who stand up for their own and others' dignity.

Ben Hecht (1893-1964)
Journalist, playwright, and novelist, moved to Chicago from New York as a child; worked as a newspaperman on the *Chicago Journal* and the *Chicago Daily News,* wrote the novels *Erik Dorn* and *Gargoyles* and the collection *1001 Afternoons in Chicago,* and, with Charles MacArthur, the play *The Front Page.*

Larry Heinemann (1944-)
Novelist and former teacher at Columbia College; American Book Award, 1987, *Paco's Story;* works include *Close Quarters* and *Cooler By the Lake.*

Kenan Heise (1933-)
Author, former *Chicago Tribune* journalist, and owner of Chicago Historical Bookworks in Evanston; wrote *Chaos, Creativity, and Culture: A Sampling of Chicago in the Twentieth Century,* a decade-by-decade examination of Chicago's cultural development, and several works of local interest.

Ernest (Miller) Hemingway (1899-1961)
Journalist, novelist, short story writer; wrote about politics, human brotherhood; Pulitzer Prize, 1952, *The Old Man and the Sea;* Nobel Prize in Literature, 1954.

Robert Herrick (1868-1938)
Novelist born in Cambridge, Massachusetts; wrote unflattering "fictional" portraits of the University of Chicago, where he was a professor of English for 30 years, such as the novels *Chimes* and *The Web of Life*.

Paul Hoover (1946-)
Poet in residence at Columbia College in Chicago; writings include *Hairpin Turns* and *Saigon, Illinois*.

(James) Langston Hughes (1902-1967)
Poet; used rhythms of blues and jazz to write about tribulations and joys of American blacks; was poet-in-residence at University of Chicago.

Ringold Wilmer "Ring" Lardner (1885-1933)
Humorist, short story writer; covered sports for *The Chicago Tribune* before becoming a columnist who sketched American life with the vernacular of sports players and working people; covered Black Sox Scandal of 1919.

Vachel Lindsay (1879-1931)
Born in Springfield, Illinois, and studied at the Art Institute of Chicago; known for poems such as "The Congo" and "General William Booth Enters Into Heaven."

Charles MacArthur (1895-1956)
Journalist, playwright; husband of actress Helen Hayes; co-author of the classic Chicago newspaper play *The Front Page*.

Archibald MacLeish (1892-1982)
Poet, dramatist, and critic, born in Glencoe, Illinois; Pulitzer Prize, 1932, *Conquistador*, and 1958, *J.B: A Play in Verse*.

David Mamet (1947-)
Prominent playwright and screenwriter born and raised in Chicago; Pulitzer Prize, 1984, *Glengarry Glen Ross;* helped found the St. Nicholas Players Theater Company.

Edgar Lee Masters (1868-1950)
Poet, playwright; wrote about village life in Midwest and the epic poem *Spoon*

River Anthology; practiced law in Chicago for 30 years.

Cris Mazza (1956-)
Fiction writer, lives in Elmhurst and teaches at the University of Illinois at Chicago; author of several books of fiction, including the PEN/Nelson Algren Award winning novel *How To Leave a Country.*

Barbara Mertz (1929-)
a.k.a. Elizabeth Peters and Barbara Michaels; mystery writer, grew up in a small Illinois town and later lived in the Chicago suburbs; attended the University of Chicago, where she obtained a doctorate at the Oriental Institute.

Sue Miller (1943-)
Born on the South Side of Chicago; her father taught at the University of Chicago; author of the novels *Family Pictures, The Good Mother,* and *Inventing the Abbotts.*

Harriet Monroe (1860-1936)
Editor, poet; founded *Poetry* magazine in Chicago in 1912.

Frank Norris (1870-1902)
Born in Chicago and moved to California at age 14; author of *The Octopus, The Pit,* and *McTeague.*

Sara Paretsky (1947-)
Mystery writer, born in Ames, Iowa, lives in Chicago with her husband Courtenay Wright and their three sons; earned both Master's and Doctor's degrees from the University of Chicago .

Sterling Plumpp (1940-)
Poet and professor at the University of Illinois at Chicago.

Philip Roth (1933-)
Student at the University of Chicago in the 1950s; novels *Letting Go* and *Zuckerman Bound* both mention the University.

Carl Sandburg (1878-1967)
Journalist; wrote poems, children's books, folklore collection, biographies;

topics included industrial and agricultural America, American geography and landscape, great figures in American history, the common man; Pulitzer Prize, 1939, *Abraham Lincoln: The War Years;* Pulitzer Prize, 1950, *Complete Poems.*

Upton Sinclair (1878-1968)

Born in Baltimore; wrote *The Jungle* about the Chicago stockyards, as well as other novels and nonfiction concerned with social and political problems.

Susan Sontag (1933-)

Essayist, novelist, and critic; born in New York City; graduated from the University of Chicago with a Bachelor's degree at age 18.

Louis "Studs" Terkel (1912-)

Born and raised on the west side of Chicago; had his own television show, *Studs' Place,* which was produced in Chicago in the 1950s; radio broadcaster for WFMT-FM for many years; his many books include *Division Street: America, Talking to Myself, The Good War, Working,* and *The Spectator.*

Scott Turow (1949-)

Born in Chicago and grew up on the North Shore; practicing lawyer, as well as the author of such novels as *One L, Presumed Innocent,* and *Burden of Proof.*

Thorstein Veblen (1857-1929)

Born in Wisconsin; became an associate professor of economics at the University of Chicago in 1906; wrote *The Theory of the Leisure Class* and other works.

Margaret Walker (1915-1998)

Poet and novelist, born in Alabama, graduated from Northwestern University in 1935, and joined the Chicago Writers' Project, part of the Works Progress Administration (WPA); author of the novel *Jubilee,* five books of poetry, and a biography of black novelist Richard Wright.

Richard (Nathaniel) Wright (1908-1960)

Novelist; described the ways blacks have been shaped and misshaped by white society; works include *Native Son* and *Black Boy.*

Notes

Introduction

1. Don't hang me for this. I counted all of the bookstores in the Yellow Pages phone books of these three cities. This includes stores that sell rare books, travel books, religious books, and "adult" books as well. As I said, it's not scientific.
2. Carl N. Smith, *Chicago and the American Literary Imagination, 1880-1920*, p. ix.
3. *The Smart Set*, June 1921.
4. Sherwood Anderson, *Sherwood Anderson's Memoirs*, p. 199.
5. Rudyard Kipling, *From Sea to Sea: Letters of Travel*, p. 139.
6. Anderson, *Memoirs*, p. 109.
7. Studs Terkel, *Chicago*, p. 11.

Downtown

1. Daniel H. Burnham and Edward H. Bennett, *Plan of Chicago*, p. 50.
2. Harriet Monroe, *A Poet's Life*, p. 454.
3. Theodore Dreiser, *The Financier*, pp. 334-335.
4. James T. Farrell, *The Young Manhood of Studs Lonigan*, p. 39.
5. Melvin Van Peebles, *The True American*, p. 67.
6. Ben Hecht, *1001 Afternoons in Chicago*, p. 232.
7. Connie Goddard and Bruce Hatton Boyer, *The Great Chicago Trivia & Fact Book*, p. 67.
8. Ernest Hemingway, *A Moveable Feast*, p. 13.
9. Willa Cather, *Later Novels*, p. 657.
10. Frank Norris, *The Pit*, p. 79.
11. James T. Farrell, *Judgment Day*, p. 43.
12. Ana Castillo, *Sapogonia*, p. 122.
13. Margaret Anderson, *My Thirty Years' War*, p. 61.
14. Louis Sullivan, *The Autobiography of an Idea*, p. 197.
15. Henry Regnery, *The Cliff-Dwellers: The History of a Chicago Cultural Institution*, p. 33.
16. Harriet Monroe, Introduction to Lindsay's *The Congo and Other Poems*, p. vi.
17. John Jakes, *Homeland*, p. 169.
18. Marge Piercy, *Going Down Fast*, p. 195.
19. Carlos Baker, *Ernest Hemingway: A Life Story*, p. 76.

Near North Side

1. *Chicago Daily News*, 11 February 1882.
2. Lloyd Lewis, *Oscar Wilde Discovers America*, p. 178.
3. Ibid., p. 169.
4. Finis Farr, *Chicago*, p. 131.
5. Harriet Monroe, *A Poet's Life*, p. 362.
6. Ibid., p. 287.
7. Peter Griffin, *Along With Youth*, p. 147.
8. Ibid., p. 152.
9. Ben Hecht, *Charlie: The Improbable Life and Times of Charles MacArthur*, p. 69.
10. Letter to M. Finley, quoted in William A. Sutton, *The Road to Winesburg*, pp. 314-315.
11. George Swank, *Carl Sandburg: Galesburg and Beyond*, p. 65.
12. Kenny J. Williams, *Sherwood Anderson: A Storyteller and a City*, p. 159.
13. William A. Sutton, *The Road to Winesburg*, p. 307.

14. Letter to Roy Jansen, April 1935, quoted in Sutton, p. 307.
15. Frank Norris, *The Pit,* p. 54.
16. Donald L. Miller, *City of the Century,* p. 524.
17. George Ade, *Stories of the Streets and of the Town,* p. 78.

West Side

1. Theodore Dreiser, *Dawn,* p. 157.
2. Interview with Ana Castillo, *Books,* March-April 2000, p. 38.
3. Ana Castillo, *Peel My Love Like an Onion,* p. 66.
4. Sherwood Anderson, *Marching Men,* p. 100.
5. Sara Paretsky, *Guardian Angel,* p. 130.
6. Jane Addams, *Twenty Years at Hull-House,* p. 97.
7. Ibid.
8. Willard Motley, *Let No Man Write My Epitaph,* p. 89.
9. W. R. Burnett, *Good-bye, Chicago,* p. 174.
10. Ana Castillo, *Loverboys,* p. 195.
11. John Jakes, *Homeland,* p. 172.

Prairie Avenue/ Near South Side

1. Eugene Izzi, *The Criminalist,* p 86.
2. Irving Wallace, "Two Nice Old Ladies," in *The Sunday Gentleman,* pp. 38-39.
3. Wallace, p. 39.
4. Herbert Asbury, *Gem of the Prairie: An Informal History of the Chicago Underworld,* p. 260.
5. Asbury, p. 259.
6. Theodore Dreiser, *Sister Carrie,* p. 112.

7. Edith Freund, *Chicago Girls,* p. 101.
8. Arthur Meeker, *Prairie Avenue,* p. 115.
9. Richard Wright, *American Hunger,* pp. 1-2.
10. Michael Fabre, *The Unfinished Quest of Richard Wright,* p. 74.
11. Ibid., p. 128.
12. Charles Fanning, *Finley Peter Dunne and Mr. Dooley,* p. 39.
13. *Chicago Magazine's Guide to Chicago,* p. 75.
14. Rudyard Kipling, *From Sea: Letters of Travel, pt. 2,* pp. 139, 153.

Near Northwest Side/Wicker Park

1. Studs Terkel, *Division Street: America,* p. xix.
2. Saul Bellow, *Humboldt's Gift* (New York: The Viking Press, 1975), p. 78.
3. "Chicago by the book," by Ted Kleine, *Chicago Tribune,* 12 June 1998 7:54.
4. Angelica Shirley Carpenter and Jean Shirley. *L. Frank Baum: Royal Historian of Oz,* pp. 9-10.
5. Carpenter and Shirley, p. 99.
6. Arnie Bernstein, *Hollywood on Lake Michigan: 100 Years of Chicago and the Movies,* pp. 26-27.
7. Nelson Algren, *Never Come Morning,* p. 215.

Lincoln Park

1. Carl Sandburg, *The Prairie Years,* pp. 153-155.
2. Alzina Stone Dale, *Mystery Reader's Walking Guide: Chicago,* p. 204.
3. Saul Bellow, *The Dean's December,* p. 283.

4. Dale, p. 217.

North Side/Carl Sandburg Country

1. Carl Sandburg, *Always the Young Strangers,* pp. 378-381.
2. George Swank, *Carl Sandburg: Galesburg and Beyond,* p. 62.
3. Carl Sandburg, "Notes for a Preface" in *Collected Poems,* p. xxii.
4. Lisel Mueller, *Learning to Play By Ear,* p. 34.
5. Margaret Anderson, *My Thirty Years' War,* p. 57.
6. Anderson, pp. 66-67.
7. Saul Bellow, *The Dean's December,* p. 282.
8. Emmett Dedmon, *Fabulous Chicago,* p. 216.
9. Dedmon, p. 218.
10. Lytton Strachey, "A Clear Case: Cyrano de Bergerac and the Prince of Cornville," in *The Bookman,* July 1902, 15:434.
11. William Maxwell, *So Long, See You Tomorrow,* p. 50.
12. Studs Terkel, *The Spectator,* p. 357.

Hyde Park

1. James T. Farrell, *My Days of Anger,* 1943, p. 297.
2. Richard Stern, *The Books in Fred Hampton's Apartment,* p. 141.
3. Clara Louis Burnham, *Sweet Clover: A Romance of the White City,* p. 26.
4. "Chicago by the book," by Ted Kleine, *Chicago Tribune,* 12 June 1998, 7:54.
5. Kleine, p. 54.
6. Harry Mark Petrakis, *Stelmark: A Family Recollection,* p. 187.
7. Edgar M. Branch, *The Studs Lonigan*

Neighborhood and the Making of James T. Farrell, p. 4.
8. James T. Farrell, *Reflections at Fifty,* p. 59.
9. A.K. Ramanujan, *Second Sight,* p. 83.
10. Andrew Greeley, *Angel Fire,* p. 47.
11. James Weber Linn, *Winds Over the Campus,* p. 47.
12. Sue Miller, *Family Pictures,* pp. 114-115.
13. Edna Ferber, *So Big,* p. 226.
14. Julie Goldsmith Gilbert, *Ferber: A Biography of Edna Ferber and Her Circle,* p. 401.

South Side

1. Harry Mark Petrakis, *Stelmark: A Family Recollection,* p. 34.
2. Saul Bellow, *Mosby's Memoirs,* p. 93.
3. Groucho Marx, *Groucho and Me,* pp. 101-102.
4. Clint C. Wilson, II, *Black Journalists in Paradox,* p. 58.
5. Gwendolyn Brooks, *Maud Martha,* p. 20.
6. James T. Farrell, *The Young Manhood of Studs Lonigan,* p. 21.
7. *New York Times Book Review,* June 20, 1954, p. 12, quoted in *Studs Lonigan's Neighborhood and the Making of James T Farrell* by Edgar M. Branch, p. iii.
8. Branch, p. 11.
9. Petrakis, p. 25.
10. Branch, p. 56.
11. James T. Farrell, *Reflections at Fifty and Other Essays,* p. 157.
12. Cyrus Colton, *The Rivers of Eros,* p. 63.
13. Clara Louise Burnham, *Sweet Clover: A Romance of the White City,* p. 123.
14. Edgar Lee Masters, *The Tale of Chicago,* p. 249.
15. Marietta Holley, *Samantha at the World's Fair,* p. 212.

16. Holley, p. xi.
17. Monroe, Harriet. *A Poet's Life,* p. 138.
18. Holley, p. 306.
19. Piercy, p. 185.
20. April Sinclair, *i left my back door open,*
p. 25.
21. Eugene Izzi, *Bad Guys,* p. 15.
22. Louis Wirth and Eleanor H. Bernert, eds.,
Local Community Fact Book of Chicago.

Oak Park

1. Quoted in *Inland Spring* magazine, 1961,
p. 13.
2. Jory Graham, *Chicago: An Extraordinary
Guide,* p. 125.
3. Anthony Burgess, *Ernest Hemingway and
His World,* p. 17.
4. Ernest Hemingway, *A Farewell to Arms,*
p. 196.

Near Chicago

1. Theodore Dreiser, *Sister Carrie,* pp. 8-9.
2. Ray Bradbury, *Fahrenheit 451,* p. 11.
3. Ray Bradbury, *Dandelion Wine,* p. x.
4. Nelson Algren, *City on the Make,* p. 25.
5. Howard Mumford Jones and Walter B.
Rideout, *Letters of Sherwood Anderson,*
pp. 63-64.
6. Sutton, Ed. *Letters to Bab,* p. 130.

Bibliography

Addams, Jane. *Twenty Years at Hull-House* (New York: The MacMillan Company, 1912).
   You can find the complete text of this classic nonfiction work at www.cs.cmu.edu/~mmbt/ women/addams/hullhouse/hullhouse.html.

Ade, George. *Stories of the Streets and of the Town: From the Chicago Record 1893-1900.* Illustrated by John T. McCutcheon and Others (Chicago: The Caxton Club, 1941).

Alger, Jr., Horatio. *Luke Walton or The Chicago Newsboy* (Philadelphia: Henry T. Coates & Co., 1889).

Algren, Nelson. *Chicago: City on the Make, with an introduction by Studs Terkel* (Chicago: The University of Chicago Press, 1987).

Algren, Nelson. *The Neon Wilderness* (Gloucester, MA: Peter Smith, 1968).

Algren, Nelson. *Never Come Morning* (New York: Harper & Brothers, 1942).

Anderson, Sherwood. *Sherwood Anderson's Memoirs* (New York: Harcourt, Brace and Company, 1942).

Andrews, Clarence A. *Chicago in Story: A Literary History* (Iowa City: Midwest Heritage Publishing Company, 1982).

Bach, Ira J. and Mary Lackritz Gray. *A Guide to Chicago's Public Sculpture* (Chicago and London: The University of Chicago Press, 1983).

Beecher, Henry Ward. *Norwood: or, Village Life in New England* (New York: Charles Scribner & Company, 1868).

Baker, Carlos. *Ernest Hemingway: A Life Story* (New York: Charles Scribner's Sons, 1969).

Bellow, Saul. *The Dean's December* (New York: Harper & Row, 1982).

Bellow, Saul. *Humboldt's Gift* (New York: The Viking Press, 1975).

Bellow, Saul. *Mosby's Memoirs and Other Stories* (New York: The Viking Press, 1968).

Bernstein, Arnie. *Hollywood on Lake Michigan: 100 Years of Chicago and the Movies* (Chicago: Lake Claremont Press, 1998).

Bradbury, Ray. *Dandelion Wine* (New York: Bantam Books, 1976).

Bradbury, Ray. *Fahrenheit 451* (New York: Simon and Schuster, 1967).

Brooks, Gwendolyn. *Maud Martha* (New York: Harper & Brothers, Publishers, 1953).

Burnett, W. R. *Good-bye, Chicago* (New York: St. Martin's Press, 1981).

Burnett, W. R. *Little Caesar* (New York: The Dial Press, Inc. 1929).

Burnham, Clara Louise. *Sweet Clover: A Romance of the White City* (Boston and New York: Houghton, Mifflin and Company, 1894).

Carpenter, Angelica Shirley and Jean Shirley. *L. Frank Baum: Royal Historian of Oz* (Minneapolis: Lerner Publications Company, 1992).

Castillo, Ana. *Loverboys* (New York: W. W. Norton and Company, 1996).

Castillo, Ana. *Sapogonia* (New York: Anchor Books, 1990).

Castillo, Ana. *Peel My Love Like an Onion* (New York: Doubleday, 1999).

Cather, Willa. *Later Novels* (New York: Library Classics of the United States, Inc., 1990).

Colter, Cyrus. *The Beach Umbrella* (Iowa City: University of Iowa Press, 1970).

Colter, Cyrus. *The Rivers of Eros* (Chicago: The Swallow Press, 1972).

Conrow, Robert. *Field Days: The Life, Times & Reputation of Eugene Field* (New York: Charles Scribner's Sons, 1974).

Stone Dale, Alzina. *Mystery Reader's Walking Guide: Chicago* (Lincolnwood, IL: Passport Books, 1995).

De Voto, Bernard. *We Accept with Pleasure* (Boston: Little, Brown and Company, 1934).

Dreiser, Theodore. *Dawn: An Autobiography of Early Youth* (Santa Rosa: Black Sparrow Press, 1998).

Drew, Bettina. *Nelson Algren: A Life On the Wild Side* (New York: Putnam, 1989).

Dubkin, Leonard. *Wolf Point: An Adventure in History* (New York: G. P. Putnam's Sons, 1953).

Dybek, Stuart. *Childhood and Other Neighborhoods* (New York: The Viking Press, 1980).

Dybek, Stuart. *The Coast of Chicago* (New York: Vintage Books, 1991).

Fabre, Michael. *The Unfinished Quest of Richard Wright* (New York: William Morrow & Company, Inc., 1973).

Farrell, James T. *Reflections at Fifty and Other Essays* (New York: The Vanguard Press, Inc., 1954).

Ferber, Edna. *Mother Knows Best* (Garden City, NY: Doubleday, Page, and Co., 1927).

Ferber, Edna. *Show Boat* (Garden City, NY: Doubleday, Page, and Co., 1926).

Ferber, Edna. *So Big* (Garden City, NY: Doubleday & Company, Inc., 1924).

Freund, Edith. *Chicago Girls* (New York: Poseidon Press, 1985).

Gilbert, Julie Goldsmith. *Ferber: A Biography of Edna Ferber and Her Circle* (Garden City, NY: Doubleday & Company, 1978).

Goddard, Connie, and Bruce Hatton Boyer. *The Great Chicago Trivia & Fact Book* (Nashville: Cumberland House Publishing, Inc., 1996).

Goudge, Elizabeth. *Green Dolphin Country* (London: Hodder and Stoughton, 1944).

Graham, Jory. *Chicago: An Extraordinary Guide* (Chicago: Rand McNally & Company, 1968).

Greeley, Andrew M. *St. Valentine's Night* (New York: Warner Books, 1989).

Griffin, Peter and Jack Hemingway. *Along With Youth: Ernest Hemingway, The Early Years* (Oxford: Oxford University Press, 1985).

Howland, Bette. *Blue in Chicago* (New York: Harper & Row, 1978).

Hecht, Ben. *A Thousand and One Afternoons in Chicago* (Chicago & London: The University of Chicago Press, 1992).

Hecht, Ben. *Charlie: The Improbable Life and Times of Charles MacArthur* (New York: Harper and Brothers, 1957).

Hemingway, Ernest. *A Farewell to Arms* (New York: Charles Scribner's Sons, 1929).

Hemingway, Ernest. *A Moveable Feast* (New York: Charles Scribner's Sons, 1964).

Holley, Marietta. *Samantha at the World's Fair, illustrated by Baron C. De Grumm* (New York: Funk & Wagnalls Company, 1893).

Hughes, Langston. *Not Without Laughter* (New York: Simon & Schuster, Scribner Paperback Fiction, 1995).

Izzi, Eugene. *Bad Guys* (New York: St. Martin's Press, 1988).

Izzi, Eugene. *The Criminalist* (New York: Avon Books, 1998).

Jakes, John. *Homeland* (New York: Doubleday, 1993).

Jones, Howard Mumford, in association with Walter B. Rideout. *Letters of Sherwood Anderson* (Boston: Little, Brown and Company, 1953).

Kipling, Rudyard. *From Sea to Sea: Letters of Travel, Part Two* (Toronto: G. N. Morang & Co., 1899).

Kogan, Herman and Lloyd Wendt. *Chicago: A Pictorial History* (New York: Bonanza Books).

Levin, Meyer. *The Old Bunch* (Secaucus, NJ: Citadel Press, 1985).

Lindsay, Vachel. *The Congo and Other Poems* (New York: The Macmillan Company, 1918).

Linn, James Weber. *Winds Over the Campus* (New York: The Bobbs-Merrill Company, 1936).

Lund, Roslyn Rosen. *The Sharing* (New York: William Morrow and Company, 1978).

Masters, Edgar Lee. *The Tale of Chicago* (New York: G. P. Putnam's Sons, 1933).

Meeker, Arthur. *Prairie Avenue* (New York: Houghton Mifflin Company, 1949).

Michaels, Barbara. *Search the Shadows* (New York: HarperPaperbacks, 1999).

Miller, Donald L. *City of the Century: The Epic of Chicago and the Making of America* (New York: Touchstone [an imprint of Simon & Schuster], 1997).

Marx, Groucho. *Groucho and Me* (New York: Da Capo Press, 1995).

Miller, Sue. *Family Pictures* (New York: Harper & Row, Publishers, Inc., 1990).

Monroe, Harriet. *A Poet's Life: Seventy Years in a Changing World* (New York: The Macmillan Company, 1938).

Mueller, Lisel. *Learning to Play by Ear: Essays and Early Poems* (La Crosse, WI: Juniper Press, 1990).

Norris, Frank. *The Pit: A Story of Chicago* (New York: Doubleday, Page & Co, 1903).

Paretsky, Sara. *Guardian Angel* (New York: Delacorte Press, 1992).

Petrakis, Harry Mark. *Stelmark: A Family Recollection* (New York: David McKay Company, Inc., 1970).

Piercy, Marge. *Going Down Fast* (New York: Trident Press, 1969).

Pirsig, Robert M. *Zen and the Art of Motorcycle Maintenance: An Inquiry Into Values* (New York: William Morrow & Company, 1974).

Ramanujan, A. K. *Second Sight* (Delhi: Oxford University Press, 1986).

Regnery, Henry. *The Cliff Dwellers: The History of a Chicago Cultural Institution* (Chicago: Chicago Historical Bookworks, 1990).

Roe, E. P. *Barriers Burned Away* (New York: Dodd, Mead and Company, 1872).

Roth, Philip. *Letting Go* (New York: Random House, 1962).

Sandburg, Carl. *Collected Poems* (New York: Harcourt, Brace and Company, 1950).

Sawyers, June Skinner. *Chicago Sketches: Urban Tales, Stories, and Legends from Chicago History* (Chicago: Wild Onion Books, 1995).

Sheeran, James Jennings. *Chicago Facts & Fancies, Caprices & Curiosities* (Palm Beach: Palm Beach Publishing Group, 1996).

Sinclair, April. *ain't gonna be the same fool twice* (New York: Hyperion, 1996).

Sinclair, April. *i left my back door open* (New York: Hyperion, 1999).

Smith, Alson J. *Chicago's Left Bank* (Chicago: Henry Regnery Company, 1953).

Smith, Carl N. *Chicago and the American Literary Imagination 1880-1920* (Chicago and London: University of Chicago Press, 1984).

Spencer, Scott. *The Endless Love* (Hopewell, NJ: The Ecco Press, 1999).

Stenerson, Douglas C. *H. L. Mencken: Iconoclast from Baltimore* (Chicago and London: The University of Chicago Press, 1971).

Stern, Richard. *The Books in Fred Hampton's Apartment* (New York: E. P. Dutton, Inc., 1973).

Stern, Richard. *Noble Rot: Stories 1949-1988* (Chicago: Another Chicago Press, 1989).

Sullivan, Louis. *The Autobiography of an Idea* (New York: Dover Publications, Inc., 1953).

Sutton, William A., ed. *Letters to Bab: Sherwood Anderson to Marietta D. Finley, 1916-33* (Urbana and Chicago: University of Illinois Press, 1985).

Sutton, William A. *The Road to Winesburg: A Mosaic of the Imaginative Life of Sherwood Anderson* (Metuchen, NJ: The Scarecrow Press, Inc., 1972).

Terkel, Studs. Chicago (New York: Pantheon Books, 1986).

Terkel, Studs. *Division Street: America* (New York: Pantheon Books, 1967).

Terkel, Studs. *The Spectator : Talk About Movies and Plays With the People Who Make Them* (New York: The New Press, 1999).

Turow, Scott. *Burden of Proof* (New York: Farrar Straus Giroux, 1990).

Van Peebles, Melvin. *The True American: A Folk Fable* (Garden City, NY: Doubleday & Company, Inc., 1976).

Williams, Kenny J. *A Storyteller and a City: Sherwood Anderson's Chicago* (DeKalb, IL: Northern Illinois University Press, 1988).

Wilson, Clint C., II. *Black Journalists in Paradox: Historical Perspectives and Current Dilemmas* (New York: Greenwood Press, 1991).

Wirth, Louis and Bernert, Eleanor H., eds. *Local Community Fact Book of Chicago* (Chicago: The University of Chicago Press, 1949).

Index

Also from Lake Claremont Press

"The Movies Are": Carl Sandburg's Film Reviews and Essays, 1920-1928
ed. by Arnie Bernstein,
introduction by Roger Ebert

Hollywood on Lake Michigan: 100 Years of Chicago and the Movies
by Arnie Bernstein

The Chicago River: A Natural and Unnatural History
by Libby Hill

Ticket to Everywhere: The Best of *Detours* Travel Column
by Dave Hoekstra

Graveyards of Chicago: The People, History, Art, and Lore of Cook County Cemeteries
by Matt Hucke and Ursula Bielski

Chicago Haunts: Ghostlore of the Windy City
by Ursula Bielski

More Chicago Haunts: Scenes from Myth and Memory
by Ursula Bielski

Haunted Michigan: Recent Encounters with Active Spirits
by Rev. Gerald S. Hunter

A Native's Guide to Chicago
by Sharon Woodhouse, with South Side coverage by Mary McNulty

A Native's Guide to Chicago's Northern Suburbs
by Jason Fargo

A Native's Guide to Chicago's Northwest Suburbs
by Martin A. Bartels

A Native's Guide to Chicago's Western Suburbs
by Laura Mazzuca Toops and John W. Toops, Jr.

A Native's Guide to Chicago's South Suburbs
by Christina Bultinck and Christy Johnston-Czarnecki

Coming Soon

A Native's Guide to Northwest Indiana
by Mark Skertic

Great Chicago Fires
by David Cowan

Slaying that Dragon: Struggles for Community on Chicago's Near West Side
by Carolyn Eastwood

Treading on Ancient Ground
by Christina and Nicole Bultinck

Chicago Haunts
(Spanish Edition)
by Ursula Bielski

Lake Claremont Press is . . .

Regional History

The Chicago River: A Natural and Unnatural History
by Libby Hill

When French explorers Jolliet and Marquette used the Chicago portage on their return trip from the Mississippi River, the Chicago River was but a humble, even sluggish, stream in the right place at the right time. That's the story of the making of Chicago. This is the *other* story—the story of the making and perpetual re-making of a river by everything from geological forces to the interventions of an emerging and mighty city. Author Libby Hill brings together years of original research and the contributions of dozens of experts to tell the Chicago River's epic tale—and intimate biography—from its conception in prehistoric glaciers to the glorious rejuvenation it's undergoing today, and every exciting episode in between. As seen in the *Chicago Tribune, Chicago Sun-Times, Chicago Reader*, and Lerner newspapers, and heard on WGN radio.

1-893121-02-X, August 2000, softcover, 78 maps and photos, $16.95

"The Movies Are":
Carl Sandburg's Film Reviews and Essays, 1920-1928
Edited and with historical commentary by Arnie Bernstein
Introduction by Roger Ebert

During the 1920s, a time when movies were still considered light entertainment by most newspapers, the *Chicago Daily News* gave Sandburg a unique forum to express his views on the burgeoning film arts. *"The Movies Are"* compiles hundreds of Sandburg's writings on film including reviews, interviews, and his earliest published essays of Abraham Lincoln—which he wrote for his film column. Take a new look at one of Hollywood's most exciting periods through the critical perspective of one of America's great writers. A passionate film advocate, Sandburg early on grasped and delighted in the many possibilities for the new motion picture medium, be they creative, humanitarian, or technological; intellectual, low-brow, or merely novel. In doing so, he began defining the scope and sophistication of future film criticism.

1-893121-05-4, October 2000, softcover, 397 pages, 72 photos, $17.95

Hollywood on Lake Michigan: 100 Years of Chicago and the Movies
by Arnie Bernstein
with foreword by *Soul Food* writer/director George Tillman, Jr.
This engaging history and street guide finally gives Chicago and Chicagoans due credit for their prominent role in moviemaking history, from the silent era to the present. With trivia, special articles, historic and contemporary photos, film profiles, anecdotes, and exclusive interviews with dozens of personalities, including Studs Terkel, Roger Ebert, Gene Siskel, Dennis Franz, Harold Ramis, Joe Mantegna, Bill Kurtis, Irma Hall, and Tim Kazurinsky. **Winner of an American Regional History Publishing Award: 1st Place—Midwest!**
0-9642426-2-1, December 1998, softcover, 364 pages, 80 photos, $15

Ghosts and Graveyards

Chicago Haunts: Ghostlore of the Windy City
by Ursula Bielski
From ruthless gangsters to restless mail order kings, from the Fort Dearborn Massacre to the St. Valentine's Day Massacre, the phantom remains of the passionate people and volatile events of Chicago history have made the Second City second to none in the annals of American ghostlore. Bielski captures over 160 years of this haunted history with her unique blend of lively storytelling, in-depth historical research, exclusive interviews, and insights from parapsychology. Called "a masterpiece of the genre," "a must-read," and "an absolutely first-rate-book" by reviewers, *Chicago Haunts* continues to earn the praise of critics and readers alike.
0-9642426-7-2, October 1998, softcover, 277 pages, 29 photos, $15

More Chicago Haunts: Scenes from Myth and Memory
by Ursula Bielski
Chicago. A town with a past. A people haunted by its history in more ways than one. A "windy city" with tales to tell . . . Bielski is back with more history, more legends, and more hauntings, including the personal scary stories of *Chicago Haunts* readers. Read about the Ovaltine factory haunts, the Monster of 63rd Street's castle of terror, phantom blueberry muffins, Wrigley Field ghosts, Al Capone's yacht, and 45 other glimpses into the haunted myths and memories of Chicagoland.
1-893121-04-6, October 2000, 312 pages, 50 photos, $15

Haunted Michigan: Recent Encounters with Active Spirits

by Rev. Gerald S. Hunter

Within these pages you will not find ancient ghost stories or legendary accounts of spooky events of long ago. Instead, Rev. Hunter shares his investigations into modern ghost stories—active hauntings that continue to this day. *Haunted Michigan* uncovers a chilling array of local spirits in its tour of the two peninsulas. Wherever you may dwell, these tales of Michigan's ethereal residents are sure to make you think about the possibility, as Hunter suggests, that we are not always alone within the confines of our happy homes. So wait until the shadows of night have cast a pall over the serenity of your peaceful abode. Then snuggle into your favorite overstuffed chair, pour yourself a bracing bolt of 80-proof courage, and open your mind to the presence of the paranormal which surrounds us all.

1-893121-10-0, October 2000, 207 pages, 20 photos, $12.95

Graveyards of Chicago:
The People, History, Art, and Lore of Cook County Cemeteries

by Matt Hucke and Ursula Bielski

Like the livelier neighborhoods that surround them, Chicago's cemeteries are often crowded, sometimes weary, ever-sophisticated, and full of secrets. They are home not only to thousands of individuals who fashioned the city's singular culture and character, but also to impressive displays of art and architecture, landscaping and limestone, egoism and ethnic pride, and the constant reminder that although physical life must end for us all, personal note—and notoriety—last forever.

0-9642426-4-8, November 1999, softcover, 228 pages, 168 photos, $15

Guidebooks by Locals

Ticket to Everywhere: The Best of *Detours* Travel Column

by Dave Hoekstra

with foreword by Studs Terkel

Chicago Sun-Times columnist Dave Hoekstra has compiled over 50 of his best road trip explorations into the offbeat people, places, events, and history of the greater Midwest and Route 66 areas. Whether covering the hair museum in Independence, Missouri, Wisconsin's "Magical Mustard Tour," the Ohio Tiki bar on the National Register of Historic Places, Detroit's polka-dot house, or Bloomington, Illinois—home to beer nuts, Hoekstra's writings will delight readers and instruct tourists.

1-893121-11-9, November 2000, softcover, photos, $15.95

A Native's Guide to Chicago, 3rd Edition
by Sharon Woodhouse,
with expanded South Side coverage by Mary McNulty
Venture into the nooks and crannies of everyday Chicago with this unique, comprehensive budget guide. Over 400 pages of free, inexpensive, and unusual things to do in the Windy City make this the perfect resource for tourists, business travelers, visiting suburbanites, and resident Chicagoans. Called the "best guidebook for locals" in *New City*'s 1999 "Best of Chicago" issue!
0-9642426-0-5, January 1999, softcover, 438 pages, photos, maps, $12.95

Whether you're a life-long resident, new in town, or just passing through, let the Native's Guide series for Chicago's suburban regions be your personal tour guides of the best our suburbs have to offer.

A Native's Guide to Chicago's Northern Suburbs
by Jason Fargo
0-9642426-8-0, June 1999, softcover, 207 pages, photos, maps, $12.95

A Native's Guide to Chicago's Northwest Suburbs
by Martin A. Bartels
1-893121-00-3, August 1999, softcover, 315 pages, photos, maps, $12.95

A Native's Guide to Chicago's Western Suburbs
by Laura Mazzuca Toops and John W. Toops, Jr.
0-9642426-6-4, August 1999, softcover, 210 pages, photos, maps, $12.95

A Native's Guide to Chicago's South Suburbs
by Christina Bultinck and Christy Johnston-Czarnecki
0-9642426-1-3, June 1999, softcover, 242 pages, photos, maps, $12.95

A Native's Guide to Northwest Indiana
by Mark Skertic
1-893121-08-9, Spring 2001

Full of the fascinating sights, places, stories, and facts that sometimes even locals don't know about, the Native's Guide series equips you with everything you need to enjoy and navigate Chicago and its suburbs like a true insider.

ORDER FORM

Literary Chicago	_____ @ $15.95 =	_____
"The Movies Are"	_____ @ $17.95 =	_____
Hollywood on Lake Michigan	_____ @ $15.00 =	_____
The Chicago River	_____ @ $16.95 =	_____
Chicago Haunts	_____ @ $15.00 =	_____
More Chicago Haunts	_____ @ $15.00 =	_____
Graveyards of Chicago	_____ @ $15.00 =	_____
Ticket to Everywhere	_____ @ $15.95 =	_____
A Native's Guide to Chicago	@ $12.95 =	_____
_____	_____ @ $ ____ =	_____
_____	_____ @ $ ____ =	_____

Subtotal: _____

Less Discount: _____

New Subtotal: _____

8.75% Sales Tax for Illinois Residents: _____

Shipping: _____

TOTAL: _____

Name_____

Address_____

City_____**State**_____**Zip**_____

Please enclose check, money order, or credit card information.

Visa/Mastercard#_____**Exp.** _____

Signature_____

Discounts when you order multiple copies!
2 books—10% off total, 3-4 books—20% off,
5-9 books—25% off, 10+ books—40% off

—Low shipping fees—
$2 for the first book and $.50 for each additional book, with a maximum charge of $5.

Order by mail, phone, fax, or e-mail.
All of our books have a no-hassle, 100% money back guarantee.

LAKE CLAREMONT PRESS

4650 N. Rockwell St.
Chicago, IL 60625
773/583-7800
773/583-7877 (fax)
lcp@lakeclaremont.com
www.lakeclaremont.com

Greg Holden has lived in the Chicago area all his life. He grew up in the suburbs, and for nearly twenty years has lived on the city's North Side. He studied literature and writing at the University of Illinois at Chicago, where he obtained a Master's Degree in English and Writing in 1982.

For many years Holden has worked as a writer himself. He was a reporter for a suburban group of newspapers, and later worked as an editor and writer at the University of Chicago. During his time at the University, Greg began to study with Molly Daniels, a novelist and director of the Clothesline School of Writing. Greg has read from his own poems and stories at Jimmy's Woodlawn Tap in Hyde Park, as well as other locations around the city.

Since 1996, Holden has been a full-time writer of books, articles, and columns on computer and Internet-related topics. He has written nine titles, including *Creating Web Pages for Kids & Parents, Small Business Internet for Dummies,* and *Starting an Online Business for Dummies.*

To take a break from the computer, he likes to go to coffeehouses and bookstores. He also enjoys visiting antique malls, where he often adds to his collections of items such as fountain pens, old watches, and hats. He continues to rehab his house and stocks with fish a pond in his backyard that he made himself. He is an active member of Jewel Heart, a Tibetan Buddhist meditation and study group based in Ann Arbor.

For updates and further information, visit the *Literary Chicago* Web site, www.literarychicago.com, or e-mail the author at gholden@literarychicago.com.